DESIGN WRITING RESEARCH

Writing on Graphic Design

Dedicated to our son, JAY LUPTON MILLER, born September 10, 1994.

DESIGN WRITING RESEARCH

Writing on Graphic Design

Ellen Lupton and J. Abbott Miller

A KIOSK BOOK

PRINCETON ARCHITECTURAL PRESS

NEW YORK 1996

PUBLISHED BY
KIOSK
214 Sullivan Street
New York, New York 10012
Phone 212 228 6787
Fax 212 228 6692

DISTRIBUTED BY
PRINCETON ARCHITECTURAL PRESS
37 East 7th Street
New York, New York 10003
Phone 212 995 9620

Design, writing, research: writing on graphic design
Ellen Lupton, J. Abbott Miller

Library of Congress Catalog Card Number 95-43396 CIP

The paper in this book meets the guidelines for
permanence and durability of the Committee on
Production Guidelines for Book Longevity of the
Council on Library Resources.

KIOSK
A small structure erected in an
urban place on which advertisements and public notices are
posted. A stall or booth, often
temporary or portable, used for
vending books, magazines,
newspapers, postcards, candies,
souvenirs, and other items.

CONTENTS

ACKNOWLEDGMENTS

This book draws on over ten years of design, writing, and research. Publishing this volume enabled us to revisit and revise work initiated since the beginning of our practice, and to put into print for the first time a group of new projects.

The first section, on THEORY, considers graphic design and typography within a post-structuralist framework. These essays are rooted in our work as students at The Cooper Union School of Art (1981–1985), where we began interpreting critical theory through visual and verbal forms. Our teachers, including Hans Haacke, George Sadek, and P. Adams Sitney, encouraged us to think about art and design in terms of culture and language. The series of essays concerning non-phonetic modes of writing—from punctuation to international symbols—originates from exhibition brochures and monographs produced at The Cooper Union's Herb Lubalin Study Center for Design and Typography, 1986–1990.

"Language of Vision" was first published in 1987 in the *AIGA Journal of Graphic Design,* edited by Steven Heller. Through his role as an editor and conference organizer, Steven Heller has set the stage for contemporary design history and criticism; he provided the initial venue for many of our projects. A version of "Laws of the Letter" first appeared in *Emigre* in 1990; editor Rudy VanderLans gave us the freedom to publish an essay whose theoretical emphasis was not typical of the magazine at that time. The chapter on deconstruction is a revision of an essay published in a special issue of *Visible Language* in 1994, edited by Andrew Blauvelt. The project on Foucault appears here for the first time.

The second part of our book looks at the intersection between graphic design and MEDIA. The essay on Andy Warhol was produced in 1989 for an exhibition catalogue edited by Donna de Salvo, who generously shared interviews she had conducted with Warhol's contemporaries. The essays on Quentin Fiore, stock photography, and low and high culture are based on articles published in *Eye* magazine in the early 90s; editor Rick Poynor has created a vital forum for design criticism. The essay on newspaper design was commissioned in 1990 by *Print* magazine, whose editors have been fruitful collaborators on several projects over the past five years.

The essay on race and advertising, published here for the first time, is based on research conducted for a seminar taught by Rosalind Krauss at The Graduate Center of the City University of New York. Other professors at CUNY who encouraged our pursuit of design studies include Rosemarie Haag Bletter, Marlene Park, and Stuart Ewen.

The final section of this book looks at HISTORY through a series of short essays organized as a time line. These essays were published in 1989 in the book *Graphic Design in America,* edited by Mildred Friedman at Walker Art Center. Her decision to create the first large-scale museum exhibition on the history of graphic design in the U.S. provided an important context for a number of scholars to test ideas about writing design history. The time line is presented here in a condensed form.

We founded the studio Design/Writing/Research in 1985 as an after-hours scenario for collaborating on projects outside the strictures of our paid employment. By 1989 Design/Writing/Research had become a self-sustaining business. Many members of the studio over the past several years helped design, produce, and edit this book, including Claudia Bernheim, Paul Carlos, Deborah Drodvillo, Luke Hayman, Steven Hoskins, Tracey Hummer, Anthony Inciong, Dina Radeka, Jane Rosch, Hall Smyth, Claudia Warrak, and David Williams.

The production of this book was managed by Suzanne Salinetti and Kenneth Milford at Studley Press, who brought care and craftsmanship to its physical form.

Mohawk Paper Mills enhanced the book's physical presence and permanence by supplying a range of archival, library-quality papers. We are grateful for the advice and advocacy of Laura Shore.

Kevin Lippert and Ann Urban at Princeton Architectural Press have taught us a lot about publishing since they began distributing and publishing our books in 1991. They encouraged us to found Kiosk in 1995, an imprint devoted to research on graphic design, product design, exhibitions, and other fields outside of architectural discourse.

Our colleagues at Cooper-Hewitt, National Design Museum were supportive during the final stages of the book's creation; we thank Susan Yelavich and Dianne H. Pilgrim.

Julia Reinhard Lupton and Kenneth Reinhard helped us through numerous passages of critical theory. Many other friends and associates contributed ideas, information, and support; we thank Brian Boyce, Lise Friedman, Maud Lavin, Mike Mills, Lawrence Mirsky, Michelle Omar, Patsy Tarr, and Jennifer Tobias.

All of our work is fueled by the love of our family. The beauty of our son, Jay Lupton Miller, illuminates everything we do. Our parents encouraged us to pursue work that made us happy, even when the professional terrain was uncertain; we will always love, revere, and remember Ruby and Jerry Miller, Mary Jane Lupton and Kenneth Baldwin, and William and Shirley Lupton.

ELLEN LUPTON AND J. ABBOTT MILLER

INTRODUCTION

My first encounter with the work of Design/Writing/Research, in the late 1980s, was one of those moments that lodges in the memory, partly for itself but also because it became the starting point for my own collaboration with Ellen Lupton and Abbott Miller. I was working as an editor at *Blueprint* magazine at the time, and one of our contributors, recently back from New York, sent me a package containing six or seven small exhibition catalogues researched, written, and designed by Ellen Lupton in her role as a curator at The Cooper Union.

What still seems notable about those early pieces, looking at them again now, is the combination of playfulness and rigor with which they re-enact the graphic procedures of their own subject matter. A four-page broadsheet about *New York Times* designer Louis Silverstein is laid out using the grid of the newspaper itself. A retrospective on the pen and ink cartoons of Edward Sorel is cast in the form of a comic strip. A visual biography of Herb Lubalin threads examples of his type treatments into Lupton's elegantly spaced lines of explanatory text, so that the reader's eye runs over each image even in the act of reading about it.

Lupton and Miller's aims and process are neatly summarized in the three-noun manifesto—Design/Writing/Research—which became the name of the company they founded in 1985, and now forms the title of this book. The reversal of the usual sequence of operations (research, writing, design) in this formulation is less an attempt to overturn conventional priorities than to underscore their own primary role as designers: Lupton as curator and exhibition designer at Cooper-Hewitt, National Design Museum; Miller as director of the New York-based Design/Writing/Research. Both separately and in their continuing collaborations, their activity as designers is nourished to an unusual degree by the processes of critical reflection encouraged by writing and research. Their already sizeable body of work, though sometimes rarefied when compared to the average design studio's, is a practical, real-world proposal showing some of the ways in which the traditional divide between theory and practice might be bridged.

In their critical writing, Lupton and Miller use design itself as a tool of explication and analysis. They reject the indifferent picture-editing and semi-integration of image and text found in most graphic design publishing. Their remarkable 1991 book *The ABC's of* ▲■●: *The Bauhaus and Design Theory* used design strategies as part of a critique of modernist theory, an idea further developed in this volume. Such work anticipated by several years calls for a new kind of critical writing being made in the 1990s. In a recent issue of the journal *Visible Language,* devoted to "Critical Histories of Graphic Design" (to which Lupton and Miller also contributed), the British writer Steve Baker proposes "that the form of a writing appropriate to the study of graphic design might itself attempt to bring the visual and the verbal into a closer relation." He goes on to imagine a history-writing "consonant with the practice of graphic design" which would use graphic "interruption" to deflect and enrich the trajectory of the critical text.

Miller, in a similar vein, has spoken of his desire to "weave" words and pictures together—a metaphor that suggests a greater than usual density of connections in the wiring of verbal and visual meaning. The visual is not simply cited in passing as an example, but becomes an indispensable term in the construction of the argument. Here, as elsewhere, Lupton and Miller stress the importance of "specificity." They are interested in theory not as an end in itself but for the ways it can be related to the artifacts and practices of design. Where much recent critical writing talks, sometimes in circles, about the kinds of issues that should be addressed—post-modernism, social questions, historical context, and so on—Lupton and Miller want to weld these issues to graphic design in a concrete and vivid way.

They feel an obvious kinship with the small lineage of designer-thinkers whose practice anticipates their own. Otto Neurath, inventor of international picture signs, suggests to them a "model for the graphic designer of the next millennium, the language worker equipped to use design and theory as tools for unearthing new questions and constructing new answers." The books designed by Quentin Fiore with Marshall McLuhan and Buckminster Fuller provide a "foundation for a design practice that merges design and writing, form and content, theory and practice."

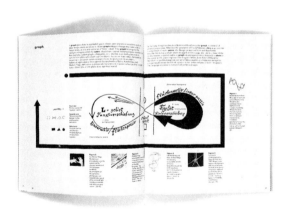

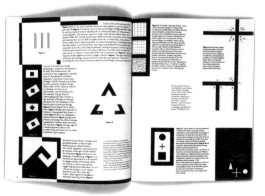

Lupton and Miller's shorter visual essays offer contemporary models for such a practice. But the small print runs of the Cooper Union catalogues and Miller's more recent monograph *Printed Letters: The Natural History of Typography* mean they have not been widely seen, particularly outside the U.S. In their updated form the early essays now share a consistent format and a single typographic voice—Martin Majoor's typeface Scala, which is also used in their books *The Bathroom, The Kitchen, and the Aesthetics of Waste* and *Mechanical Brides,* as well as in the dance journal *Dance Ink.* Forceful, quirky, contemporary and exact, Scala is becoming a Design/Writing/Research house style, an appropriation that may be without precedent in critical writing.

Book, *The ABCs of ▲■●: The Bauhaus and Design Theory*
Published by The Cooper Union and Princeton Architectural Press

As well as being revoiced, material originally written for other publications is in a more fundamental sense reclaimed in this book. I find myself in the unusual position of seeing three articles first published in the magazine I edit, *Eye,* redesigned by their authors in what presumably represents for them a definitive form. The "Graphic Design in America" time line, created for a Walker Art Center catalogue, is similarly revised and recast. Readers inclined to see such changes as only a matter of surface appearance would miss a fundamental point made by Lupton and Miller themselves in the essay "Deconstruction and Typography" about the significance of graphic structures. Devices which traditional literary and linguistic research tends to overlook—such as spacing, framing, punctuation, type style, and layout—perform a potentially "transformative" function in the articulation of meaning. To reformat a complex visual essay is almost certainly at some level to change what it "says."

Design/Writing/Research is a project of total authorship that has few direct parallels in contemporary writing about graphic design. Other designers and design thinkers also draw on the post-structuralist theory that has informed Lupton and Miller's work since the beginning. Others again are questioning the outworn tenets of an earlier design history and criticism. And many others, across the field of graphic design, are arguing that designers should take a more active and responsible role—as self-conscious authors—in the shaping of content, whether as writers themselves, or as more equal collaborators. Meanwhile, designers who write about design are increasingly anxious to design what they write.

But outside the pages of *Emigre* and the occasional exhibition catalogue, opportunities to realize such a design and media criticism remain scarce. And this, more than anything, is the aspect of Lupton and Miller's ten-year achievement that sets them apart. Working separately and together, they have discovered or devised for themselves professional spaces in which it has been possible to develop a coherent body of projects that unite their own writing and design. They have done more than simply theorized. They have turned critical reflection into a viable form of everyday practice.

RICK POYNOR

THEORY

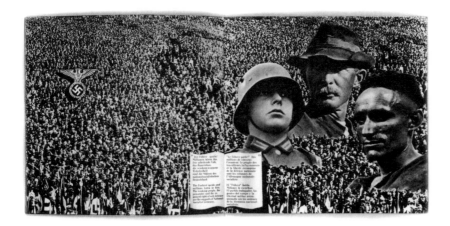

TOP Brochure, designed by
Herbert Bayer, 1934. Republished
in *Gebrauchsgrafik*, April 1936.
This Nazi publication uses the
structure of a book-within-a-book.
The shield-like book appears
against backgrounds depicting
the "folk" masses and Germany's
natural and industrial resources.

CENTER Book, *The Reign of
Narcissism*, by Barbara Bloom,
1990. Württembergischer
Kunstverein Stuttgart. Bloom
presents a literary source as a
physical artifact.

BOTTOM Catalogue, California
Institute of the Arts, designed by
Barbara Glauber and Somi Kim,
1993. A cartoon-like icon of a
book occupies the spine of the
layout.

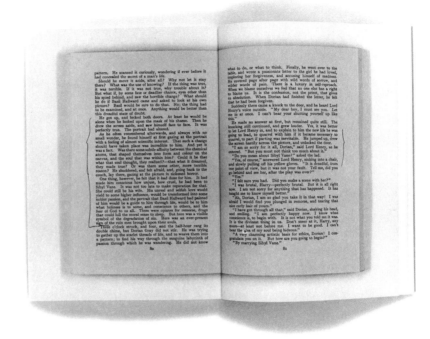

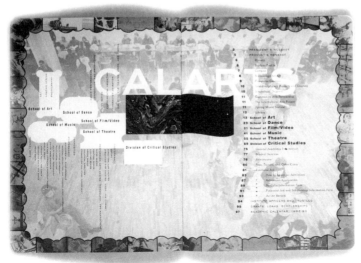

Deconstruction and Graphic Design

1 Jacques Derrida, *Of Grammatology*, trans. Gayatri Chakravorty Spivak (Baltimore: Johns Hopkins University Press, 1976). See especially Chapter 2, "Linguistics and Grammatology," 27-73.

2 Jonathan Culler explores the impact of deconstruction on literary criticism in his book *On Deconstruction: Theory and Criticism after Structuralism* (Ithaca: Cornell University Press, 1982).

Since the surfacing of the term "deconstruction" in design journalism in the mid-1980s, this suggestive word has served to label practices in architecture, graphic design, products, and fashion that favor chopped-up, layered, and fragmented forms, often imbued with ambiguous futuristic overtones. This essay looks at the reception and use of deconstruction in the recent history of design, and then considers the place of typography within the the work of Jacques Derrida, who initiated the theory of deconstruction. Derrida described deconstruction as a mode of questioning through and about the technologies, formal devices, social institutions, and central metaphors of representation. Deconstruction belongs to both history and theory. It is embedded in recent visual and academic culture, and it describes a strategy of critical form-making which is performed across a range of artifacts and practices.

Derrida introduced the concept of deconstruction in his book *Of Grammatology*, published in France in 1967 and translated into English in 1976.[1] Deconstruction became a banner for vanguard literary studies in the U.S. in the 1970s and 80s, scandalizing departments of English, French, and comparative literature. Deconstruction rejected the project of modern criticism, which had been to uncover the meaning of a literary work by studying the way its form and content communicate essential humanistic messages. Deconstruction, like critical strategies based on Marxism, feminism, semiotics, and anthropology, focuses not on the themes and imagery of its objects but rather on the linguistic and institutional systems that frame their production.[2]

In Derrida's theory, deconstruction asks how representation inhabits reality. How does the external image of things get *inside* their internal essence? How does the surface get under the skin? Western culture since Plato has been governed by such oppositions as reality/representation, inside/outside, original/copy, and mind/body. The intellectual achievements of the West—its science, art, philosophy, literature—have valued one side of these pairs over the other, allying one with truth and the other with falsehood. Deconstruction attacks such oppositions by showing how the devalued, negative concept inhabits the valued, positive one.

Consider, for example, the opposition between nature and culture. The idea of "nature" depends on the idea of "culture" in order to be understood, and yet culture is embedded in nature. It is delusionary to conceive of the non-human environment as a pristine setting untouched by the products of human endeavor—cities, roads, farms, landfills. The fact that Western societies have produced a concept of "nature" in opposition to "culture" reflects our alienation from the ecological systems that civilization depletes and transforms. Another inside/outside construction is found in the Judeo-Christian concept of the body as an external shell for the inner soul, a construction that elevates the mind as the sacred source of thought and spirit, while denigrating the body as mere mechanics. In the realm of aesthetics, the original work of art carries an aura of authenticity that its copy lacks—the original is endowed with the spirit of its maker, while the copy is mere empty matter.

Derrida asserted that an intellectual system (or *episteme*) built on the opposition between reality and representation has, in fact, depended on representations to build itself:

> External/internal, image/reality, representation/presence, such is the old grid to which is given the task of outlining the domain of a science. And of what science? Of a science that can no longer answer to the classical concept of the *episteme* because the originality of its field—an originality that it inaugurates— is that the opening of the 'image' within it appears as the condition of 'reality,' a relationship that can no longer be thought within the simple difference and the uncompromising exteriority of 'image' and 'reality,' of 'outside' and 'inside,' of 'appearance' and 'essence' (33).

A crucial opposition for Derrida is speech/writing. The Western philosophical tradition has denigrated writing as an inferior copy of the spoken word. *Speech* draws on interior consciousness, but *writing* is dead and abstract. Writing sets language adrift, untethering it from the speaking subject. In the process of embodying language, writing steals its soul. Contrary to this view, deconstruction looks at writing as an active form of representation. Writing is not merely a bad copy, a faulty transcription, of the spoken word; writing invades thought and speech, transforming the sacred realms of memory, knowledge, and spirit.

SPEECH
interior to the mind
requires no equipment
spontaneously learned
natural
original
present subject

According to Derrida, any memory system can be called a form of writing, since it records information for the purpose of future transmissions. The spoken language itself shares writing's characteristic alienation from interior consciousness, since its function depends on the repeatability of signs, and thus on a split between thought and expression, between the originality of the spontaneous utterance and the familiarity of the copy.

Derrida used the term *grammatology* to name the study of writing as a distinctive form of representation. This rather cumbersome word serves to title the book whose more infamous legacy is deconstruction. Derrida proposed grammatology as a field of inquiry for which deconstruction is a crucial mode of research, a manner of questioning that frames the nature of its object. Falling within the domain of grammatology are the material forms and processes of typography and graphic design.

If writing is but a copy of spoken language, typography is a mode of representation even farther removed from the primal source of meaning in the mind of the author. The alphabet, in principal, represents the sounds of speech by reducing them to a finite set of repeatable marks; typography is but one of the media through which this repetition occurs. The letter *a* might be carved in stone, written in pencil, or printed from an engraved block, but only the last is, properly speaking, typographic. Typographic production involves composing identical letters into lines of text. The characters might be generated from relief surfaces made of wood, metal, or rubber, or from a photographic negative, a digital code, or a paper stencil. The art of typography includes the design of letterforms for reproduction and the arrangement of characters into lines of text. Typographic features include the choice of typefaces; the spacing of letters, words, lines, and columns; and the pattern formed by these graphic distinctions across the body of a document. We will return to Derrida's own engagement with typographic forms later in this essay, but first, we will look at the life of deconstruction in design culture.

WRITING
exterior to the mind
requires equipment
culturally constructed
artificial
copy
absent subject

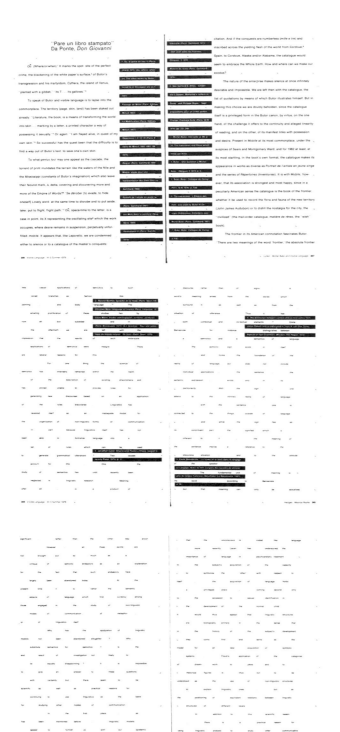

Journal, *Visible Language*, "French Currents of the Letter," designed by Richard Kerr, Alice Hecht, Jane Kosstrin, Herbert Thompson, and Katherine McCoy at Cranbrook Academy of Art, 1978. This collection of essays on French literary theory was designed as a student project. The conventional relationship between inside and outside, figure and ground, is inverted as the spaces between lines and words progressively expand and the footnotes move into the area normally reserved for the central text.

3 Post-structuralist texts widely read by students of art and design during the 1980s include Roland Barthes, *Mythologies*, trans. Annette Lavers (New York: Farrar, Straus & Giroux, 1972); Michel Foucault, *Discipline and Punish: The Birth of the Prison*, trans. Alan Sheridan (New York: Random House, 1979); and Jean Baudrillard, *For a Critique of the Political Economy of the Sign*, trans. Charles Levin (St. Louis, MO: Telos Press, 1981).

4 Books that helped popularize post-structuralism include *The Anti-Aesthetic: Essays on Postmodern Culture*, Hal Foster, ed. (Port Townsend, WA: Bay Press, 1983); and Terry Eagleton, *Literary Theory: An Introduction* (Minneapolis: University of Minnesota Press, 1983).

5 *Cranbrook Design: The New Discourse* (New York: Rizzoli, 1990), with essays by Katherine McCoy, Lorraine Wild, and others. See also Katherine McCoy, "American Graphic Design Expression," *Design Quarterly* 148 (1990): 4-22.

6 *French Currents of the Letter* includes essays on typography and deconstruction. See Andrew J. McKenna, "Biblioclasm: Derrida and his Precursors," *Visible Language* XII (Summer 1978): 289-304.

Deconstruction belongs to the broader critical field known as "post-structuralism," whose key figures include Roland Barthes, Michel Foucault, and Jean Baudrillard. Each of these writers has looked at modes of representation—from the conventions of literature and photography to the design of schools and prisons—as powerful technologies that build and remake the social world. Deconstruction's attack on the neutrality of signs is also at work in the consumer mythologies of Barthes, the institutional archaeologies of Foucault, and the simulationist aesthetics of Baudrillard.[3]

The idea that cultural forms help fabricate such seemingly "natural" categories as race, sexuality, class, and aesthetic value had profound relevance to visual artists in the 1970s and 80s. Post-structuralism provided a critical avenue into "post-modernism," posing an alternative to the period's nostalgic returns to figurative painting and neo-classical architecture. While Barbara Kruger, Cindy Sherman, and Victor Burgin were attacking media myths through their visual work, books such as Hal Foster's *The Anti-Aesthetic* and Terry Eagleton's *Literary Theory* delivered post-structuralism to artists and students in an accessible form.[4]

Graphic designers in many U.S. art programs were exposed to critical theory through the fields of photography, architecture, and performance and installation art. The most widely publicized intersection of post-structuralism and graphic design occurred at the Cranbrook Academy of Art under the leadership of co-chair Katherine McCoy.[5] Designers at Cranbrook first confronted literary criticism when they designed a special issue of the journal *Visible Language* on contemporary French literary aesthetics, published in the summer of 1978. Daniel Libeskind, head of Cranbrook's architecture program, provided the graphic designers with a seminar in literary theory that prepared them to develop their strategy: the students disintegrated the series of essays by progressively expanding the spaces between lines and words and pushing the footnotes into the space normally reserved for the main text. *French Currents of the Letter* rejected the established ideologies of problem-solving and direct communication that constituted "normal science" for modern graphic designers.[6]

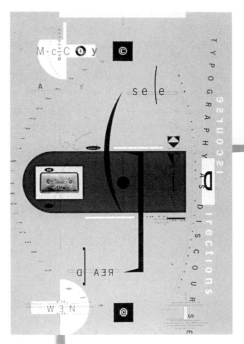

Poster, *Typography as Discourse*, designed by Allen Hori, 1989. Cranbrook Academy of Art, Michigan.

Post-structuralism re-entered discussions at Cranbrook around 1983. McCoy has credited Jeffery Keedy, a student at the school from 1983-85, with introducing fellow course members to books by Barthes and others.[7] The classes of 1985-87 and 1986-88 also actively engaged critical theory; students at this time included Andrew Blauvelt, Brad Collins, Edward Fella, David Frej, and Allen Hori. Interaction with the photography department, chaired by Carl Toth, fostered dialogue about critical theory and visual practice.[8] Post-structuralism did not serve, however, as a unified methodology at the school, even in the period of its strongest currency, but was part of an eclectic gathering of ideas. According to Keedy, his peers at Cranbrook were looking at everything from alchemical mysticism to the "proportion voodoo" of the golden section.[9]

McCoy recalled in a 1991 interview: "Theory had become part of the intellectual culture in art and photography. We were never trying to apply specific texts—it was more of a general filtration process. The term 'deconstructivist' drives me crazy. Post-structuralism is an attitude, not a style."[10] Designers at Cranbrook expressed this "attitude" in formal experiments (visual and verbal) that played with conventions of reading, and in projects that used theory as a direct source of content by collaging together quotations from various sources. Theory thus provided both an intellectual background for abstract expression and a subject for research. Allen Hori's 1989 poster *Typography as Discourse*, designed to announce a lecture by McCoy, is a manifesto for a design practice informed by literary theory. Hori's typography challenges the traditional opposition between seeing and reading by treating the surface as both theoretical content and sensual form, as both text and texture. Rather than deliver information directly, Hori's poster expects the reader to work to uncover its messages.

The response to post-structuralism at Cranbrook was largely optimistic, side-stepping the pessimism and political critique that permeates the work of Barthes, Foucault, and others. McCoy used the architectural theory of Robert Venturi and Denise Scott Brown as a "stepping stone" to post-structuralism, enabling her to merge the Pop appreciation of the commercial vernacular with post-structuralism's critique of "fixed meaning."[11] McCoy's preference for formal celebration over cultural criticism is echoed in Keedy's comment, "It was the poetic aspect of Barthes which attracted me, not the Marxist analysis. After all, we're designers working in a consumer society, and while Marxism is interesting as an idea, I wouldn't want to put it into practice."[12]

7 Katherine McCoy, interview with Ellen Lupton, February, 1991.

8 Communication with Andrew Blauvelt, June, 1994.

9 Jeffery Keedy, interview with Ellen Lupton, February, 1991.

10 Katherine McCoy, interview with Ellen Lupton, February, 1991.

11 Robert Venturi, Denise Scott Brown, and Steven Izenour, *Learning from Las Vegas* (Cambridge: MIT Press, 1972).

12 Jeffery Keedy, interview with Ellen Lupton, February, 1991.

13 Robin Kinross has blamed post-structuralism for contemporary designers' retreat into personal visions of typographic form and function. Although theory has been used this way by some designers, the post-structuralist view of the power of signs is profoundly social, yielding a critique rather than a celebration of humanist notions of taste and originality. See Kinross, *Fellow Readers: Notes on Multiplied Language* (London: Hyphen Press, 1994).

14 Philip Johnson and Mark Wigley, *Deconstructivist Architecture* (New York: Museum of Modern Art, 1988).

Post-structuralism's emphasis on the openness of meaning has been incorporated by many designers into a romantic theory of self-expression: as the argument goes, because signification is not fixed in material forms, designers and readers share in the spontaneous creation of meaning. Interpretations are private and personal, generated by the unique sensibilities of makers and readers. This approach represents a rather cheerful response to the post-structuralist theme of the "death of the author," which asserts that the interior self is constructed by external systems and technologies. According to the writings of Barthes and Foucault, for example, the citizen/artist/producer is not the imperious master of language, media, education, custom, and so forth; instead, the individual operates within the grid of possibilities these codes present. Rather than view the production of meaning as a private matter, post-structuralist theory tends to see the realm of the "personal" as structured by external signs. Invention and revolution result from tactical aggressions against the grid.[13]

"Deconstructivism" catapulted into the mainstream design press with MoMA's 1988 exhibition *Deconstructivist Architecture*, curated by Philip Johnson and Mark Wigley.[14] The curators used the term "deconstructivism" to link a range of contemporary architectural practices to Russian Constructivism, whose early years envisioned form and technology in chaotic upheaval rather than rational resolution. The MoMA exhibition located a similarly skewed variant of modernism in the work of Frank Gehry, Daniel Libeskind, Peter Eisenman, and others. Wigley wrote in his catalogue essay:

> A deconstructive architect is...not one who dismantles buildings, but one who locates the inherent dilemmas within buildings. The deconstructive architect puts the pure forms of the architectural tradition on the couch and identifies the symptoms of a repressed impurity.
> The impurity is drawn to the surface by a combination of gentle coaxing and violent torture: the form is interrogated (11).

In Wigley's view, deconstruction in architecture asks questions about modernism by re-examining its own language, materials, and processes.

Although the MoMA show described deconstruction as a *mode of inquiry* rather than a repertoire of mannerisms, the curators nonetheless framed their exhibition around a new "ism" and thus helped canonize the elements of a period style, marked by twisted geometries, centerless plans, and shards of glass and metal. This cluster of visual features quickly emigrated from architecture to graphic design, just as the icons and colors of neo-classical post-modernism had traveled there shortly before. While a more critical approach to deconstruction had reached graphic designers through the fields of photography and the fine arts, architecture provided a ready-to-use formal vocabulary that could be adopted more broadly. "Deconstruction," "deconstructivism," and just plain "decon" became design-world clichés, where they named existing tendencies and catalyzed new ones in the fields of furniture, fashion, and graphic design.[15]

In 1990 Philip Meggs published a how-to guide for would-be deconstructivists in the magazine *Step-by-Step Graphics.* Following the logic of the MoMA project, Meggs's story begins with Constructivism and ends with "deconstruction"; unlike Wigley, however, Meggs depicted early modernism as a purely rational enterprise.[16] Chuck Byrne's and Martha Witte's more analytical piece for *Print* (1990) describes deconstruction as a "zeitgeist," a philosophical germ circulating in contemporary culture that influences graphic designers even though they might not know it. Their view corresponds roughly to McCoy's sense of post-structuralism as a general "attitude" responding to the "intellectual culture" of the time. Byrne's and Witte's article identifies examples of deconstruction across the ideological map of contemporary design, ranging from the work of Paula Scher and Stephen Doyle to Lucille Tenazas and Lorraine Wild.

Today, in the mid-90s, the term "deconstruction" is used casually to label any work that favors complexity over simplicity and dramatizes the formal possibilities of digital production. The term is commonly used to invoke a generic allegiance with Cranbrook or CalArts, a gesture that reduces both schools to flat symbols by blanketing a variety of distinct practices. Our view of deconstruction in graphic design is at once narrower and broader in its scope than the view evolving from the current discourse. Rather than look at deconstruction as a historical style or period, we see deconstruction as a critical process—an *act* of questioning.

15 Michael Collins and Andreas Papadakis include a chapter on "Deconstruction, Deconstructivism, and Late-Modernism" in their book *Post-Modern Design* (New York: Rizzoli, 1989): 179-95. The book is a survey of furniture, jewelry, and other decorative arts.

16 Essays on deconstruction and graphic design include Philip Meggs, "De-constructing Typography," *Step-by-Step Graphics* 6 (February 1990): 178-181; and Chuck Byrne and Martha Witte, "A Brave New World: Understanding Deconstruction," *Print* XLIV (November/December 1990): 80-87.

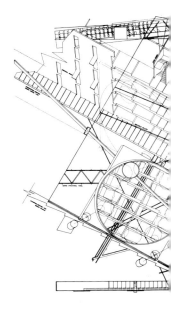

17 Ferdinand de Saussure founded structural linguistics with his *Course in General Linguistics*, Wade Baskin, trans. (New York: McGraw-Hill, 1959). See "Graphic Representation of Language," 23-32, and "General Principles," 65-100. On Saussure and critical theory, see Jonathan Culler, *Ferdinand de Saussure* (Ithaca: Cornell University Press, 1976).

BOTTOM Sections and exploded axonometric of structure and circulation, *City Edge*, designed by Daniel Libeskind, 1987. Featured in the Museum of Modern Art's 1988 exhibition *Deconstructivist Architecture*.

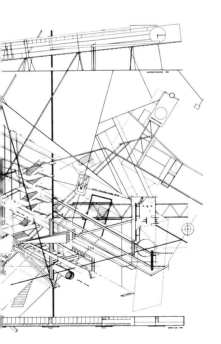

Having looked at deconstruction's life in recent design culture, we will now locate design within the theory of deconstruction. The visual resources of typography are instrumental to Derrida's dissection of Western art and philosophy. Derrida's critique of the speech/writing opposition developed out of his reading of Ferdinand de Saussure's *Course in General Linguistics*, a foundational text for structuralist linguistics, semiotics, and anthropology.[17] Saussure asserted that the meaning of signs does not reside in the signs themselves: there is no natural bond between the *signifier* (the sign's material aspect) and the *signified* (its referent). Instead, the meaning of a sign comes only from its relationship to other signs in a system. This principle is the basis of structuralism, which focuses on patterns or structures that generate meaning rather than on the "content" of a given code or custom.

Saussure argued that because the sign has no inherent meaning, it is, taken by itself, empty, void, absent. The sign has no life apart from the system or "structure" that frames it. Language is not a transparent window onto pre-existing concepts, but instead actively forms the realm of ideas. The base, material body of the signifier is not a secondary copy of the elevated, lofty realm of concepts: *both* are formless masses before the articulating work of language has sliced them into distinct pieces. Rather than think of language as a code for passively representing "thoughts," Saussure showed that "thoughts" take shape out of the material body of language.

Derrida's *Of Grammatology* points out that although Saussure was willing to reveal the emptiness at the heart of language, he became infuriated when he saw the same principle at work in *writing*, the system of signs created to represent speech. Saussure viewed writing as a copy of speech, an artificial technology for reproducing language. While the alphabet claims to be a phonetic transcription of spoken sounds, codes such as written English are full of irrational spellings: for example, words that sound the same but are spelled differently (*meet/meat*) and letter combinations with spurious pronunciations (*th-*, *sh-*, *-ght*). The tone of Saussure's critique escalates from mild irritation at the beginning of his argument to impassioned condemnation of the alphabet's violation of an innocent, natural speech: the "tyranny of writing" distorts its pristine referent through "orthographic monstrosities" and "phonic deformations" (30-2).

Saussure launched his attack on *phonetic* writing, the paradigmatic medium of communication in the West. He explicitly excluded pictographic and ideographic scripts from his critique. In Saussure's words, Chinese ideograms have fewer "annoying consequences" than the alphabet, because their users clearly understand their role as secondary signs for spoken words and not as language itself (26). The power (and seductiveness) of phonetic writing lies in its economy: a small number of characters can represent an infinite series of words. Unlike pictographic or ideographic scripts, phonetic writing represents the *signifier* of language (its material sound) rather than the *signified* (its conceptual meaning or "content"). Whereas an ideogram depicts a concept, phonetic characters merely indicate sound. The alphabet thus embraces the arbitrariness of the sign by considering the signifier independently of its meaning.

The alphabet cleaved language into an inside and an outside: the destiny of phonetic writing is to occupy and define the outside, to serve as a mechanical copy of the signifier that leaves intact a sacred interior. According to Derrida, the interiority, the fullness, of speech relies on the existence of an exterior, empty representation—the alphabet. Similarly, the notion of "nature" as an ideal realm separate from human production could only emerge as "civilization" was despoiling the ecological systems on which culture depends. To "deconstruct" the relationship between speech and writing is to reverse the status of the two terms, but not just to replace one with the other. Deconstruction aims to show that speech is, at bottom, characterized by the same failure to transparently reflect reality, by the same internal emptiness. There is no full or innocent speech. The fact that our culture developed a phonetic writing system—one that represents the material *signifier* in isolation from the sacred *signified*— is indicative of our primary alienation from the spoken language. Phonetic writing, because it exploits the gap between signifier and signified, is not simply a secondary reflection of language, but is a symptom of language's own lack of presence, its lack of interior self-completeness.

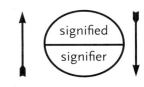

LEFT Diagram, structure of the sign, from *Course in General Linguistics*, by Ferdinand de Saussure.

RIGHT Diagram, language taking form out of the shapeless mass of sounds and concepts, from *Course in General Linguistics*, by Ferdinand de Saussure.

Derrida's final attack on the notion of writing as a secondary copy of speech is to claim, perversely, that "phonetic writing does not exist" (39). Not only does writing inhabit speech, transforming its grammar and sound, and not only does phonetic writing function as language's "own other," an "outside" manufactured to affirm its own illusory "insided-ness," but this model of the "outside" continually fails to behave in the manner expected of it. Thus where Saussure had claimed that there are only two kinds of writing—phonetic and ideographic—Derrida showed that the frontiers between them fluctuate.

Phonetic writing is full of non-phonetic elements and functions. Some signs used in conjunction with the alphabet are ideographic, including numbers and mathematical symbols. Other graphic marks cannot be called signs at all, because they do not represent distinct "signifieds" or concepts: for example, punctuation, flourishes, deletions, and patterns of difference such as roman/italic and uppercase/lowercase. What "idea" is represented by the space between two words or a dingbat at the opening of a line? Key among these non-phonetic marks are various forms of spacing—negative gaps between the positive symbols of the alphabet. According to Derrida spacing cannot be dismissed as a "simple accessory" of writing: "That a speech supposedly alive can lend itself to spacing in its own writing is what relates to its own death" (39). The alphabet has come to rely on silent graphic servants such as spacing and punctuation, which, like the frame of a picture, seem safely "outside" the internal content and structure of a work and yet are necessary conditions for making and reading.

Derrida's book *The Truth in Painting* discusses *framing* as a crucial component of works of art.[18] In the Enlightenment aesthetics of Kant, the frame of a picture belongs to a class of elements called *parerga*, meaning "about the work," or outside/around the work. Kant's list of *parerga* includes the columns on buildings, the draperies on statues, and the frames on pictures. Kant describes such framing devices as ornamental appendages to the work of art: they touch the work but remain safely outside it. Kant's aesthetics form the basis of modern art criticism, which proclaims the wholeness and self-completeness of the object.

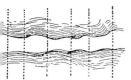

18 Derrida presents a theory of the frame in *The Truth in Painting*, trans. Geoff Bennington and Ian McLeod (Chicago: University of Chicago Press, 1987).

According to Derrida, the "quasi-detachment" and apparent self-effacement of the picture frame and other *parerga* serve both to *hide* and *reveal* the emptiness at the core of the seemingly autonomous object of aesthetic devotion. Like the non-phonetic supplements to the alphabet, the borders around images or texts are at once figure and ground, positive element and negative gap, expendable appendix and crucial support. In Derrida's words:

⌐   The *parergon*   ¬
is a form that has,
as its traditional determination,
not that it stands out
but that it disappears,
buries itself, effaces itself,
melts away at the moment it deploys its greatest energy.
The frame
is in no way a background...
but neither
is its thickness as margin a figure.
Or at least it is a figure which
⌐ comes away of its own accord (61). ¬

Spacing and punctuation, borders and frames: these are the territory of typography and graphic design, those marginal arts that render texts and images readable. The substance of typography lies not in the alphabet as such—the generic forms of characters and their conventionalized uses—but rather in the visual framework and specific graphic forms that materialize the system of writing. Design and typography work at the *edges* of writing, determining the shape and style of letters, the spaces between them, and their placement on the page. Typography, from its position at the margins of communication, has moved writing away from speech.

DESIGN AS DECONSTRUCTION

The history of typography and writing could be written as the development of formal structures that have explored the border between the inside and the outside of texts. To compile a catalogue of the micro-mechanics of publishing—indexes and title pages, captions and colophons, folios and footnotes, leading and line lengths, margins and marginalia, spacing and punctuation—would contribute to the field that Derrida called *grammatology*, the study of writing as a distinctive mode of representation. Such a history could position various typographic techniques in relation to the split between form and content, inside and outside. Some conventions have served to rationalize the delivery of information by erecting transparent "crystal goblets" around a seemingly independent, neutral body of "content." Some structures invade the sacred interior so deeply as to turn the text inside out, while others ignore or contradict the internal organization of a text in response to external pressures imposed by technology, aesthetics, corporate interests, social propriety, production conveniences, and so on.

Robin Kinross's *Modern Typography* (1992) charts the progressive rationalization of the forms and uses of letters across several centuries. Kinross's book describes printing as a prototypically "modern" process, that from its inception mobilized techniques of mass production and precipitated the mature arts and sciences. The seeds of modernization were present in Gutenberg's first proofs; their fruits are born in the self-conscious methodologies, professionalized practices, and standardized visual forms of printers and typographers, which, beginning in the late seventeenth century, replaced an older notion of printing as a hermetic art of "black magic," its methods jealously guarded by a caste of craftsmen.[19] If Kinross's history of modern typography spans five centuries, so too might a counter history of deconstruction, running alongside and beneath the erection of transparent formal structures and coherent bodies of professional knowledge.

19 Robin Kinross, *Modern Typography: An Essay in Critical History* (London: Hyphen Press, 1992). Johanna Drucker writes about the experimental and transgressive—rather than rational—side of modernism in *The Visible Word: Experimental Typography and Modern Art, 1909-1923* (Chicago: University of Chicago Press, 1994).

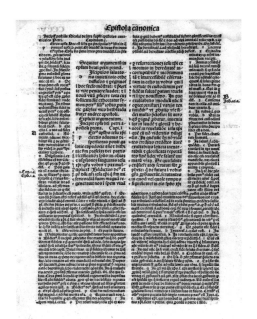

Derrida's own writing has drawn on forms of page layout from outside the conventions of university publishing. His book *Glas*, designed with Richard Eckersley at the University of Nebraska Press, consists of parallel texts set in different typefaces to suggest heterogeneous voices and modes of writing. *Glas* transforms the scholarly annotations of medieval manuscripts and the accidental juxtapositions of modern newspapers into a deliberate authorial strategy.

A study of typography and writing informed by deconstruction would examine structures that dramatize the intrusion of visual form into verbal content, the invasion of "ideas" by graphic marks, gaps, and differences. The pages at top left represent two different approaches to framing the text. In the first, the margins are a transparent border for the solid block that dominates the page. The lines of classical roman characters are minimally interrupted, preserving the text as a continuous field of letters. The second example draws on the tradition of scribal marginalia and biblical commentary. Here, typography is an interpretive medium; the text is open rather than closed. The first example suggests that the frontiers between interior and exterior, figure and ground, reader and writer, are securely defined, while the second example dramatizes such divides by engulfing the center with the edge.

Another comparison comes from the history of the newspaper, which emerged as an elite literary medium in the seventeenth century. Early English newspapers based their structure on the classical book, whose text block was designed to be read from beginning to end. As the newspaper became a popular medium in nineteenth-century Europe and America, it expanded from a book-scaled signature to a broadsheet incorporating diverse elements, from reports of crime and scandal to ads for goods and services. The modern illustrated newspaper is a patchwork of competing elements, whose juxtaposition reflects not rational hierarchies of content but struggles between editorial, advertising, and production interests. While the structure of the classical news journal aspired to the status of a coherent, complete object, the appearance of the popular paper resulted from hasty compromises and arbitrary conditions.[20]

20 On the history of the newspaper, see Allen Hutt, *The Changing Newspaper: Typographic Trends in Britain and America, 1622-1972* (London: Gordon Fraser, 1973).

21 Mitchell Stevens, "Jacques Derrida," *The New York Times Sunday Magazine* (January 23, 1994): 22-5.

Book, *Strange Attractors,* designed
by Marlene McCarty and Tibor
Kalman, 1989. The New Museum
of Contemporary Art, New York.

generic inadequation), after copulation (the positive relationship of genus to itself), another negativity works (over) the indefinite reproduction of the genus, the nonhistoricity and the faulty infinite of natural life. The genus preserves itself only by the decline and the death of individuals: old age, disease, and spontaneous death. In disease, the total organism is divided, not just differentiated, but morseled in its relationship to the inorganic, to the inorganic *Potenz*. Entering into conflict with this inorganic *Potenz*, one of the individual's systems or organs separates itself from the whole, acquires a kind of abnormal independence that injures the "fluidity" of the whole, the circulation of inner exchanges. The cause of this is an external attack originating from the inorganic, a heterogeneous "excitement (*Erregung*)." Such an appendix, laden with an enormous culture, goes back to Herodotus and Heraclitus's aphorisms on fever, makes use of all the medical learnings of the epoch, [*genre, Art*] of diseases, those of the soul, which are peculiar to man (the *Encyclopedia* proposes a discourse on madness or insanity and refers to Pinel), which can arise from fear or grief and can go even to the point of death.

The recovery process is disease itself. As for the treatise on the remedy, it largely overlaps [*déborde*] that of the illness. Like disease, the remedy is an *Erregung*, an external and aggressive excitement [*stimulation*]. The remedy always remains difficult to assimilate, is the organism's other. A counterexcitement destined to "relieve" the first attack, the remedy ought to be analyzed under the category of digestion: by essence the remedy is indigestible, "intolerable." A medicament is not digested more or less well, as the organism's absolute other, it is never digested. This limit is that of the speculative dialectics of digestion and of interiorization. The more one is raised in(to) the differentiating hierarchy of animalness, the more the easily digestible can be heterogenous to the organism, the more the organism is capable of assimilating foreign bodies or differentiated organic totalities. Conversely, at the bottom of the ladder, in the vegetal or animal life incapable of "difference in (it)self," the easily digestible can be only the homogeneous, homogeneous to (it)self, homogeneous in (it)self: water for the plants, mother's milk (predigested element) for the nurslings. The more differentiation increases, the more the stimulus must be differentiated and heterogeneous in (it)self for the organism to support it. The stimulus can be homogeneous to the organism only to the rate of an equal degree of heterogeneity: thus maternal milk, like water, would be badly tolerated by the adult. That is what Hegel says. Logically, this leads to food composed of meat for man, and even to anthropophagy: anthropophagy is conceptually required by speculative idealism. Speculative idealism even reaches its highest point in anthropophagy at the opening of *Sa*.

He makes himself "as supple as possible," twists around himself, *E tu, lenta ginestra*

The line of the parting in two not only encircles the neck [*cou*] severed by the guillotine; it overlaps the edge of the cordon (of police) that separates him, detaches him from the remain(s) of his mother to which he was nonetheless (this hanging counterpart) bound again. It/she delimits the scaffold.

Remain(s)—the mother.

However, (this hanging counterpart) two pages

example of the counsels for reading I efface all the time; as I do not cease to decapitate metalanguage; or rather to replunge its head into the text in order to extract it from the text, regularly, the interval of a respiration whoever reads *page* must gather up all that is in bed there. For example: "A while ago, in my cell, the two pimps said: 'We're making the pages.' They meant they were going to make the beds [*lits*], but a kind of luminous idea transformed me there, with my legs spread apart [*écartées*], into a husky guard or a palace groom who 'makes' a palace page just as a young man makes a chick.

—To hear this boasting made Divine swoon with pleasure, as when she disentangled—it seemed to her that she was unbuttoning a fly, that her hand, already inside, was pulling up the shirt—certain pig-latin words from their extra syllables, as an adornment [*parure*] or fancy dress [*travesti*] edbay, allbay

further on, at the penultimate sentence of the book, 'The rest, the remain(s), is unsayable'"

Book, *Glas*, by Jacques Derrida. French edition, above right, published by Éditions Galilée, Paris, 1974. English edition, left, published by University of Nebraska Press, 1986; designed by Richard Eckersley.

Book, *The Telephone Book*, by Avital Ronal, designed by Richard Eckersley, 1989. University of Nebraska Press. For one spread, Eckersley deliberately riddled the block of text with vertical gaps— such openings, called "rivers" in the argot of typography, are seen as flaws in conventional book design, which aspires to evenly colored fields of text.

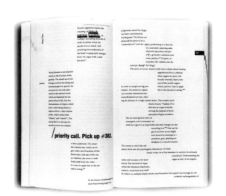

Visual "dictionaries" of page design featuring schematic diagrams of typical layouts have been a common theme in the trade literature of twentieth-century design. Jan Tschichold's 1934 manifesto "The Placing of Type in a Given Space" charts a range of subtle variations in the location of headings and body copy, while Don May's 1942 manual *101 Roughs* depicts variants of commercial page design. While Tschichold charted minor differences among clearly ordered elements, May accommodated the diverse media and competing messages found in advertising. Both theorists presented a series of formal containers for generic bodies of "content," but with a difference: Tschichold's structures aspire to be neutral frames for dominant textual figures, while May's patterns are active grounds that ignore conventional hierarchies. Included among May's deranged structures are *"Four point:* The layout touches all four sides of the space once and only once," and *"Center axis:* The heading copy, illustration, and logotype flush on alternate sides of axis."

If one pursued the study of grammatology proposed by Derrida, the resulting catalogue of forms might include the graphic conditions outlined above. In each case, we have juxtaposed a coherent, seemingly self-complete artifact with a situation where external forces interfere with content. A history of typography informed by deconstruction would show how graphic design has revealed, revised, or ignored the accepted rules of communication. Such interventions can represent either deliberate, critical confrontations or haphazard, casual encounters with the social, technological, and aesthetic pressures that shape the making of texts.

In a 1994 interview, Derrida was asked about the purported "death" of deconstruction on North American campuses. He answered, "I think there is some element in deconstruction that belongs to the structure of history or events. It started before the academic phenomenon of deconstruction, and it will continue with other names."[21] In the spirit of this statement, we are interested in de-periodizing the relevance of deconstruction. Instead of viewing it as an "ism" of the late-80s and early-90s, we see it as part of the ongoing development of design and typography as distinctive modes of representation.

21 Mitchell Stevens, "Jacques Derrida," *The New York Times Magazine* (January 23, 1994): 22-5.

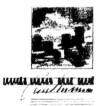
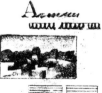
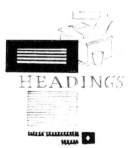
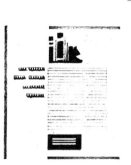

HEADINGS

TOP Page diagrams, designed by Jan Tschichold, from "The Placing of Type in a Given Space," 1934. Reprinted in *Jan Tschichold, Typographer*, Ruari McClean, ed. (Boston: David R. Godine, 1975).

BOTTOM Page diagrams, designed by Don May, 1942. From *101 Roughs* (Chicago: Frederick J. Drake & Co.).

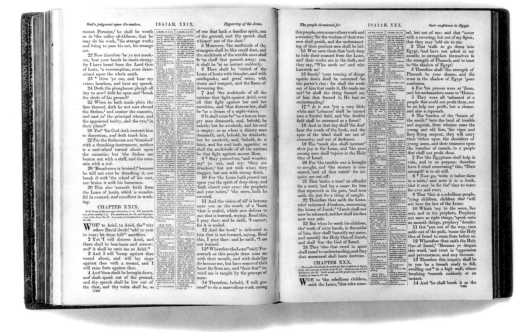

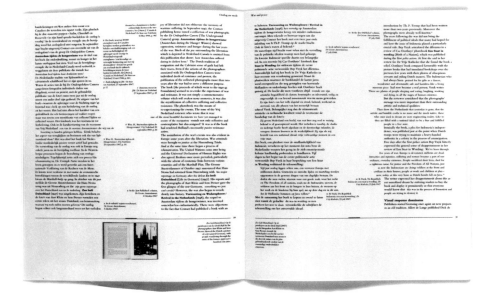

TOP Book, *The Imperial Family Bible*, 1854. Blackie and Son, Glasgow. Marginal commentary runs down the center of the page.

BOTTOM *Photography Between Covers: The Dutch Documentary Photobook after 1945,* designed by Fred Struving, 1989. Fragment Uitgeverij, Amsterdam. In this bilingual book, footnotes and other marginalia occupy the center.

But deconstruction also belongs to culture: it is an operation that has taken a name and has spun a web of influence in particular social contexts. Deconstruction has lived in a variety of institutional worlds, from university literature departments to schools of art and design to the discourse of popular journalism, where it has functioned both as a critical activity and as a banner for a range of styles. We will close our essay with an example of graphic design that directly critiques contemporary media.

Vincent Gagliostro's cover for *NYQ*, a gay and lesbian news magazine, was designed in November, 1991, in response to basketball star Magic Johnson's announcement that he is HIV-positive. Gagliostro imposed *NYQ*'s own logo and headline over a *Newsweek* cover of Magic Johnson, his arms upheld in a gesture of saintly sacrifice and athletic vigor. "He is not *our* hero," wrote NYQ over the existing text. While Gagliostro's layering and splicing of type and image are shared with more aestheticized, individualized gestures found elsewhere in contemporary design, his design did not aim to trigger an infinite variety of "personal" interpretations but instead explicitly manipulated a cultural artifact. Gagliostro's act of rewriting is a powerful response to the ubiquity of normative sign systems, showing that the structures of mass media can be reshuffled and reinhabited. The *NYQ* cover reveals and exploits the function of framing as a transformative process that refuses to remain outside the editorial content it encloses.

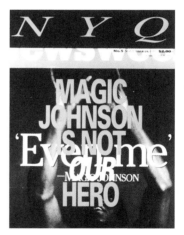

Magazine cover, *NYQ*, designed by Vincent Gagliostro, New York, 1991.

Spacing, framing, punctuation, type style, layout, and other nonphonetic structures of difference constitute the material interface of writing. Traditional literary and linguistic research overlooks such graphic forms, focusing instead on the Word as the center of communication. According to Derrida, the functions of repetition, quotation, and fragmentation that characterize writing are conditions endemic to all human expression—even the seemingly spontaneous, self-present utterances of speech or the smooth, naturalistic surfaces of painting and photography. Design can critically engage the mechanics of representation, exposing and revising its ideological biases; design also can remake the grammar of communication by discovering structures and patterns within the material media of visual and verbal writing.

Counting Sheep

A Brief History of Written Numbers

One way to write a number is to spell it out in alphabetic characters, just as one would write any other word: o-n-e. Other methods of numerical notation, however, include non-phonetic signs, which, unlike the alphabet, do not aim to reproduce the spoken word. This essay is about the relation between writing and numbers: to examine the history of numerical notation is to challenge a few basic assumptions about the nature of writing.

Many historians view phonetic scripts as the most advanced stage in the development of writing. The roman alphabet is an attempt to analyze the innumerable sounds of speech into a couple dozen signs, suited to being carved in stone or drawn on paper, and capable of indefinite preservation. Most definitions of writing take the physical permanence and phonetic fidelity of the alphabet as their model: a form of communication only qualifies as "writing" if it is a representation of speech, capable of being read back orally, as a series of words, one after the other. Writing is assumed to be *graphic,* consisting of lines drawn on a flat plane.

Techniques for visualizing numbers tend to appear in cultures long before efforts to reproduce the full spoken language. A look at several early forms of numerical notation reveals a fluid range of forms through which human cultures have attempted to depict the order—numerical and linguistic—of the world. Many of these visualizations employ concrete objects rather than graphic marks, including sticks, stones, beads, furniture, and the human body. Writing is commonly described as an inferior, secondary copy of the immediate, intuitive spoken word; some early representations of number, however, show that a culture's choice of symbols helps structure its verbal number sequence. In these cases, writing helps *give form* to the spoken language, rather than passively reproducing it.

Since the Renaissance, the infrastructure of Western civilization has consisted largely of paper. Modern Hindu-Arabic numerals appeared in India between the sixth and eighth centuries A.D., but they did not begin to compete with finger counting and the abacus in Europe until the fifteenth century: calculations on paper ultimately replaced calculations with objects. The fifteenth century also witnessed the introduction of movable type in Europe, and with it, the rise of the book and a growing dependency on paper. During the twentieth century, radio, television, and electronic media have shaken the supremacy of the book. We may find, in the multiple modes of representing numbers, an expanded definition of writing.

The English word *score* means "a cut or indentation;" it also refers to the number twenty. The word gets it double meaning from an object called a tally stick, a length of wood or bone marked with a series of scratches ▦▦▦▦▦▦. The twentieth cut on a tally stick is sometimes called a score. Tally sticks have appeared in literate and non-literate cultures from prehistory to the present; they keep time, count objects, and record credits and debts.

In the simplest form of tally, one notch is made for each item recorded: to count five sheep 🐑 🐑 🐑 🐑 🐑, a shepherd might make five scratches on a stick ▦▦▦. This principle is called *ordering*: there is a one-to-one correspondence between the set of symbols and the set of objects counted. Ordering is also at work in modern dice, where ⚄ equals five, and in playing cards, where 🂵 is the five of diamonds.

The principle of *grouping* arranges an ordered collection of signs into smaller sets. Groups on a tally stick might be indicated with larger and smaller cuts ▦▦▦, or straight lines and diagonals ▦▦▦. In a tally convention familiar today, 卌 represents five single strokes grouped in a bundle.

The ancient principles of ordering and grouping have no relation to spoken numbers, arising not from the will to record speech but from the need to keep track or "keep score" of objects or events. Whereas the Hindu-Arabic symbol 3 corresponds with the spoken number "three," a particular tick on a score pad, such as the third mark in the series 卌 , is a graphic substitute for an event (the counting of a 🐑). Linguists call this kind of mark *indexical*: there is a relationship of cause and effect between the sign and its referent, as in foot prints ⟨image⟩ or a curve mapped on a graph ⟨image⟩. The figure X, for example, is not only a phonetic letter but a sign it its own right, serving as a record or "index" of events: X stands for a signature ⟨image⟩, or X signals an act of ⟨image⟩ selection or an act of del⟨image⟩tion. X is also the roman numeral for ten.

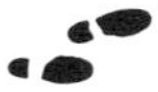

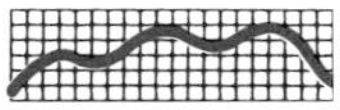

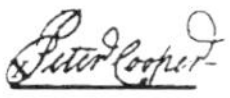

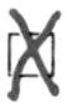

Roman numerals were the dominant written numbers in Europe from the period of the Roman empire until the rise of the Hindu-Arabic system. Employing the principles of ordering and grouping, roman numerals consist of a graphic symbol for each power of ten (I, X, C, M), and for each subdivision of five (V, L, D). The numeral III represents three as one one one, and CCC represents three hundred as hundred hundred hundred.

The forms of the roman numerals coincide with the characters of the roman alphabet, but they may actually derive from tally markings. In tallies, a single vertical mark ⟨image⟩ commonly represents one, while two diagonal cuts, such as ⟨image⟩ or ⟨image⟩, stand for five, and a crossed stroke, such as ⟨image⟩ or ⟨image⟩, indicates ten. The roman numeral D is half of the symbol ⟨image⟩, an ancient form of the sign for one thousand. The roman numerals may thus originate from a pre-alphabetic style of writing.

"After all the natural way to count is not that

one and one make two

but to go on counting by one and one....

One and one and one and one.

That is the natural way to go on counting."

GERTRUDE STEIN

The English word *calculate* comes from the Latin *calculus*, meaning "small stone." Like tally sticks, stones are an ancient counting tool which, in their simplest application, require no verbal number sequence to operate: one stone is collected 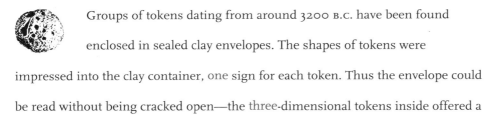 for every object counted . A counting technique used by the Sumerians beginning around 8000 B.C. involved small "tokens" manufactured out of clay . Invented during the period when agriculture was supplanting an economy of hunting and gathering, tokens probably recorded business transactions between such parties as the temple government and a shepherd in charge of some .

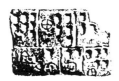

Groups of tokens dating from around 3200 B.C. have been found enclosed in sealed clay envelopes. The shapes of tokens were impressed into the clay container, one sign for each token. Thus the envelope could be read without being cracked open—the three-dimensional tokens inside offered a hidden guarantee for the graphic signs on the outside.

Soon, however, the marks impressed into the envelopes replaced the tokens altogether, and records were kept on small clay tablets instead. The production of tokens appears to have ceased around 3100 B.C., when a system for graphically recording the spoken language was emerging in Sumeria. The new script retained some symbols from the older token system, but a basic conceptual change took place.

"What is logic?
To me two and two equals twenty-two, not four."

MAN RAY

Each token had represented a quantity of a particular product: a clay disc marked ⊕, for example, stood for 🐑, and could not be used to count any other kind of object. The collection ⊕ ⊕ ⊕ ⊕ ⊕ signified 🐑🐑🐑🐑🐑: number and object were fused together. The new writing system, however, paired a separate number symbol with a sign for the object, so that ⟦⊕⟧ meant five 🐑. The number symbol, meaning five, might be paired with the sign for any object. Number was now independent from things: with the rise of written language came a move away from concrete thought and toward abstraction.

Modern English contains a few words that signify a plurality of particular objects: a flock of 🐑🐑🐑, a herd of 🐄🐄🐄, or a school of 🐟🐟🐟. The English word *pair* names objects or groups of objects to which doubleness is a natural state: a pair of 👢👢, a pair of ◁◁, a pair of ⚬⚬. Modern Japanese has separate "number classes" for different objects; words called "counters" are inserted between the number word and the name of the object counted: for example, *dai* for vehicles, *hai* for glassfuls, *ma* for rooms, *mai* for thin, flat objects, *hon* for long, cylindrical objects, *go o-sya* for train car numbers, and so on. Linguists consider conventions such as these remnants of an older, less abstract stage of thought, which conceived of number as an integral characteristic of the objects being counted.

"The depicting of objects
            is appropriate to a savage people;
            signs of words to a barbaric people;
            and the alphabet to a civilized people."

J.J. ROUSSEAU

Most verbal number sequences are organized into groups of ten; they are called "base ten." A number sequence can be devised with any other base, such as five or twelve; digital computers, for example, use base two numbers, which employ the most minimal set of symbols possible, zero and one, on and off. Yet no culture has been known to spontaneously generate binary numbers; most cultures use ten. Why would the human mind be almost universally compelled to generate number sequences 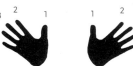 with a base ten structure? The answer lies not in the mind but in the body.

Human hands, equipped with ten fingers, are convenient devices for counting and calculating. Numerous cultures use the hands and feet, fingers and toes, as the basis of number systems. Aztec numeration is base twenty; thus thirty is expressed verbally as "twenty plus one," and forty is "two times twenty." The modern French word 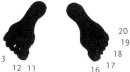 *quatre-vignt*, which means "four twenties," is equivalent to the English eighty. The human body readily suggests counting in fives, tens, and twenties: our word *digit* comes from the Latin *digitus,* meaning "finger or toe."

Europeans initially distrusted the zero.
A fifteenth-century French writer complained,

"Just as the rag doll wanted to be an eagle,

the donkey a lion,

and the monkey a queen,

the *cifra* [zero] put on airs and pretended to be

a digit."

The whole body can become a set of symbols for representing numbers. A technique used by the Papuan natives of the Torres Strait assigns numerical values to positions on the body. The verbal words identifying the numbers are each names for body parts, and some of the words appear more than once.

For example, the word *doro* refers to fingers from both the right and left hands, and thus its numerical value in any instance would be made evident only if the "speaker" were also pointing to a body part. Thus the verbal names have a nonverbal source, and cannot function alone.

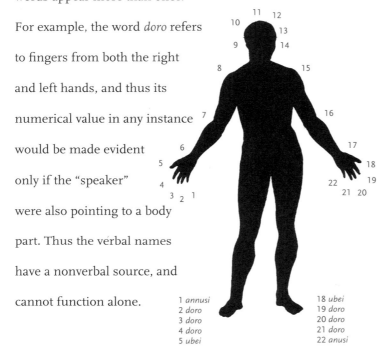

1 *annusi*
2 *doro*
3 *doro*
4 *doro*
5 *ubei*

18 *ubei*
19 *doro*
20 *doro*
21 *doro*
22 *anusi*

In its simplest form, finger counting relies on the principle of ordering: seven fingers for seven sheep. In the body system at left, each body part stands for a unique step in a sequence; it represents a *position* in a series rather than a concrete object.

In Europe, hand counting systems capable of representing numbers in the thousands and tens of thousands were widely used until the ascendence of Hindu-Arabic numerals; the body provided a numerical vocabulary "spoken" by hand in both the monastery and the marketplace. Writing is generally defined as a method for depicting *speech*, yet the recurrence of the base ten sequence suggests that when representing numbers, speech followed an example offered by non-verbal expression.

ABACUS

The *abacus,* used for counting and computing in ancient Greece and Rome, remained powerful until the rise of Hindu-Arabic numerals during the Renaissance. The abacus has had a longer life in China and Japan, where it is still used alongside the electronic calculator.

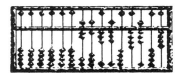

7 6 3, 8 0 4, 8 0 4

On an abacus, each string of beads represents a power of ten, and each bead is a unit. The horizontal division indicates groups of five, allowing a number to be represented with fewer beads. Adding and subtracting with an abacus involves manipulating physical objects rather than abstract signs—the concreteness of the abacus makes it useful for teaching children arithmetic. The Latin word *abacus* also means "table": an abacus often consisted of a table that was cut with grooves or simply marked with chalk lines, on which discs called "counters" were

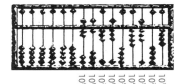

moved about. Called "counting tables," such numerical furniture was used widely throughout Europe for both commercial and scholarly arithmetic. Like Hindu-Arabic numerals, an abacus indicates powers of ten by position. A major difference between the abacus and Hindu-Arabic numerals is how to represent the *absence* of digits in a power of ten. The abacus achieved this quite sensibly: an empty column. The Hindu-Arabic system could not use an empty column, however, because a gap in a row of digits would indicate two distinct numbers.

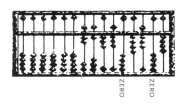

ZERO ZERO

Thus a symbol was invented to represent an empty set: the zero. The Hindu-Arabic system became the numerical equivalent of the alphabet: abstract, concise, graphic. With the rise of the new numerals, the tradition of "writing" with objects began to disappear.

SOURCES This essay relies on Georges Ifrah, *From One to Zero: A Universal History of Numbers* (New York: Viking Penguin, 1981, 1985), and Karl Menninger, *Number Words and Number Symbols: A Cultural History of Numbers* (Cambridge: MIT Pres, 1958, 1969). On Sumerian tokens, see Denise Schmandt-Besserat, "Tokens: Facts and Interpretations," *Visible Language*, Vol. XX, No. 3 (Summer 1986): 250-273.

Learning of the Latin and Greek Languages, the Knowledge of which, is abfolutely neceffary for fome Profeffions in civil Life, as well as for Perfons intended for the Service of the Church ; and ought to be the Study of every Gentleman, as he cannot be faid to have a liberal Education, or a Place among the Learned, who is a Stranger to them.   But what I would (agreeable to the moft judicious Writers on Education) contend for, is, that there is Time enough for teaching Youth the dead Languages, without neglecting the Study of their own, or excluding real and ufeful Knowledge ; and that of all Grammars that of their own Language ought chiefly to be minded.

Let us hear what the judicious Author of an anonymous Letter in Turnbull's Obfervations on a liberal Education fays, concerning the Study of the Englifh Language.   Speaking of the Education of Greece, whofe Youth were taught to write their own Language more accurately than we are Latin and Greek, afks, " But where is " Englifh taught at prefent ? Who thinks it " of Ufe to ftudy correctly that Language " which he is to ufe every Day in his Life, " be his Station ever fo high, or ever fo " infignificant.   It is in this the Nobility " and Gentry defend their Country, and " ferve their Prince in Parliament ; in this " the Lawyers plead, the Divines inftruct, " and

" and all Ranks of People write their Let- " ters, and transact all their Affairs ; and " yet who thinks it worth his Learning to " write this even accurately, not to fay po- " litely ? Every one is fuffered to form his " Style by Chance ; to imitate the firft " wretched Model that falls in his Way, " before he knows what is Faulty, or can " relifh the Beauties of a juft Simplicity. " Few think their Children qualified for a " Trade, till they have been whipped at a " Latin School for five or fix Years to " learn a little of that which they are " obliged to forget, when in thofe Years " right Education would have improved " their Minds, and taught them to acquire " Habits of writing their own Language " eafily under right Direction ; and this " would have been ufeful to them as long " as they lived."

The fame Writer, after making Obfervations on fome other effential Parts of Education, refumes the Subject of an Englifh one, as an Affair of the utmoft Confequence.   " Particularly, fays he, I fhould " think teaching them to write and fpeak " correctly and fluently in their own Lan- " guage, is the moft important Inftruction. " One Exercife fhould be daily to write a " Page of Englifh, and after that to exa- " mine every Word by the Grammar " Rules ; and in every Sentence they have " compofed

Book, *The British Grammar*, by James Buchanan. Published by A. Millar in the Strand, London, 1762. Reproduced in facsimile by Scolar Press, Menston, England, 1968. The use of quotation marks to frame a field of quoted matter was common in eighteenth-century typography.

Period Styles

A Punctuated History

GREEK AND LATIN MANUSCRIPTS WERE USUALLY WRITTEN WITH NO SPACE BETWEEN WORDS UNTIL AROUND THE NINTH CENTURY AD ALTHOUGH· ROMAN·INSCRIPTIONS·LIKE·THE·FAMOUS·TRAJAN·COLUMN·SOMETIMES· SEPARATED·WORDS·WITH·A·CENTERED·DOT·   EVEN AFTER SPACING BECAME COMMON IT REMAINED HAPHAZARD   FOREXAMPLE OFTEN A PREPOSITION WAS LINKEDTO ANOTHER WORD   EARLY GREEK WRITING RAN IN LINES ALTERNATING FROM LEFT TO RIGHT AND RIGHT TO LEFT   THIS CONVENTION WAS CALLED BOUSTREPHEDON MEANING AS THE OX PLOWS   IT WAS CONVENIENT FOR LARGE CARVED MONUMENTS   BUT BOUSTREPHEDON HINDERED THE READING AND WRITING OF SMALLER TEXTS AND SO THE LEFT TO RIGHT DIRECTION BECAME DOMINANT   A CENTERED DOT DIVID· ED WORDS WHICH SPLIT AT THE END OF A LINE IN EARLY GREEK AND LATIN MANUSCRIPTS   IN THE ELEVENTH CENTURY A MARK SIMILAR TO THE MOD- ERN HYPHEN WAS INTRODUCED   MEDIEVAL SCRIBES OFTEN FILLED‡°/‡°(;](;] SHORT LINES WITH MARKS AND ORNAMENTS   THE PERFECTLY JUSTIFIED LINE BECAME THE STANDARD AFTER THE INVENTION OF PRINTING THE EARLIEST GREEK LITERARY TEXTS WERE DIVIDED INTO UNITS WITH A HORIZONTAL LINE CALLED A PARAGRAPHOS   PARAGRAPHING REMAINS OUR CENTRAL METHOD OF ORGANIZING PROSE AND YET ALTHOUGH PARAGRAPHS ARE ANCIENT THEY ARE NOT GRAMMATICALLY ESSENTIAL THE CORRECTNESS OF A PARAGRAPH IS A MATTER OF STYLE HAVING NO STRICT RULES

LATER GREEK DOCUMENTS SOMETIMES MARKED PARAGRAPHS BY PLACING THE FIRST LETTER OF THE NEW LINE IN THE MARGIN   THIS LETTER COULD BE ENLARGED COLORED OR ORNATE

TODAY THE OUTDENT IS OFTEN USED FOR LISTS WHOSE ITEMS ARE IDENTIFIED ALPHABETICALLY AS IN DICTIONARIES OR BIBLIOGRAPHIES ¶ A MARK CALLED CAPITULUM WAS INTRODUCED IN EARLY LATIN MANUSCRIPTS ¶ IT FUNCTIONED VARIOUSLY AS A POINTER OR SEPARATOR ¶ IT USUALLY OCCURRED INSIDE A RUNNING BLOCK OF TEXT WHICH DID NOT BREAK ONTO A NEW LINE ¶ THIS TECHNIQUE SAVED SPACE ¶ IT ALSO PRESERVED THE VISUAL DENSITY OF THE PAGE WHICH EMULATED THE CONTINUOUS UNBROKEN FLOW OF SPEECH

BY THE SEVENTEENTH CENTURY THE INDENT WAS THE STANDARD PARAGRAPH BREAK IN WESTERN PROSE THE RISE OF PRINTING ENCOURAGED THE USE OF SPACE TO ORGANIZE TEXTS A GAP IN A PRINTED PAGE FEELS MORE DELIBERATE THAN A GAP IN A MANUSCRIPT BECAUSE IT IS MADE BY A SLUG OF LEAD RATHER THAN A FLUX IN HANDWRITING

EVEN AFTER THE ASCENDENCE OF THE INDENT THE CAPITULUM REMAINED IN USE FOR IDENTIFYING SECTIONS AND CHAPTERS ALONG WITH OTHER MARKS LIKE THE SECTION § THE DAGGER † THE DOUBLE DAGGER ‡ THE ASTERISK ＊ AND NUMEROUS LESS CONVENTIONAL ORNAMENTS § SUCH MARKS HAVE BEEN USED SINCE THE MIDDLE AGES FOR CITING PASSAGES AND KEYING MARGINAL REFERENCES † THE INVENTION OF PRINTING MADE MORE ELABORATE AND PRECISE REFERENCING POSSIBLE BECAUSE THE PAGES OF A TEXT WERE CONSISTENT FROM ONE COPY TO THE NEXT ‡

ALL PUNCTUATION WAS USED IDIOSYNCRATICALLY UNTIL AFTER THE INVENTION OF PRINTING WHICH REVOLUTIONIZED WRITING BY DISSEMI-

NATING GRAMMATICAL AND TYPOGRAPHICAL STANDARDS BEFORE PRINTING PUNCTUATION VARIED WILDLY FROM REGION TO REGION AND SCRIBE TO SCRIBE THE LIBRARIAN AT ALEXANDRIA WHO WAS NAMED ARISTOPHANES DESIGNED A GREEK PUNCTUATION SYSTEM CIRCA 260 BC HIS SYSTEM MARKED THE SHORTEST SEGMENTS OF DISCOURSE WITH A CENTERED DOT · CALLED A COMMA · AND MARKED THE LONGER SECTIONS WITH A LOW DOT CALLED A COLON . A HIGH DOT SET OFF THE LONGEST UNIT · HE CALLED IT PERIODOS · THE THREE DOTS WERE EASILY DISTINGUISHED FROM ONE ANOTHER BECAUSE ALL THE LETTERS WERE THE SAME HEIGHT · PROVIDING A CONSISTENT FRAME OF REFERENCE · LIKE A MUSICAL STAFF ·

ALTHOUGH THE TERMS COMMA · COLON · AND PERIOD PERSIST · THE SHAPE OF THE MARKS AND THEIR FUNCTION TODAY ARE DIFFERENT · DURING THE SEVENTH AND EIGHTH CENTURIES NEW MARKS APPEARED IN SOME MANUSCRIPTS INCLUDING THE SEMICOLON ; THE INVERTED SEMI-COLON ; AND A QUESTION MARK THAT RAN HORIZONTALLY ⸴ A THIN DIAGONAL SLASH / CALLED A VIRGULE / WAS SOMETIMES USED LIKE A COMMA IN MEDIEVAL MANUSCRIPTS AND EARLY PRINTED BOOKS . SUCH MARKS ARE THOUGHT TO HAVE BEEN CUES FOR READING ALOUD ; THEY INDICATED A RISING , FALLING , OR LEVEL TONE OF VOICE . THE USE OF PUNCTUATION BY SCRIBES AND THEIR INTERPRETATION BY READERS WAS BY NO MEANS CONSISTENT , HOWEVER , AND MARKS MIGHT BE ADDED TO A MANUSCRIPT BY ANOTHER SCRIBE WELL AFTER IT WAS WRITTEN .

EARLY PUNCTUATION WAS LINKED TO ORAL DELIVERY. FOR EXAMPLE THE TERMS COMMA, COLON, AND PERIODOS, AS THEY WERE USED BY ARISTO-PHANES, COME FROM THE THEORY OF RHETORIC, WHERE THEY REFER TO RHYTHMICAL UNITS OF SPEECH. AS A SOURCE OF RHETORICAL RATHER THAN

GRAMMATICAL CUES, PUNCTUATION SERVED TO REGULATE PACE AND GIVE EMPHASIS TO PARTICULAR PHRASES, RATHER THAN TO MARK THE LOGICAL STRUCTURE OF SENTENCES. MANY OF THE PAUSES IN RHETORICAL DELIVERY, HOWEVER, NATURALLY CORRESPOND WITH GRAMMATICAL STRUCTURE: FOR EXAMPLE, WHEN A PAUSE FALLS BETWEEN TWO CLAUSES OR SENTENCES.

THE SYSTEM OF ARISTOPHANES WAS RARELY USED BY THE GREEKS, BUT IT WAS REVIVED BY THE LATIN GRAMMARIAN DONATUS IN THE FOURTH CENTURY A.D. ACCORDING TO DONATUS PUNCTUATION SHOULD FALL WHEREVER THE SPEAKER WOULD NEED A MOMENT'S REST; IT PROVIDED BREATHING CUES FOR READING ALOUD. SOME LATER WRITERS MODIFIED THE THEORIES OF DONATUS, RETURNING TO A RHETORICAL APPROACH TO PUNCTUATION, IN WHICH THE MARKS SERVED TO CONTROL RHYTHM AND EMPHASIS. AFTER THE INVENTION OF PRINTING, GRAMMARIANS BEGAN TO BASE PUNCTUATION ON STRUCTURE RATHER THAN ON SPOKEN SOUND: MARKS SUCH AS THE COMMA, COLON, AND PERIOD SIGNALLED SOME OF THE GRAMMATICAL PARTS OF A SENTENCE. THUS PUNCTUATION CAME TO BE DEFINED ARCHITECTURALLY RATHER THAN ORALLY. THE COMMA BECAME A MARK OF SEPARATION, AND THE SEMICOLON WORKED AS A JOINT BETWEEN INDEPENDENT CLAUSES; THE COLON INDICATED GRAMMATICAL DISCONTINUITY: WRITING WAS SLOWLY DISTANCED FROM SPEECH.

RHETORIC, STRUCTURE, AND PACE ARE ALL AT WORK IN MODERN ENGLISH PUNCTUATION, WHOSE RULES WERE ESTABLISHED BY THE END OF THE EIGHTEENTH CENTURY. ALTHOUGH STRUCTURE IS THE STRONGEST RATIONALE TODAY, PUNCTUATION REMAINS A LARGELY INTUITIVE ART. A WRITER CAN OFTEN CHOOSE AMONG SEVERAL CORRECT WAYS TO PUNCTUATE A PASSAGE, EACH WITH A SLIGHTLY DIFFERENT RHYTHM AND MEANING.

THERE WAS NO CONSISTENT MARK FOR QUOTATIONS BEFORE THE SEV-
ENTEENTH CENTURY. DIRECT SPEECH WAS USUALLY ANNOUNCED ONLY BY
PHRASES LIKE HE SAID. ,,SOMETIMES A DOUBLE COMMA WAS USED IN MAN-
USCRIPTS TO POINT OUT IMPORTANT SENTENCES AND WAS LATER USED TO
ENCLOSE "QUOTATIONS." ENGLISH PRINTERS BEFORE THE NINETEENTH
" CENTURY OFTEN EDGED ONE MARGIN OF A QUOTE WITH DOUBLE COMMAS.
" THIS CONVENTION PRESENTED TEXT AS A SPATIAL PLANE RATHER THAN A
" TEMPORAL LINE, FRAMING THE QUOTED PASSAGE LIKE A PICTURE.
" PRINTING, BY PRODUCING IDENTICAL COPIES OF A TEXT, ENCOURAGED
" THE STANDARDIZATION OF QUOTATION MARKS. PRINTED BOOKS COM-
" MONLY INCORPORATED MATERIAL FROM OTHER SOURCES.

BOTH THE GREEK AND ROMAN ALPHABETS WERE ORIGINALLY MAJUS-
CULE: ALL LETTERS WERE THE SAME HEIGHT. greek and roman minuscule
letters developed out of rapidly written scripts called cursive, which were
used for business correspondence. minuscule characters have limbs
extending above and below a uniform body. alcuin, advisor to charle-
magne, introduced the "carolingian" minuscule, which spread rapidly
through europe between the eighth and twelfth centuries. during the dis-
semination of the carolingian script, condensed, black minuscule styles of
handwriting, now called "gothic," were also developing; they eventually
replaced the classical carolingian.

A carolingian manuscript sometimes marked the beginning of a
sentence with an enlarged letter. This character was often a majuscule,
presaging the modern use of minuscule and majuscule as double features
of the same alphabet. Both scripts were still considered separate manners
of writing, however.

"As he Sets on, he [the printer] considers
how to Point his Work,
viz. when to Set, where; where. where to make ( ) where [ ]
and when to make a Break....
When he meets with proper Names of Persons or Places
he Sets them in Italick...
and Sets the first Letter with a Capital,
or as the Person or Place he finds
the purpose of the Author to dignifie, all Capitals;
but then, if he conveniently can,
he will Set a Space between every Letter...
to make it shew more Graceful and Stately."

JOSEPH MOXON 1683

In the fifteenth century, the Carolingian script was revived by the Italian humanists. The new script, called "lettera antica," was paired with classical roman capitals. It became the basis of the roman typefaces, which were established as a European norm by the mid-sixteenth century. The terms "uppercase" and "lowercase" refer to the drawers in a printing shop that hold the two fonts. Until recently, Punctuation was an Intuitive Art, ruled by convenience and Intuition. A Printer could Liberally Capitalize the Initial of Any word She deemed worthy of Distinction, as well as Proper Names. The printer was Free to set some Words entirely in C A P I T A L S and to add further emphasis with extra S P A C E S.

The roman typefaces were based on a formal script used for books. *The cursive, rapidly written version of the Carolingian minuscule was employed for business and also for books sold in the less expensive writing shops. Called "antica corsiva" or "cancelleresca," this style of handwriting was the model for the italic typefaces cut for Aldus Manutius in Venice in 1500. Aldus Manutius was a scholar, printer, and businessman. Italic script conserved space, and Aldus developed it for his internationally distributed series of small, inexpensive books. The Aldine italic was paired with Roman capitals. The Italian typo-*

grapher Tagliente advocated Italic Capitals in the early sixteenth century. Aldus set entire books in italic; it was an autonomous type style, unrelated to roman. In France, however, the roman style was becoming the neutral, generic norm, with *italic* played against it for *contrast*. The pairs UPPER-CASE/lowercase and roman/*italic* each add an inaudible, non-phonetic dimension to the alphabet. Before *italic* became the official auxiliary of roman, scribes and printers had other techniques for marking emphasis, including enlarged, **heavy**, colored, or **gothic** letters. Underlining appeared in some medieval manuscripts, and today it is the conventional substitute for italics in handwritten and typewritten texts. S p a c e is sometimes inserted between letters to declare e m p h a s i s in German and Eastern European book t y p o g r a p h y . **Boldface** fonts were not common until the nineteenth century, when display advertising created a demand for **big, black** types. Most book faces designed since the early twentieth century belong to families of four: roman, *italic*, **bold roman**, and ***bold italic***. These are used for systematically marking different kinds of copy, such as headings, captions, body text, notes, and references.

Since the rise of digital production, printed texts have become more visually elaborate—typographic variations are now routinely available to writers and designers. Some recent fonts contain only ornaments and symbols; Carlos Segura's typeface Dingura (𐊶𐊢 𐊱𐊪𐊤𐊽 𐊲𐊢 𐊹𐊾 𐊿 𐊹𐊤 𐊢𐊾 𐊾) consists of mysterious runes that recall the era of manuscript production. During the e-mail incunabula, writers and designers have been using punctuation marks for expressive ends. Punctuated portraits found in electronic correspondence range from the simple "smiley" :-) to such subtle constructions as $-) [yuppie] or :-I [indifferent].

Otto Neurath, *International Picture Language*, 1936. Modeling Isotype after language, Neurath showed how to build compound signs out of elementary units. Neurath's work extended beyond the design of symbols, however, to include the use of icons in statistical charts. His theory of information design included the search for ways to organize information that maximize their visual impact. Collection of Smithsonian Institution Libraries, Cooper-Hewitt, National Design Museum.

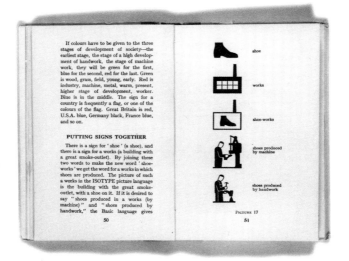

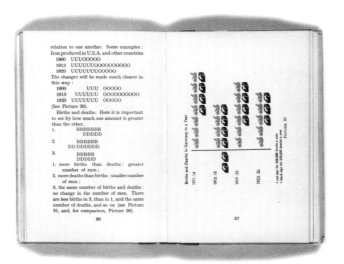

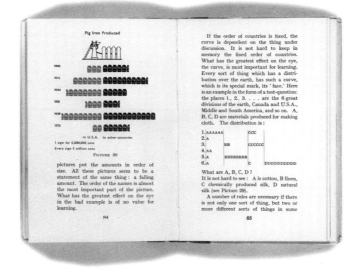

Modern Hieroglyphs

[symbol] and [symbol] are from the standard symbol set designed by Cook & Shanosky Associates in collaboration with the American Institute of Graphic Arts in 1974. [symbol] and [symbol] are endorsed by the U.S. Department of Transportation (D.O.T.). They belong to an international hiero-glyphics of public infomation.* Their ancestors, [symbol] and [symbol], were created by the Viennese philosopher and social scientist Otto Neurath in the 1920s. Neurath and his colleagues con-structed a universe of people [symbol], [symbol], [symbol], [symbol], [symbol], places [symbol], objects [symbol], [symbol], [symbol], and actions [symbol], [symbol], [symbol]. He called his system Isotype [symbol], the International System of TYpographic Picture Education.**

Although Neurath advocated the use of [symbol] in transportation signs, his primary interest was in presenting social statistics in textbooks, posters, and educational museums. In Neurath's charts, a given symbol, such as [symbol], represented a quantity of people or things; a series ([symbol] [symbol] [symbol] [symbol]) of symbols represented a larger number of objects. Thus a visual, perceptual Gestalt replaced abstract numerals in [symbol] charts. Anticipating Edward Tufte's later writings on the display of data, Neurath developed practical guides for representing **#**'s in a visually accessible way.

As a member of the Vienna Circle of philosophers in the 1920s, Otto Neurath was a founder of logical positivism, a theory that brought together two opposing modes of inquiry: *rationalism*, which studies reality through logic, geometry, and mathematics; and *empiricism* (or positivism), which claims that observation is the key to knowledge. ✱✱✱ The ◁ and its associated equipment—such as ⚗ and 🔬—are the primary tools of empirical knowledge. The logical positivists attempted to analyze language into a minimal set of direct experiences, claiming that all languages can be reduced to a core of observations, such as big, small, ᵘᵖ, ₍down₎, red, or **black**. With 🔲, Neurath translated a philosophical theory into a visual practice. The sign 👤 is *positive* because as a picture, it is based in observation; 👤 is *logical* because it concentrates the details of experience into a schematic mark. Neurath aimed to combine the mechanical empiricism of photography 🖼 with the rational structures of mathematics and geometry ●.

Although Neurath believed that pictures are objective and universal, the meanings of international signs are culturally specific. We understand, for example, that 👤 and 👩 represent *lavatory for men* and *lavatory for women*. Yet the reference to toilets is left unstated. A functional description, such as 👤 and 🚻, might denote the difference between these facilities more directly, but the signs' conventional meaning still would have to be learned.

We distinguish 👤 as male because he is contrasted against the figure 👩, whose gender is marked by a stylized reference to a garment sometimes worn by Western women. In the D.O.T. system, 👤 refers to "people" in general except where he is contrasted with 👩. Thus 🚰 does not mean *drinking fountain for men;* nor does 🛗 mean *elevator for men;* and nor does the sign 🪑 mean *waiting room for men*—👤 stands in for *man* generically. The only place 👩 appears in the D.O.T. system besides on lavatory doors is in 🎫, the sign for *ticket sales.* Here, where one person is offering a service to another, the designers deemed it appropriate to show 👩 assisting 👤.

The stylistic principles of Neurath's 🏛 remain the basis of international pictograms today: *reduction* and *consistency*. Many Isotype signs are flat shapes with little or no interior detail, as in 🔨, 🐓, and ☎. These flat silhouettes suggest a rationalized theater of shadows, in which signs appear to be the natural imprints of material objects—Plato's cave renovated into an empiricist 🔬 laboratory. When depth is expressed in 🏛, isometric drawings 📚 are used instead of traditional perspective. Parallel lines do not converge, and dimension is fixed from foreground 🕯 to background.

Consistency governs the stylistic uniformity of a symbol set. The D.O.T. system, for example, is a world of coordinated objects, including 🚬, 🚕, 🚗, 🍴, and 🛏. The sign system designed for the Munich Olympics in 1972 was the semiotic climax of international pictures: a geometric body alphabet 🏃 is deployed on a consistent grid: 🤼, 🏃, 🏊, 🤸, 🤼, 🤾, and 🤹.

The reduction and consistency of international pictures heighten their alphabetic quality. Neurath's 🚶 and 🧍 were a critique of writing that resembled writing, a utopian effort to transcend the limitations of letters by exploiting the visual characteristics of typography. **★★★★** Neurath's preferred typeface was **Futura**, designed by Paul Renner around 1926-27. Paralleling the machine aesthetic in architecture and industrial design, **Futura** is stripped of references to handicraft and calligraphy. Neurath conceived of 🏛 as clean, logical, free of redundancy: writing as a machine 🛁 for living in.

The current figure 🚶 might be called **Helvetica Man**, his style coordinating with the favorite typeface of post-war institutional design culture. A more inclusive pictographic landscape might be inhabited by variants of **Helvetica Man** that harmonize with other typefaces, such as Serif Man ⋔, *Italic Man* ⋔ and *Cursive Man* ⋔.

⋔ and ⋔ are neither universal, self-evident, nor purely informational—like linguistic signs, they must be learned; like other styles of drawing, they are culturally specific. When we see ⋔ engraved over an airport door, we know she belongs to the language of public information, not the language of commerce. Thus we do not mistake ⋔ for, say, *brothel*, where ⋔ might purchase the services of ⋔. The clean, geometric character of ⋔ and ⋔ is loaded with cultural associations—"public," "neutral," "modern."

An international picture functions as a memento, a token for memory, a souvenir for words. ⅋ is *restaurant* as ⅄ is *Paris*. The very American Ⅴ is hardly the geometric essence of *drinking alcohol in airports*, but like ⅄, a cocktail is a useful cliché for storing a range of experiences. Likewise, ⅋, ⅋, ⅋, ⅋, ⅋ and ⅋, taken from different international picture sets, are helpful tags for remembering objects we tend to forget.

Otto Neurath believed that ⅋ could transcend national boundaries and unify global social life. By translating a philosophical theory into a popular medium, he fathered a new breed of **ABCs**, whose progeny have populated public spaces across the industrial world. Since the birth of Neurath's ⅋ and ⅋, designers and critics have framed new questions about visual and verbal writing that acknowledge the cultural basis of images, symbols, and experience. As we rethink the boundaries between words and pictures, Otto Neurath could serve as a model for the graphic designer of the next millennium, ⅋ the language worker equipped to use design and theory as tools for unearthing new questions and ⅋ constructing new answers. **★★★★★**

✳ This essay is based on research and writing initiated at The Cooper Union in 1986, with the exhibition *Global Signage: Semiotics and the Language of International Pictures*, curated by Ellen Lupton. The essay "Reading Isotype" was published in *Design Issues* III/2 (1986): 47-58; and in *Design Discourse*, ed. Victor Margolin (Chicago: University of Chicago Press, 1989). The global iconography of pictograms and logotypes was further explored by Ellen Lupton and J. Abbott Miller in "Critical Wayfinding," *The Edge of the Millennium*, ed. Susan Yelavich (New York: Whitney Library of Design, 1993), 220-32.

The pictorial symbols endorsed by the D.O.T. are documented in *Symbol Signs* (New York: American Institute of Graphic Arts, 1974). International symbols became a major interest of modernist graphic designers during the 1960s and 70s. Martin Krampen surveyed the theory and practice of the movement in "Signs and Symbols in Graphic Communication," *Design Quarterly* 62 (1965). *Print* devoted a special issue to the subject, November/December, 1962. On signage for the Olympic games, see Heiner Jacob and Masaru Katzumie, "Sign Systems for International Events," *Print* (November/December 1969): 40. The industrial designer Henry Dreyfuss published the encyclopedic *Symbol Source Book: An Authoritative Guide to International Graphic Symbols* in 1972 (New York: McGraw-Hill); an archive of his research materials is housed at Cooper-Hewitt, National Design Museum.

✳✳ Otto Neurath's colleagues included his wife, Marie Neurath, the Dutch graphic designer Gerd Arntz, and the American graphic designer Rudolf Modley, who brought Isotype to the United States after working with Neurath in Vienna. The Otto and Marie Neurath Collection is housed at the Reading University Library, Reading, Great Britain. Neurath's writings on Isotype include *International Picture Language* (Reading: Reading University, 1980), facsimile of the 1936 edition; *Basic by Isotype* (London: Kegan Paul, 1937); and "From Vienna Method to Isotype," in *Empiricism and Sociology*, ed. Marie Neurath and Robert S. Cohen (Dordrecht, Holland: D. Reidel, 1973). Critical works on Neurath and Isotype include *Graphic Communication through Isotype*, ed. Michael Twyman (Reading: Reading University, 1975), 7-17; and Robin Kinross, "On the Influence of Isotype," *Information Design Journal* II/2 (1981): 122-30. Works by Rudolf Modley include *How to Use Pictorial Statistics* (New York: Harper and Brothers, 1937); *A History of the War, In Maps, In Pictographs, In Words* (New York: Penguin, 1943); and *Handbook of Pictorial Symbols* (New York: Dover, 1976).

✳✳✳ Neurath explained his philosophy in "Empirical Sociology: The Scientific Content of History and Political Economy," in *Empiricism and Sociology*, cited above. On logical positivism, see Peter Halfpenny, *Positivism and Sociology: Explaining Social Life* (London: George Allen and Unwin, 1982).
On Neurath and his context, see William M. Johnston, "The Eclipse of a Universal Man," in *The Austrian Mind: An Intellectual and Social History, 1848-1938* (Berkeley: University of California Press, 1972), 192-95.

✳✳✳✳ Attempts to reform the alphabet into a more accurate reflection of speech were documented by Herbert Spencer in *The Visible Word* (New York: Hastings House, 1968). Herbert Bayer discussed his own writing reform efforts in "Basic Alphabet," *Print* (May/June 1964): 16-20. Charles Bliss proposed a new hieroglyphic script in which each character would "show the outline of the real thing, directly connected with meaning" in *Semantography (Blissymbolics)* (Coogee, Australia: Semantography Publications, 1949).

✳✳✳✳✳ Whereas Otto Neurath saw pictorial communication as an antidote to writing, other writers and designers have addressed the overlaps between visual and verbal forms. On rhetoric and visual practices, see Roland Barthes, "The Rhetoric of the Image," in *Image/Music/Text*, trans. Stephen Heath (New York: Hill and Wang, 1977); Gui Bonsieppe, "Visual/Verbal Rhetoric," *Ulm* 14/16 (1965): 23-40; Hanno Ehses and Ellen Lupton, *Design Papers 5: Rhetorical Handbook* (Halifax: Nova Scotia College of Art and Design, 1988); and Katherine McCoy and David Frej, "Typography as Discourse," *I.D.* 35 (March/April 1988): 34-7.

Language of Dreams

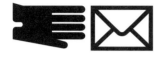

According to Freud, dreams are organized or "written" according to the principle of the rebus, a form of expression employing both words and pictures. An image of a glove might stand for another object with a similar structure, such as a sock or an envelope, or it might stand for a memory associated with gloves, such as bad weather or polite manners. The dream-glove might stand also for a word whose sound or spelling resembles the name glove, such as love or grove. Freud argued that to decipher a dream one must exchange the direct, literal meaning of its images for indirect substitutions.

This principle, called the *rebus*, is a feature of numerous written languages, from Egyptian hieroglyphics to modern Japanese. According to many historians, writing naturally evolves from pictographs through various phonetic systems, climaxing in the alphabet, which analyzes the sounds of a spoken language into tiny repeatable elements. Discovery of the rebus principle enables a culture to invent a phonetic script.[1]

Japanese writing is built upon that of Chinese, a logographic system that has separate symbols for words and parts of words, resulting in over 40,000 signs. Chinese has numerous words that sound the same but have different meanings, called homophones. Thus Chinese writing, while it appears cumbersome to Westerners, is well-suited to the Chinese language, because even though many of its characters have similar or identical pronunciations, they are graphically distinct.

1　Comparative studies of writing include I.J. Gelb, *A Study of Writing* (Chicago: University of Chicago Press, 1952, 1963); Albertine Guar, *A History of Writing* (London: The British Library, 1984); and Roy Harris, *The Origin of Writing* (La Salle, IL: Open Court, 1986).

精神分折学の創始者シブモント・フロイトによると夢とは「リーブス」の法則(rebus＝判じ絵)、すなわち言語と絵とを使った表現の仕方によって、構成あるいは「書かれて」います。手袋のイメージが、例えばくつ下、封筒等他の構成がよく類似した物を意味しているかもしれません。又は、悪天候や上品なマナー等、手袋と関連した個人的な想い出に関係があるのかもしれません。夢の中の「手袋(glove)」は又、「言葉」の音と読みが似ている「愛(love)」や「小さい森(grove)」を意味するかもしれません。フロイトは夢を解読する為には直接的である夢のイメージの文学上の意味を間接的な代用物に交換することが必要だと論じています。

リーブスの法則はエジプトの象形文字から現代の日本語へと、色々な文語の特色となっています。数々の西洋の言語の歴史家によると、書法は多くの異なった音声法を通した象形文字から自然に発展したものです。その頂点がアルファベットで、口語の音声を分折してこまかい操り返し可能な要素となったものです。リーブスの法則の発見によって音声筆記体活字の発明が可能になりました。

日本語の書法は記号を語、又は語の一部に分類した語標法である中国語を基礎に出来た言語です。そしてこの結果として莫大な(4万個以上の)個々の記号になりました。中国語では「同音異義語」といって同じ音で異なる意味の単語が数多くあります。すなわち西洋人には見た目はわずらわしい中国語書法も中国語という言語面から見ると良く出来ているということになります。なぜなら、良く似たり同じ「発音」の言葉は多くても、図解的には見分けることが出来るからです。

The Chinese script already had been in use for around 2,000 years when Korean scholars introduced it to the Japanese court in the fourth and fifth centuries AD (Western time). The Japanese acquired deep respect for Chinese civilization, and some took on the ambitious task of learning its script. Initially, the Japanese used Chinese characters to read and write in Chinese, which became the official written language of Japan's imperial court. By the seventh century, however, more attempts were made to write the *Japanese* language with Chinese characters.[2]

This was no simple task. The Japanese and Chinese spoken languages are totally different in their grammar and phonology. While many Chinese characters could be exchanged directly for Japanese words, some features of Japanese are impossible to translate. For example, Japanese is heavily inflected, meaning that the basic form of a noun, verb, or modifier changes in different grammatical settings. Chinese, in contrast, has few inflections. In this sense, Japanese resembles Latin more than Chinese! The principle of the rebus arose to address such difficulties of translation: a Chinese character could be used to stand for a Japanese word or syllable unrelated in *meaning* but similar in *sound*.

中国書体は4、5世紀に韓国の学者によって日本の皇室に紹介されるすでに2千年程前から存在していました。日本人は中国の文明に強い尊敬の念をいだいていました。そこで中国書体を習得しようという希望を持った人が何人か出てきたのです。初めに、日本の皇室公認の文語になった漢字は、日本人が中国語で読み書きするのに使われました。しかし7世紀に入ると、漢字を使って「日本語」を書くことが試みられました。

これは容易い作業ではありませんでした。日本語と中国語の話し言葉では、文法と音声学が全く違うのです。多くの漢字はそのまま日本語に置き代えられますが、日本語の特徴として漢字に置きかえることは不可能なものもあります。例をあげると、日本語は語尾の変化が激しい。つまり基本形の名詞、動詞、又は修飾語句が異なる文法の状況によって変化するということです。これに比べると中国語には語尾変化はほとんどありません。いわば日本語は中国語よりもラテン語に似ているということです。リーブスの法則はこれらの難しい訳に着手する為に発生したのです。すなわち意味的には関係がないのに「音」が似ているために、日本語一語や一音節を一つの漢字で表すことが出来るということです。

2 For discussions of the Japanese script, see Yaeko Sato Habein, *The History of the Japanese Written Language* (Tokyo: University of Tokyo Press, 1984); Wolfgang Hadminsky and Mark Spahn, *Kanji and Kana: A Handbook and Dictionary of the Japanese Writing System* (Rutland, VT and Tokyo: Charles E. Tuttle Company, 1981); and Roy Andrew Miller, *The Japanese Language* (Chicago: University of Chicago Press, 1967), Chapter 3, "Writing Systems," 91-140.

The chart at right is a thought game that invites the English reader to imagine designing a written form for English if the Latin alphabet did not exist. Imagine that a sophisticated neighboring civilization has a writing system, but that we have none. We will call this writing system Airport-*moji* (or Airport-script). We will pretend to invent an English writing system out of these hieroglyphs.

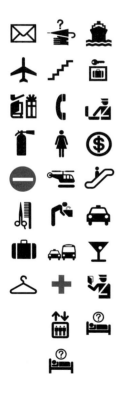

pictograph 象形文字	ideograph 表意文字
man and woman 女と男	toilets トイレ
knife and fork フォークとナイフ	restaurant レストラン
a man dreams of a question 質問を夢みる人	hotel information ホテル インフォメーショ
a car dreams of a key 鍵を夢みる車	car rental レンタカー

We begin our task by trying to guess the meaning of Airport-*moji*. Some of the characters appear to be simple, direct depictions of objects (man and woman, or knife and fork). Others, however, are more obscure. Consider, for example, the character that shows a giant key floating above a car: if we interpreted this sign as a literal depiction of a scene, we might read "a car dreams of key." A figurative sign interpreted for its literal meaning is called a pictograph. A pictograph does not refer to a word in a particular language, but to a physical object in the real world.

While such fanciful scenarios as "a car dreaming of a key" have an appealing charm, we would find little use for such a specific sign in writing the English language.

Perhaps instead we should combine the individual meanings of the two pictures (car and key) to create a third meaning. The whole sign could mean car key, parking, or "Please lock your car," but upon consulting with native writers of Airport-*moji*, we discover that the real meaning of the sign is car rental. Such a sign is called an ideograph, because it stands for a concept or "idea" rather than a material object.

Chinese characters borrowed to write the Japanese language are called *kanji*. A *kun* reading of *kanji* employs the Chinese character for its Chinese meaning, but assigns it a Japanese pronunciation.

「空港文字」の意味をあてることから作業を始めてみましょう。単純に物をそのまま表わした文字もありますが、意味がはっきりしないものもあります。例えば巨大な鍵が車の上に浮かんでいる文字を考察してみると、その現場（鍵を夢みる車）をそのまま表わした様に解釈できます。そのまま事実に忠実な意味を解釈した形象的な記号を「象形文字」といいます。「鍵を夢みる車」の様な空想上のシナリオは、魅力的ですが、実際に英語の文語としてはほとんど使い道がありません。

その代わりに2つの絵の個々の意味をまとめた文字から他の意味に訳してみるべきでしょう。その文字は「車の鍵」、「駐車場」又は「車の鍵をしめてください」という意味になります。しかし、この「空港文字」の筆者たちによりますと、この文字の本当の意味はレンタカーだということです。この様な文字は「表意文字」と呼ばれます。概念又は「アイディア」を表わしているからです。

日本語が借りた中国文字は「漢字」と呼ばれています。「漢字」の「訓読み」とは、その文字が中国語の意味を使い日本語読みをすることをいいます。

rebus	syllabary	alphabet
リーブス（判じ絵）	音節文字	象形文字

	rebus		syllabary		alphabet
🚶	john ジョン	🚗	car カー	🍸	A is for alcohol アルコールのA
🚶←	knee ニー（ひざ）	☕	cup カップ	🚢	B is for boat ボートのB
🚗	car カー	✂	cut カット（切る）	🔑	C is for car (and key) カー（とキー）のC
👶	son サン（息子）	🐕	cat キャット（猫）	🚬	C is for cigarette (and smoke) シガレット（とスモーク）のC

We soon run into difficulty, however, using Airport-*moji* to write English. Consider, for example, the familiar English proper name Johnny Carson. Rather than invent a new ideograph for it, we could use existing characters to stand for the sounds of the spoken name. (The rebus above relies on an English slang word for toilet — john.) The whole rebus reads "john-knee car-son."

In Japanese, some readings of *kanji* (called *on* readings) employ the Chinese rather than the Japanese pronunciation of the character. For example, the *on* reading of the *kanji* for "mountain" is *san*, a Chinese word, while the *kun* reading of the same character is *yama*, the Japanese word for "mountain."

By employing the drawing of a car to stand for the English syllable *car*, we begin to create a syllabary, a set of symbols representing all the consonant-vowel pairs of a language.

Modern Japanese *katakana* and *hiragana* (together called *kana*) are indigenous phonetic sign systems used in addition to the Chinese *kanji*. Both *katakana* and *hiragana* are syllabaries.

In theory, *kana* could have replaced the unwieldy collection of *kanji*, but because of Japan's continued respect for Chinese culture and attachment to the subtle connotations and graphic variety enabled by its characters, *kanji* have remained a central element of Japanese writing.

An alphabet abstracts the sounds of a spoken language into even smaller units, assigning separate symbols to consonants and vowels. Western culture reveres its alphabet as the most rational of all writing systems, but in practice, the Latin alphabet is full of irregularities: The letter C, for example, can sound like the initial letters in either car and key or cigarette and smoke.

Attempts to reform such irregularities in English, like efforts to eliminate *kanji* from Japanese, have largely failed. It is unlikely that our spelling system will ever become more rational. The alphabet is not the perfect climax of writing's "natural" evolution, but it has seeped into the pores of our culture.

「空港文字」を使い英語を書くのは困難だと間もなくわかるでしょう。「ジョニー カーソン」という英語で実在する名前を例にとって考察してください。新しい表意文字を発明する代わりにすでに存在する英語の名前の「音」を使用して「ジョニー カーソン」という言葉を表現することができます。（上記の判じ絵の「ジョン」とは英語の口語でトイレの另（John-knee Car-son）絵をつなぐと「ジョニー カーソン（John-knee Car-son）」と読めます。

日本語では漢字の読み方（音読み）がリーブスの法則にしたがうことがあります。音読みは漢字の発音をつかいます。例えば「音読み」の「山」は中国読みで「さん」、「訓読み」では日本読みで「やま」と読まれます。

もし英語の「車（car）」という「音節」を車のドローイングに毎回おきかえて使うとすると、「音節文字」、すなわちその言語のすべての音節を代表することのできる記号の一組みを作ることが可能です。

現代日本語の「片仮名」と「平仮名」（双方はまとめて仮名と呼ばれています）は中国の「漢字」に加えた日本国産の文字の集まりです。個々は音節文字で日本語の音節を表わしています。

理論上では仮名は、使用しにくい「漢字」の全てに代わって使うことができたはずですが、日本の中国文化に対する尊敬の念と、「漢字」によって微妙な語感と写実的、図解的変化に富む事が可能になったので「漢字」は日本の文語の中心として残ることになったのです。

アルファベットとは口語の音をもっと小さな単位で抽象的に表わしたもので、子音と母音を別々の記号で割りあてたものです。西洋文化では全ての文語の中でアルファベットが一番合理的であると尊敬されていますが、実際問題としてラテンアルファベットには多くの変則があります。たとえばCは「車（カー）」と鍵（キー）又は「たばこ（シガレット）」と「煙（スモーク）」のようによく似て聞こえます。

日本語から漢字を減らそうとした様に英語から変則を改正しようという試みは大きな失敗におわりました。我々のつづりの法則がもっと合理的になるということはないでしょう。それはアルファベットが文語の「自然」進化の完璧な最高頂のものであるからではなく、私たちの文化の底辺まで行き渡ったからです。

Body of the Book

In the 1920s Laszlo Moholy-Nagy saw the camera as an extension of the human body, an instrument that allows the frail biological eye to halt time, cross extreme distances, magnify invisible landscapes, and penetrate opaque structures.[1] All objects manufactured for use are extensions of the body; food, furniture, shelter, and tools do not lie in a region safely "outside" the body, but instead are continuations of the body, turning it inside out. As Elaine Scarry has written, there is no fundamental difference between an object that is as external and disposable as a glove and one as internal and permanent as an artificial organ: both become part of the body.[2]

What might be the relationship, then, between writing, typography, and the body? In the West, writing has historically been seen as secondary to speech: while speech appears to give an immediate voice to the interior self, writing is an external device, an intellectual technology employing an artificial code. Speech appears to be naturally birthed by the biological organs of the body, while writing depends on the mediation of external tools: chisel, stylus, pencil, keyboard. Every culture instinctively produces some form of speech; a system of writing, in contrast, must be deliberately designed.

But what if one were to see writing as an extension of the body, no different in essence from an artificial limb or a contact lens? Like a chair supporting the human skeleton, writing supplements the body's capacity to speak: it is permanent rather than ephemeral, it withstands movements in place and time, and it remains readable in the absence of its author.

There is another way in which writing extends the body: it is a physical by-product, a material trace of human activity.[3] Unlike speech, writing leaves behind a visible mark. As the end-product of the so-called "thought process," writing thus resembles excrement. It is also akin to hair, finger nails, and the surface of the skin—each is a part of the body that is continually regenerated yet biologically dead, detachable, disposable. Writing is like blood, sweat, semen, saliva, and other substances that the body periodically produces and eliminates.

1 Laszlo Moholy-Nagy, *Painting Photography Film* (Cambridge: MIT Press, 1969). First published in 1925.

2 Elaine Scarry, *The Body in Pain: The Making and Unmaking of the World* (New York: Oxford University Press, 1985).

3 Jacques Derrida has discussed speech as a physical, material by-product of the mouth rather than a purely phonic, abstract signal: "The text is spit out. It is like a discourse in which the unities model themselves after an excrement, a secretion." Quoted in Gregory Ulmer, *Applied Grammatology: Post(e) Pedagogy from Jacques Derrida to Joseph Beuys* (Baltimore: Johns Hopkins University Press, 1985): 55.

head
1. The upper division of the body that contains the brain, mouth, and chief sense organs.
2. A word or series of words, often distinguished typographically, placed at the beginning of a passage or
at the top of a page in order to introduce or categorize.

gloss From the Greek *glossa, glotta,* meaning tongue. 1. A brief explanation (as in the margins or between the lines of a text) of a difficult or obscure word or expression. 2. A false and often willfully misleading interpretation. 3. A continuous commentary accompanying a text. A *gloss* could be an official element of a page or a handwritten remark. Library books are often defiled by the *glosses* of several readers. A book is thus not only read by many, but written by many.

In the language of publishing and typography, we refer to the body of a work as its "main part," its central, substantial core. When we refer to the "body" of a person, we invoke a division between inside and outside: body and soul, body and mind. Similarly, the typographic term "body" suggests a division between inside and outside, between that which properly belongs to a text and the secondary limbs attached to it: glosses, footnotes, heads and subheads, figures, appendices. One of the graphic designer's tasks is to articulate visually the differences between these secondary elements and the "body" of the text. But do such limbs remain safely "outside" the text? Instead we could see these seemingly detachable, external parts as *internal* organs, life-support systems fundamental to the shape of meaning. As an extension of the text, an element such as a gloss, footnote, figure, or appendix is an integral part of the body, opening up the skin of the text, turning it inside out.

body 1. The organized physical substance of an animal or plant, whether living or dead. 2. The dead organism: CORPSE. 3. The trunk of a person or a tree, as distinct from its head, limbs, branches, or roots. 4. The main part of a literary or journalistic work: TEXT.

Whereas the "body" of a text is typically assigned to a single author, notes, glosses, figures, and appendices are organs for importing material from the outside, for exchanging discourse with other documents. Such organs nourish, impregnate, and sometimes deface, infect, the internal body.

The valves of these organs serve not only to absorb, but also to expel, excrete. They generate substances, leaving a mark, a trail of argument in excess of the seemingly self-contained "body" of the work. The organs of the text are sites for elaboration, expansion, overflow, like the body's periodic release of semen or blood. For example, footnotes support the text from below; they represent the foundation of research. They do not constitute a merely passive base or pedestal, however, but rather a vital root system that feeds the work through a subterranean web of other texts. Footnotes can serve as minimal anchors or as loquacious networks that grossly enlarge the reach of the body. By documenting the exchange of fluids between texts, footnotes diagram the paternity of ideas.

figure 1. Bodily shape, especially of a person. 2. A diagram or illustration supporting a text.

foot 1. The terminal part of the vertebrate leg upon which an individual stands. 2. Something resembling a foot in appearance or use.

footnote 1. A note of reference, explanation, or comment, placed below the text on a printed page. 2. Something that is subordinately related to a larger work: COMMENTARY.

appendix 1. A bodily outgrowth or process, specifically the organ VERIFORM APPENDIX, commonly subject to surgical removal. 2. Supplementary material attached to the end of a piece of writing, often consisting of tables, diagrams, glossaries, etc.

Antique

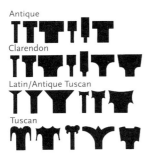

Clarendon

Latin/Antique Tuscan

Tuscan

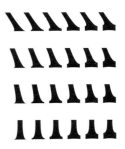

Typographic historian Rob Roy Kelly has classified nineteenth-century ornamental letters, showing how designers elaborated a huge variety of styles around a few basic structures. *American Wood Type, 1828-1900* (New York: Van Nostrand Reinhold, 1969).

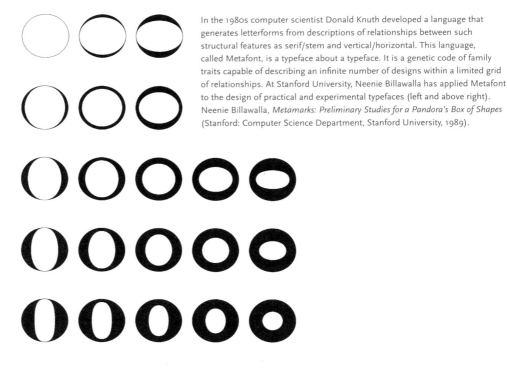

In the 1980s computer scientist Donald Knuth developed a language that generates letterforms from descriptions of relationships between such structural features as serif/stem and vertical/horizontal. This language, called Metafont, is a typeface about a typeface. It is a genetic code of family traits capable of describing an infinite number of designs within a limited grid of relationships. At Stanford University, Neenie Billawalla has applied Metafont to the design of practical and experimental typefaces (left and above right). Neenie Billawalla, *Metamarks: Preliminary Studies for a Pandora's Box of Shapes* (Stanford: Computer Science Department, Stanford University, 1989).

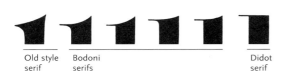

Old style serif   Bodoni serifs   Didot serif

The serifs designed by Bodoni and Didot in the late eighteenth century rejected calligraphy as the basis for typographic form. Bodoni and Didot constructed serifs as pure geometric elements distanced from the gestures of the hand. Frank Denman, *The Shaping of Our Alphabet* (New York: Alfred Knopf, 1955).

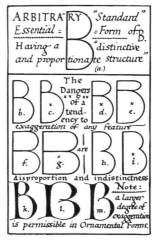

At the turn of the twentieth century, design reformers condemned the structural manipulation of letterforms as evidence of typographic decadence. Edward Johnston's 1906 diagram of "essential" characters was based on Roman inscriptions. While deriding commercial display faces, Johnston accepted similar devices in manuscript initials, reflecting the Arts and Crafts tolerance for all things medieval. Edward Johnston, *Writing & Illuminating & Lettering* (London: Sir Isaac Pitman & Sons, 1932).

Laws of the Letter

What sort of sign system is typography? Is the history of letterforms a logical evolution toward perfect shapes, or a string of responses to the changing philosophy, technology, and social uses of writing? This essay, which considers typography in relation to structuralist theory, charts a shift from the humanist understanding of printed letters as reflections of handwritten marks or classical proportions toward the modernist view of typography as the endless manipulation of abstract elements. In modern typography, systematic relations across the body of the alphabet took precedence over the "character" of individual letterforms.

Structuralism emerged from the teachings of Ferdinand de Saussure in the early twentieth century. Saussure's theory of language infused many later currents of thought, including the anthropology of Claude Levi-Strauss, the philosophy of Jacques Derrida, and the social mythology of Roland Barthes. These writers have looked at the products of human culture—from marriage rituals to soap bubbles— in terms of systems of opposition, patterns of difference that generate meaning.

Saussure attacked the assumption that language exists to represent ideas. Against the common sense view of language as a passive collection of names assigned to pre-existing concepts, Saussure argued that both thought and sound are shapeless masses before the acquisition of speech. Without language, the realm of potential human sounds is just a field of noise; the plane of concepts is an equally vague nebula of emotions and perceptions. Language links these two layers and cuts them up into discrete, repeatable segments, or signs. "Ideas" emerge only when both of these formless slabs are sliced into units.

For Saussure, the most troublesome feature of the linguistic sign was its *arbitrariness:* there is no resemblance between the sound "horse" and the concept of a horse. No natural link binds the material, phonic aspect of the sign (the *signifier*) to the mental concept (the *signified*): only a social agreement appears to hold the two elements together. If the connection between the signifier and signified, the sound and the concept, is arbitrary, what, then, binds the two together? If there is no iconic, natural relationship between the sound "horse" and the concept it invokes, why is the link between them so reliable?

To explain this link, Saussure introduced the principle of linguistic *value.* The identity of a sign rests not in the sign itself, but on its relation to other signs in the system. The sound *horse* is recognizable only in opposition to other English sounds: *horse* is distinct from *morse, force, bourse, house, hearse,* etc. Likewise the concept "horse" has identity only in opposition to other concepts, such as "cow," "antelope," and "pony." The meaning of a sign does not reside within the sign itself, but is generated from the surrounding system. The sign alone is empty.

Renaissance theorists sought to derive roman letters from the proportions of the human body and from mathematical relationships endowed with divine signficance. See Millard Meiss, "The First Alphabetical Treatises in the Renaissance," *Visible Language* III, 1 (January 1969): 3-30.

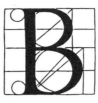

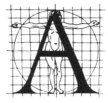

The fusion of rationalism and mysticism is seen in the theoretical constructions of Geofroy Tory, 1529.

The italic version of the king's alphabet was generated by shifting the underlying grid. This abstract, geometric method of constructing the italic form anticipated mechanical and digital manipulations of letterforms.

In 1693, a committee of the Académie des Sciences commissioned a study of roman letters constructed on a rational grid. A typeface based on these diagrams was designed by Philippe Grandjean around 1700. Called the *romain du roi,* it was endorsed by Louis XIV.

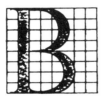

The geometrical constructions of the Renaissance and Enlightenment distanced the printed letter from the gestures of the hand. In the typefaces designed by Giambattista Bodoni in Parma in the late eighteenth century, the serif is a flattened, attenuated slab.

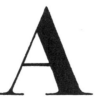

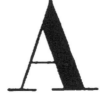

The French typefounder François Ambroise Didot, a contem-porary of Bodoni, produced a typeface in 1784 that surpassed Bodoni's in articulating the serifs as discrete structural elements detachable from the stem.

STRUCTURALIST TYPOGRAPHY

What sort of semiotic system is typography? The alphabet is designed to represent speech. Writing is thus a language depicting another language, a set of signs for representing signs. The design of letterforms is removed one step farther: it is a medium whose signified is not words but rather the alphabet.

"You have two goblets before you. One is of solid gold, wrought in the most exquisite patterns. The other is of crystal-clear glass, thin as a bubble, and as transparent...[an] amateur of fine vintages...will choose the crystal, because everything about it is calculated to reveal rather than to hide the beautiful thing which it was meant to contain.
...the virtues of the perfect wine glass also have a parallel in typography"
BEATRICE WARDE, *The Crystal Goblet*, 1932

In what ways has typography responded to its alphabetic signified? While Gutenberg's fonts naturalistically simulated the variety and aura of handwriting, humanist designers at the turn of the sixteenth century distanced the letter from calligraphy by constructing roman alphabets with the tools of geometry. The letterform was no longer thought of as a sequence of manual pen strokes, but as a conceptual ideal bound to no particular technology. This Platonic structure became typography's new signified.

A committee established by Louis XIV in 1693 further idealized the alphabet. Embracing the current passion for scientific method, the *romain du roi* imposed an orthogonal grid over the organic forms of traditional lettering. Italic letters were generated by shifting the grid, a procedure divorced from calligraphy and prophetic of the mathematical distortions enabled by nineteenth- and twentieth-century technologies. The grid was seen as an objective field on which to glimpse the ideal shadow of the alphabet, cast as clearly as the image on the gridded glass of a *camera obscura*.

Bodoni and Didot completed the typographic erasure of calligraphy; these faces polarized letterforms into extremes of thick and thin and reduced serifs to wafer-thin slices. While the humanists had hoped to discover absolute proportions legislating the forms of letters, and the creators of the *romain du roi* pursued a norm grounded in scientific and bureaucratic legality, Bodoni and Didot reduced the alphabet to a system of oppositions—thick and thin, vertical and horizontal, serif and stem. Typography was no longer compelled to refer back to an ideal canon of proportions: instead, letterforms were understood as a set of elements open to manipulation. While Bodoni and Didot called their work *classic*, typographers since the early nineteenth century have classified these typefaces as *modern*, for they completed a development away from the organic origins of written forms.

Modern typography replaced idealism with relativism. The notion of a direct ancestral bond between contemporary typefaces and a divine classical past was displaced by a code of relationships that could yield infinite variations. The alphabet had lost its center: operating in its place was a mode of designing letters that we call *structuralist typography*.

The radical classicism of Bodoni and Didot opened the way for inventive manipulations of the alphabet's linguistic elements by designers of advertising display faces.

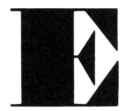

Beginning in the early ninteenth century, Fat Face fonts exaggerated Bodoni's polarization of letterforms into thick and thin elements.

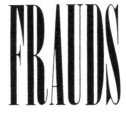

Severe condensing was another popular form of manipulation. The effect is particularly startling in the letter *A* in this sample from an 1870 wood type catalogue.

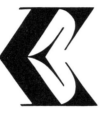

The wholly vertical stress of Bodoni replaced the oblique stress of old-style fonts, which were modelled on calligraphy. This Roman Grotesque, published in 1838, adds a second and more shocking twist to the geometric regularity of modern faces.

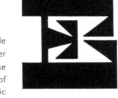

The Italian style is another perverse exploration of linguistic possibility, turning serifs inside out and rotating the thick strokes from vertical to horizontal.

The sans serif display fonts of the nineteenth century are linguistic manipulations in which the serif axis and the contrast axis have been reduced to zero. This font was published in 1834.

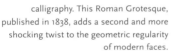

Egyptian or Antique fonts shift the linguistic function of the serif from a passive, ornamental ending to an active, load-bearing structure.

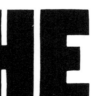

TYPOGRAPHIC NOVELTY

The break initiated by Didot and Bodoni triggered a population explosion in nineteenth-century commercial typography. A profusion of bizarre new specimens rejected classical norms in favor of the incessant pursuit of novelty. Technology encouraged the spawning of new fonts. The introduction of the combined pantograph and router in 1834 revolutionized wood-type manufacture. The pantograph is a tracing device which, when linked to a router for carving letters out of wood or metal, allows different sizes and styles of a font to be generated from a single parent drawing, eliminating the painstaking task of cutting individual punches by hand. This automated approach to type design led the historian Daniel Berkeley Updike to later denounce the pantograph for its tendency to "mechanize the design of types."

"Abominable are the tumblers into which he [the bartender] pours his poison. Though true cylinders without—within, the villainous green goggling glasses deceitfully tapered downwards to a cheating bottom. Parallel meridians rudely pecked into the glass surround these goblets. Fill to *this* mark, and your charge is but a penny; to *this*, a penny more; and so on to the full glass...which you may gulp down for a shilling."
HERMAN MELVILLE, *Moby Dick*, 1851

The programmatic shifts in scale enabled by the pantograph encouraged an understanding of the alphabet as a flexible system, susceptible to systematic variations divorced from a calligraphic origin. The swelling population of typographic mutants—compressed, expanded, outline, inline, shadowed, extruded, faceted, floriated, perspective, bowed—signaled a shift in the "signified" of typography. The notion of letterforms as essential, archetypal structures gave way to a recognition of letters as units within a larger system of formal features (weight, stress, cross-bars, serifs, angles, curves, ascenders, descenders, etc.). The relationships between letters within a font became more important than the identity of individual characters. The variety of nineteenth-century display faces suggested that the "alphabet" is a flexible system of differences, not a pedigreed line of fixed symbols.

The proliferation of typefaces available for use in books and advertising led the American Typefounders Company (ATF) to organize fonts into "type families" in the early twentieth century. Each family consists of variations of a single parent design—book, italic, bold, condensed, etc. This system—still in use today—encouraged printers and their clients to use genetically related characters rather than combining fonts of mixed heritage. The use of type families, claimed ATF, had "added dignity and distinction...to commercial printing." It also reflected the structuralist view of a typeface as a set of genetic traits that could be translated across a series of offspring.

MODERNISM

Avant-garde designers produced fonts in the early twentieth century that tested the structural limits of the alphabet.

RBCDEFGHIJ ΛBCDEFG

Theo van Doesburg's 1919 font and Bart van der Leck's 1941 design for Het Vlas are typographic translations of the geometric principles of De Stijl painting.

abcdefghijklmnopqrstuv

The stencil construction of Josef Albers's 1925 stencil typeface generates an alphabetic ensemble out of a restricted repertoire of elementary shapes.

abcdefghijklmnopqrstuvwxyz

Similarly, Herbert Bayer's 1925 "universal," designed at the Bauhaus, relies on interchangeable geometric parts to produce a self-consciously rational font.

An even more radical reduction is Wladyslav Strzeminski's 1931 font, which generates letterforms out of right angles and the arcs of a single circle.

The formal parameters of these avant-garde typefaces suppress the individuality of letters by forcing attention to the system—the discrete figures in Strzeminski's font, for example, are indecipherable apart from the surrounding code. These fonts are a typographic analogue for structuralist philosophy and linguistics, which seeks to find, as Derrida has written, "a form or function organized according to an internal legality in which elements have meaning only in the solidarity of their correlation or opposition."

Structuralist typography was inaugurated by Bodoni and Didot and was continued by the designers of advertising display faces. By shifting the emphasis from the individual letter to the overall *series* of characters, structuralist typography exchanged the fixed identity of the letter for the relational system of the font. In the twentieth century, modernism invested this mode of formal manipulation with ideological significance by replacing the solicitous novelty of advertising display faces with a visual assault on mass culture and the middle classes.

The modernism of De Stijl, Dada, Futurism, Constructivism, and the Bauhaus aimed to "defamiliarize" writing. Defamiliarization, as theorized by the Russian formalist critic Victor Shklovsky in the 1910s, held that the everyday world is invisible until we are forced to see it differently, and that art is a primary means for "making strange" the already-seen and already-known. Cinematic shock techniques, the "New Vision" in photography, and typographic experimentation were facets of the modernist attack on the familiar.

NEO-MODERNISM

Designers have continued to invent typefaces that manipulate the formal system of the alphabet and attempt to defamiliarize the experience of reading.

AaBbCcDdEeFfGgHhIiJj AaBbCcDdEeFfGgHh

Zuzana Licko's font Emperor, 1985, embraces the limits of coarse-resolution output. Jeffrey Keedy's 1989 font NeoTheo is an homage to the early avant-garde.

ABCDEFGHIJKLMNOPQRSTUVWXYZ

The reduced template of angles behind Max Kisman's 1988 Zwartvet is akin to the minimal geometric vocabulary used in Albers's 1925 stencil letters.

AabbcddefgghijkLMNoppaqrrsst

The emphatic constructedness of Licko's 1988 Variex family shares the fascination with system and geometry found in Bayer's 1925 "universal."

AaBbCcDdEeFfGgHhIiJjKkLlMmNnOoPp

These neo-avant-garde fonts do not take the structuralist idea to the extremes approached by the historical avant-gardes. Licko's 1989 Lunatix, for example, conserves the conventional core of the alphabet, while in contrast, Strzeminski's elliptical font expresses a vast range of functional roles with minimal elements. Like the fonts of the historical avant-gardes, many of these neo-modern typefaces look to technology for aesthetic cues, rather than imitating traditional typographic forms. In the 1920s Bayer and others saw industry as the foundation for a universal and democratic society. A similar technological optimism appears to inform many neo-modern typefaces; these were produced, however, in a post-industrial world where technology is no longer seen as a benign source of liberation.

abcdefghijkl abcdefghijklmn

The roots of neo-modern typographers' celebration of digital technology can be seen in the typeface New, constructed by the Dutch designer Wim Crouwel in 1967. Embracing the limitations of CRT display terminals, Crouwel substituted the curves and diagonals traditionally used to construct the alphabet with a minimal array of perpendicular elements. In addition to such serious interpretations of "high" technology, Crouwel's work includes designs linked to the low culture and low technology of Pop. His font Oldenburg (above right) translated the artist's "soft alphabet" into the medium of type. While this second font shares the systematic character of the typeface New, it introduced irony, narrative, and figurative representation into a traditionally abstract realm of communication.

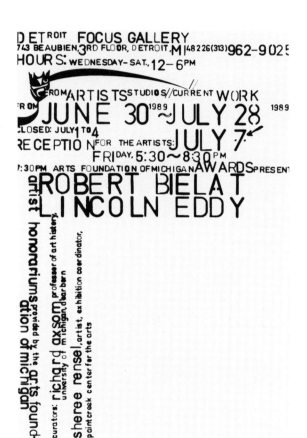

DETROIT FOCUS GALLERY
743 BEAUBIEN, 3RD FLOOR, DETROIT, MI 48226 (313) 962-9025
HOURS: WEDNESDAY-SAT., 12-6 PM

FROM ARTISTS STUDIOS//CURRENT WORK
JUNE 30 1989 ~ JULY 28 1989
CLOSED: JULY 1 TO 4
RECEPTION FOR THE ARTISTS: JULY 7
FRIDAY, 5:30 ~ 8:30 PM
7:30 PM ARTS FOUNDATION OF MICHIGAN AWARDS PRESENT
ROBERT BIELAT
LINCOLN EDDY

artist honorariums provided by the arts foundation of michigan

curators: richard axsom professor of art history, university of michigan, dearborn
sheree rensel, artist, exhibition coordinator, paintcreek center for the arts

Of Light/Primitive Processes:

Dorothy Potter Barnett

Daniel G. Pohlman
Jack O. Summers

October 13-November 11, 1989

Sponsorship of Artists:
Seaman Patrick Paper
O'Leary Paint
Koenig Art let Supplies

Adray Appliance Photo & Sound Center
AIN Plastic
Calumet Photo graphic
Graphic Systems Supply

Curator:
Carlos
Diaz
Gallery
Talk:
Bill
Rauhauser

Detroit Focus Gallery
743 Beaubien, 3rd Floor
Phone: (313)962-9025   Hours: Wednesday—Saturday, Noon-6:00pm

Detroit, Michigan 48226

Opening Reception: Friday, October 13th 5:00-7:30 p.m.

The work of Ed Fella has broadly influenced recent developments in type design. Fella's posters for the Detroit Focus Gallery, produced between 1987 and 1990, feature damaged and defective forms—from third-generation photocopies to broken pieces of transfer type. These imperfect elements are meticulously assembled by hand into free-form compositions. Fella's experiments inspired other designers to construct digital fonts with battered features and hybrid origins. Collection Cooper-Hewitt, National Design Museum.

POST-STRUCTURALISM

Post-structuralist theory built upon and revised Saussure's ideas by questioning the supremacy of the system as the generator of meaning. While Saussure faulted writing for not being a transparent medium or "crystal goblet" for conveying speech, Derrida challenged this devaluation by foregrounding the typographic and rhetorical materiality of writing. Derrida and other writers have provoked suspicion of coherent "master-codes," such as Marxism or functionalism, that try to ground meaning in a totalizing structure or theory. This destabilizing (de-structuring, deconstructing) approach to language and culture has been called *post-structuralism*.

Template Gothic

AaBbCcDdEeFfGgJjKkLlMmNnO

Dead History

AaBbCcDdEeFfGgHhIiJjKk

Beowolf

AaBbCcDdEeFfGgHhIiJjKkLl

Narly

AaBbCcDdEeFfGgHhIiJjK

The field of typographic design has seen a shift from the structuralist approach of modernism and neo-modernism to a more skeptical and inclusive view of digital technology. Template Gothic, designed by Barry Deck in 1990, mixes references to hand-made and machine-made forms, low and high technologies. In contrast with Albers's 1925 stencil characters, which celebrated industrial production and standardization, Deck's Template refers to an imperfect matrix yielding irregular yet mechanically mediated characters. Dead History, designed by P. Scott Makela in 1990, splices the traditional serif font Centennial with the rounded sans serif VAG, commonly used in packaging and advertising. Dead History grafts the classical with the Pop, the sharp with the blunt. Beowolf, designed by Erik von Blokland and Just van Rossum in Holland in 1990, is a randomized typeface whose edges change each time the letters are printed. Beowolf exploits digital technology not as a means for seamless reproduction but as a channel for injecting chance and uncertainty into the tidy typographic world. Narly, designed by Zuzana Licko in 1993, is a jubilantly organic revision of structuralist typography. Licko, one of the first designers to match neo-modernism with the Mac, is now breeding new life forms in her typographic hothouse. Strange organisms spawn along the limbs of her letters, from tendrils of ornament to knobby, crusty growths.

These typefaces have exchanged the clean, mechanical paradigm of structuralism for a model that merges biology and technology. Such narrative, referential typographic practices have participated in the broader cultural re-evaluation of modernism. While the avant-garde institutionalized the "shock of the new," post-modernism replaced this faith in renewal with parody, quotation, pastiche, and an uneasy alliance with technology.

Language of Vision

"Design history" should be understood not as a catalogue of styles or a canon of formal rules, but as a complex enterprise that engages political, economic, and intellectual culture. The renewed interest in history has provoked an emerging interest in theory, a concern for identifying general principles that inform the practice of design. The body of theory established within the modernist pedagogical tradition is intrinsically hostile to an historical approach to graphic design. In our profession, as in architecture and the fine arts, the move toward greater historical awareness is linked to a revision of modernism.

The institution of graphic design emerged out of the modern art movement in the early twentieth century and was consolidated into a profession over the last fifty years. Its theoretical base comes out of avant-garde movements and organizations such as Constructivism, de Stijl, and the Bauhaus. Elements of these critical, reform-minded practices were codified by art schools after World War II. Many design textbooks, produced across the history of the profession, reproduce a core of theoretical principles based on abstract painting and gestalt psychology. Gyorgy Kepes's *Language of Vision* (1944), Rudolph Arnheim's *Art and Visual Perception* (1954), and Donis Dondis's *A Primer of Visual Literacy* (1973) contain recurring themes in modern design theory.

Pervading these works is a focus on *perception* at the expense of *interpretation*. "Perception" refers to the subjective experience of the individual as framed by the body and brain. Aesthetic theories based on perception favor sensation over intellect, seeing over reading, universality over cultural difference, physical immediacy over social mediation. Modern design pedagogy, an approach to form-making validated by theories of perception, suggests a universal faculty of vision common to all humans of all times, capable of overriding cultural and historical barriers. A study of design oriented around interpretation, on the other hand, would suggest that the reception of a particular image shifts from one time or place to the next, drawing meaning from conventions of format, style, and symbolism, and from its association with other images and with words. While modern design theory focuses on perception, an historically and culturally self-conscious approach would center on interpretation.

Kepes, Dondis, and Arnheim each employed "gestalt psychology," a theory developed by German scientists during the 1920s. For all three of these writers, as for numerous others working in this tradition, design is, at bottom, an abstract, formal activity; text is secondary, added only after the mastery of form. A theory of design that isolates visual perception from linguistic interpretation encourages indifference to cultural meaning. Although the study of abstract composition is unobjectionable in itself, design's linguistic and social aspects are trivialized or ignored when abstraction is made the primary focus of design thinking.

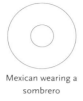

Mexican wearing a
sombrero

In *Art and Visual Perception,* Arnheim defined his term "visual concept" as a mental image of an object that is built out of purely visual experiences of it from many angles. In a humorous tone, he explained that this picture of a Mexican is not a valid representation, because it does not refer to the true "visual concept" of a Mexican. In other words, it requires textual information— a caption—in order to be understood.[1] But what indeed would qualify as the "visual concept" of a Mexican? The sombrero is already a cultural sign, a tourist's cliche. The "visual concept" of a Mexican would consist of more stereotypes, gathered not only from one's experience of real Mexicans, but from movies, television, and books; a big moustache, a bright poncho, leather boots.

Arnheim's example was intended to be funny. He aimed to extend the premise of his joke, however, to experience at large, suggesting that one's understanding of the world is assembled out of purely "visual" perceptions, with language playing the role of a subservient filing system for sense data. In the practice of daily life, however, perception is filtered by culture. A concept of an object is both visual (spatial, sensual, pictorial) and linguistic (conventional, determined by social agreement). The concept of a thing is built up from conventional views and attributes, learned from education, art, and the mass media.

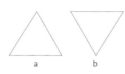

a   b

Arnheim explained that although these two triangles are geometrically identical, they are perceived as different shapes due to the shift in orientation; one is stable, the other unstable. The change is owed to the psychology and physiology of the brain. Triangle B is "unstable," however, only if it is removed from any situation of use and judged as purely abstract form, as in the contextual vacuum of a psychological test or a basic design class, where one is asked to look at the shape "for itself." If the triangle appeared in a geometry book, its rotation would be described mathematically. If the triangle were used as an arrow, its pointing function would make its "instability" irrelevant.

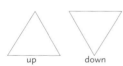

up   down

Basic design courses routinely turn culturally meaningful images into abstract shapes. Type, photographs, and simplified object drawings are cropped, angled, colored, and textured into pleasing arrangements. Abstraction is the first lesson for many design students. It remains a primary assumption behind later work, a staple design "idea." A design theory oriented toward cultural interpretation rather than universal perception would consciously address the conventional, historically changing aspect of words and images in design problems.

The term *visual language* is a common metaphor in modern design textbooks: a "vocabulary" of design elements (dots, lines, shapes, textures, colors) is organized by a "grammar" of contrasts (instability/balance, asymmetry/symmetry, soft/hard, heavy/light). This theory was elaborated in Johannes Itten's Basic Course at the Bauhaus, initiated in Weimar in 1919. A similar program was continued by Kandinsky and Moholy-Nagy at Dessau. Books like *Language of Vision* by Gyorgy Kepes, a teacher at the New Bauhaus in Chicago in the 1940s, further developed the theory of design as a "language" founded in abstraction. Kepes wrote, "Just as the letters of the alphabet can be put together in innumerable ways to form words to convey meanings, so the optical measures and qualities can be brought together...and each particular relationship generates a different sensation of space."[2] Kepes's visual language has a purely sensual meaning.

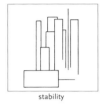 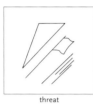 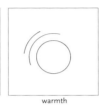

stability   threat   warmth

In her *Primer of Visual Literacy,* Donis Dondis explained that each of the abstract compositions at left has a universal "meaning" that appeals directly to human perception.[3] Yet the brain of a medieval villager would interpret these pictures differently from the brain of a contemporary New Yorker, who might see lower Manhattan in the design for "stability." Dondis replaced concrete, culturally relative meaning with a vague, universalizing mood.

Perhaps Dondis's ideal of "visual literacy," the capacity to perceive and produce abstract compositions, depends on a prior foundation in *verbal* literacy. In a study by the anthropologist A.R. Luria, inhabitants of a remote Russian village were asked to identify drawings of abstract shapes. Some of these villagers knew how to read or write while others did not.

square

Those who were literate interpreted the images as abstract geometric shapes, and they identified them by name: circle, square, triangle. The nonliterate villagers, on the other hand, associated the drawings with objects from their everyday environments: a circle might be a plate, bucket, watch, or moon; a square could be a mirror, door, or house. Luria's research suggests that the ability to see visual forms as "abstract," i.e. disengaged from a context of social use and figurative communication, is a sophisticated skill rather than a universal faculty of perception. It requires the rational, analytical thought processes which characterize literate cultures.[4]

mirror
door
house

The term "visual language" is a metaphor. It compares the structure of the picture plane to the grammar or syntax of language. The effect of this comparison is to segregate "vision" from "language." The two terms are set up as analogous but irreconcilable opposites, parallel realms that will never converge. Theories of visual language and the educational practices based on them close off the study of social and linguistic meaning by isolating visual expression from other modes of communication.

In the interest of interpretation over perception, "language" can be understood inclusively rather than exclusively. Words, images, objects, and customs, insofar as they enter into the process of communication, do not occupy separate classes, but participate in the culturally and historically determined meaning that characterizes verbal language. One of the most influential theorists of this model is Roland Barthes, whose writings in the 1950s and 60s have had a continuing impact on literature, architecture, and film. In graphic design, Herb Lubalin is famous for using words as pictures and pictures as words, and for juxtaposing images and texts to produce new content. He saw no strict barrier between visual and verbal communication.

If Lubalin and other protagonists of the "big idea" approach to design worked intuitively, why, then, does theory matter? Many educators and designers avoid explicit principles in favor of intuitive, pragmatic "common sense."[5] But this anti-theoretical approach is still theoretical. Any position is conditioned by intellectual structures, however vaguely they are defined. By refusing to analyze its own prejudice, pragmatism reinforces the main bias of modernist theory: it suppresses the conscious analysis of design's place in history and culture. Common sense pedagogy limits discussion to the immediate formal and practical success of a project, making the broader social context of design seem irrelevant and secondary.

Theory can function both constructively, as a tool for generating design ideas, and analytically, as an evaluation method. Hanno Ehses, director of the visual communications program at Nova Scotia College of Art and Design, has formed an educational method based on classical rhetoric, the vocabulary used by the ancient Greeks to produce persuasive language. Ehses has applied terms that normally describe writing, like "pun" or "metaphor," to graphic design, giving students a way to recognize and then produce visual/verbal "arguments" and figures of speech. Victor Burgin and other artists have used semiotics and psychoanalysis to study images from painting, film, and advertising. By employing theory to connect rather than disengage visual and verbal expression, we can intensify and direct the cultural meaning of our work.

1 Rudolph Arnheim, *Art and Visual Perception: A Psychology of the Creative Eye* (Berkeley: University of California Press, 1954).

2 Gyorgy Kepes, *Language of Vision* (Chicago: Paul Theobold, 1944), 23.

3 Donis Dondis, *A Primer of Visual Literacy* (Cambridge: MIT Press, 1973), 106.

4 Luria's study is discussed in Walter Ong, *Orality and Literacy: The Technologizing of the Word* (New York and London: Metheun, 1982), 49-52.

5 Paula Scher, "Back to Show and Tell," *AIGA Journal of Graphic Design*, 4, 1 (1986).

Disciplines of Design

Writing with Foucault

A *discipline* is the range of objects, practices, and information that define a field of knowledge. A discipline such as law, medicine, art, or philosophy embraces modes of learning and obeying, knowing and conforming. The boundaries of a discipline mark not only what falls *within* its breadth but also what the field *excludes*, what it bars. The study of disciplines was central to the work of Michel Foucault, who examined the exercise of power through bodies of knowledge (such as psychiatry or political science) and the institutions they authorize (such as hospitals, prisons, or schools).

In a 1982 interview published in the design tabloid *Skyline,* Foucault was asked whether architecture can be a technique of domination or a tool of liberation.[1] In response, Foucault refused to say that architecture is, by itself, either oppressive or liberating; instead, design becomes powerful only when it enters the domain of *other* discourses: for example, when governments look at the structure of the city as a model for the state, or when criminal justice looks at the arrangement of prisons as a means of controlling inmates, or when medicine looks at sanitary housing as a technique for preventing disease.[2]

Foucault elaborated this approach in *The Archaeology of Knowledge,* which asks how it is possible to speak of a discipline such as "medicine" or "economics" or "biology" as a coherent subject.[3] One might also ask, what is the nebulous cultural entity we call design? How can this inconsistent series of objects, people, and practices be grouped under one name?

To open his discussion of disciplines, Foucault looked at the apparent physical unity of the printed book as a prototype for the unity of a professional discourse. A book, while appearing to be a complete, self-contained object—a model of thingness—is, in fact, dispersed across a network of other texts. Likewise, the cumulative knowledge of a discipline is not an "enormous book that is gradually and continuously being written," but is, instead, a "system of dispersion" (37).

"The frontiers of a book
are never clear-cut:
beyond the title, the first lines,
and the last full stop,
beyond its internal configuration
and its autonomous form,
it is caught up in a
system of references to
other books, other texts,
other sentences;
it is a node within a network....
The book is not simply an object
that one holds in one's hands;...
its unity is variable and relative.
As soon as one questions that unity,
it loses its self-evidence;
it indicates itself, constructs itself,
only on the basis of a
complex field of discourse" (23).

1 "Power and Knowledge," *Skyline* (March 1982).

2 Michel Foucault, *Discipline and Punish: The Birth of the Prison,* trans. Alan Sheridan (New York: Vintage Books, 1977).

3 Michel Foucault, *The Archaeology of Knowledge,* trans. M. Sheridan Smith (New York: Pantheon, 1972).

Foucault was fascinated with such spatialized forms of text as the table, the index, and the list. The essay we have constructed on the following pages re-reads passages from *The Archaeology of Knowledge* by substituting the word design where Foucault refers to "madness" and "medicine." We have positioned design as both sickness and cure: it is the object of a pathologist's study (madness) and the subject of specialized knowledge (medicine).

Looking at the history of mental illness, Foucault asked whether "psychiatry" is unified across time because it has always referred to the same mental condition: madness. Rather than consider madness to be a coherent, stable entity, Foucault addressed the interplay of legal and medical discourses that enabled it to become visible as a distinct phenomenon, an object.

If a discipline is not unified by its *object*, then perhaps, Foucault suggested, it is unified by a particular *subject*: an expert, such as the medical doctor, who is qualified to exercise the authority of the field. Foucault argued that while the doctor appears uniquely sanctioned to apply the knowledge of medicine, his authority is dispersed across various institutional sites—the hospital, the laboratory, the library—that challenge the singularity of his judgment.

Modern design emerged in response to the Industrial Revolution, when reform-minded artists and artisans tried to impart a critical sensibility to the making of objects and media. Design took shape as a critique of industry, yet it gained its mature and legitimate status by becoming an agent of machine production and mass consumption. Today, the electronic offshoots of the Machine Age threaten to dissolve design's authority as a definitive sequence of objects and subjects. Design is dispersed across a network of technologies, institutions, and services that define the discipline and its limits.

"But need we dispense forever
with the *'oeuvre,'* the 'book,' or
even such unities as 'science'
or 'literature' [or design]?
Should we regard them as
illusions, illegitimate constructions,
or ill-acquired results?...
What we must do, in fact,
is tear ourselves away
from their virtual self-evidence,
and free the problems that they pose....
[What is design?]
What distinct types of law
can [design] obey?
What articulation is [design] capable of?
What sub-groups can [design]
give rise to?
What specific phenomena does [design]
reveal in the field of discourse?....
In short, [design] requires a theory,
and this theory cannot be constructed
unless the *field* of the facts of discourse
on the basis of which those facts
are built appears in its non-synthetic
purity" (26).

DESIGN AS MADNESS

	"If, in a particular period
	in the history of our society,
the delinquent	[the designer]
	was
psychologized	[professionalized
and pathologized	and aestheticized],
	if
criminal behavior	[visual production]
	could give rise to...objects of knowledge,
	this was because a group of particular relations
	was adopted for use in
psychiatric discourse	[design discourse]....
	The relation between
the authority of	[the conditions of
medical decision	industrial production and popular consumption]
	and
the authority of	[the morality of
judicial decision	materials, styles, and modes of construction]....
	The relation between
therapeutic confinement	[commercial production
in a hospital	in the workshop, printshop, and factory]...
	and
punitive confinement	[critical production
in a prison	by the journal, academy, and design council]...
	These are relations that, operating in
psychiatric discourse	[design discourse],
	have made possible the formation of
	a whole group of various objects....
	These relations are not present in the object....
	They do not define its internal constitution,
	but what enables it to appear..." (43-5).

"We are not trying to find out

who was mad   [who was a designer]

at a particular period, or in what his

madness   [practice]

consisted, or whether his

disturbances   [practices]

were identical with those known to us today.

We are not asking ourselves whether

witches   [job printers, sign painters, typesetters, or graffiti writers]

were unrecognized and persecuted

madmen and madwomen   [designers],

or whether, at a different period, a

mystical or aesthetic   [naïve or primitive]

experience was not unduly

medicalized   [professionalized].

We are not trying to reconstitute what

madness itself   [design itself]

might be....What, in short, we wish to do

is to dispense with 'things'....

To substitute for the enigmatic treasure of

'things' anterior to discourse,

the regular formation of objects that emerge

only in discourse....

To write a history of

discursive objects   [design practices]

that does not plunge them into the common

depth of a primal soil, but deploys

the nexus of regularities

[popular/elite, formal/informal, center/edge,

strange/familiar, radical/traditional]

that govern their dispersion" (47-8).

DESIGN AS MEDICINE

"The status of
the doctor [the designer]
is generally a rather special one...
Medical statements [Design services]
cannot come from anybody;
their value...cannot be dissociated from
the statutorily defined [the professionally qualified]
person who has some right to make them...
We must...describe the
institutional sites from which
the doctor [the designer]
makes his discourse...
In our societies, these sites are:
the hospital [the corporation]...
the private practice [the design consultancy]...
the laboratory [the art school]...
the library [museums, magazines, trade annuals, clip art]...
The doctor himself [The designer himself]
has gradually ceased to be the locus of
medical judgment [design practice].
Beside him, outside him, there have appeared
masses of documentation
[styles, symbols, surfaces, typefaces],
instruments of correlation
[laser printers, service bureaus, copy shops],
and techniques of analysis
[templates, guide books, trade shows, night schools],
which, of course, he makes use of,
but which modify his position as
an observing subject [an expert endowed with the power to
create form, solve problems, pass judgment,
and confer meaning]" (51-2;33-4).

MEDIA

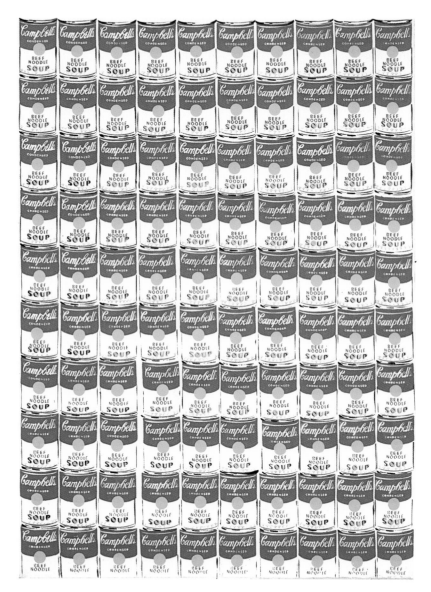

Andy Warhol
One Hundred Cans, 1962
Synthetic polymer paint and silkscreen ink on canvas
Collection Albright-Knox Art Gallery, Buffalo, New York
Gift of Seymour Knox, 1963

Line Art

Andy Warhol and the Commercial Art World of the 1950s

While Pop Art brought the banality of graphic design into the context of painting, Warhol's commercial illustrations were deliberately individualistic.

While Pop Art brought the banality of graphic design into the context of painting, Warhol's commercial illustrations were deliberately individualistic.

While Pop Art brought the banality of graphic design into the context of painting, Warhol's commercial illustrations were deliberately individualistic.

While Pop Art brought the banality of graphic design into the context of painting, Warhol's commercial illustrations were deliberately individualistic.

While Pop Art brought the banality of graphic design into the context of painting, Warhol's commercial illustrations were deliberately individualistic.

While Pop Art brought the banality of graphic design into the context of painting, Warhol's commercial illustrations were deliberately individualistic.

While Pop Art brought the banality of graphic design into the context of painting, Warhol's commercial illustrations were deliberately individualistic.

While Pop Art brought the banality of graphic design into the context of painting, Warhol's commercial illustrations were deliberately individualistic.

While Pop Art brought the banality of graphic design into the context of painting, Warhol's commercial illustrations were deliberately individualistic.

While Pop Art brought the banality of graphic design into the context of painting, Warhol's commercial illustrations were deliberately individualistic.

While Pop Art brought the banality of graphic design into the context of painting, Warhol's commercial illustrations were deliberately individualistic.

While Pop Art brought the banality of graphic design into the context of painting, Warhol's commercial illustrations were deliberately individualistic.

While Pop Art brought the banality of graphic design into the context of painting, Warhol's commercial illustrations were deliberately individualistic.

While Pop Art brought the banality of graphic design into the context of painting, Warhol's commercial illustrations were deliberately individualistic.

While Pop Art brought the banality of graphic design into the context of painting, Warhol's commercial illustrations were deliberately individualistic.

Andy Warhol was a successful commercial illustrator before he launched his second career as a fine artist. These two practices occupied different aesthetic and cultural realms, and yet were linked in fundamental ways. Warhol's flamboyant style of illustration was deliberately expressive and "artistic," and yet it was firmly grounded in the technologies of mechanical reproduction.

The printing term "line art" refers to an image consisting of pure black and white, with no tonal gradations. For any image to be reproduced through offset or letterpress printing, it must meet the conditions of "line art." While type or an ink drawing are by nature composed of black marks, the continuous tones of a photograph or a wash illustration must be translated into the dot pattern of a half-tone. An ink drawing is "camera-ready." Because the mediation of the half-tone screen is unnecessary for reproducing it, the process is both economically expedient and visually direct, the copy closely resembling its original.

A typical Warhol illustration of a shoe, created for a fashion magazine, demonstrates how a two-color image was reproduced from "line art." A base layer carries an ink drawing of a patterned shoe, and a second layer, on a transparent overlay, contains the pattern. The printer would have photographed the two drawings, each of which represents a separate color; the crossed marks on each layer allowed them to be realigned into one two-color image. Silkscreen printing demands the same process of separating a picture into layers of "line art."

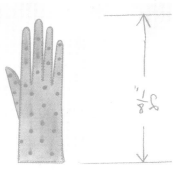

Before the introduction of the half-tone process in the 1880s, wood engravers reproduced photographs by translating them by hand into patterns of black marks. Photographic processes were also widely used in the printing of line drawings. For example, an illustrator could prepare a drawing of arbitrary dimensions, which could then be photographically reduced.[1] With the rise of half-tone reproduction, continuous-tone photography became a medium of commercial representation. Some illustrators continued to approximate the realism of photography, but many commercial artists worked to define the products of the hand against those of the camera, marketing drawings that were stylistically distinct.[2]

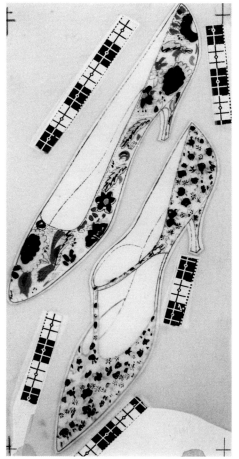

Andy Warhol
Untitled (Shoes with registration marks), c. 1955-60
Ink and acetate over ink and tempera collage on board
© 1995 The Andy Warhol Foundation, Inc.

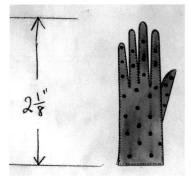

Andy Warhol
Polka dot glove with measurements, n. d.
Ink on paper
Collection The Andy Warhol Foundation, Inc.

While "artistic" illustration fostered the associations of originality attached to painting, it still had to accommodate the techniques of photo-mechanical reproduction. During the 1950s, line drawing became an aesthetically and technically economical solution to the twin demands of reproduction and artistic singularity: it served as a "signature" or record of the artist's personality, and it also provided the printer with camera-ready art.

Illustrators for advertising and editorial design enjoyed a period of influence and affluence during this period. In the juried exhibition *Illustrators '59,* one criterion for judgement was, "Could a camera have done it?"[3] The winning entries were realistically rendered scenes inflected with the cachet of expressionist gesture and impressionist atmosphere.

1 On graphic arts technology, see Estelle Jussim, *Visual Communications and the Graphic Arts: Photographic Technologies in the Nineteenth Century* (New York: R. R. Bowker Co., 1974).

2 No trends in advertising and design are "universal," and as this essay aims to point out, the commercial art world in which Andy Warhol was a successful player occupied the sophisticated "cutting edge" of the trade, and not the mainstream of consumer graphics. A 1957 study conducted by the magazine *Art Direction* found that many of the "trends" discussed by art directors were difficult to quantify. "1937 to 1957: A Contrast in Consumer Ads, What's Different Today and Why," *Art Direction,* 9, 10 (January 1958): 76-79, 125.

3 "Illustrators '59," *Art Direction,* 10, 11 (February 1959): insert.

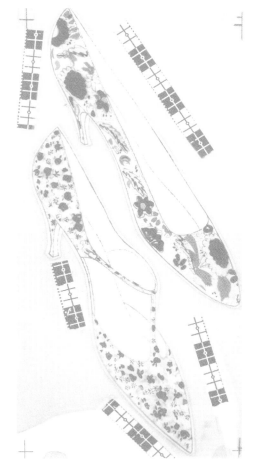

Andy Warhol
Rheumatoid Arthritis, 1952
The Upjohn Company, Kalamazoo, Michigan
Printed promotional brochure
Collection The Andy Warhol Foundation, Inc.

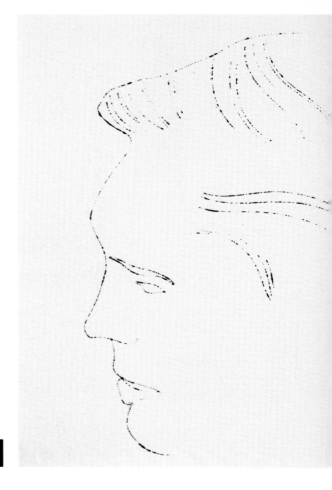

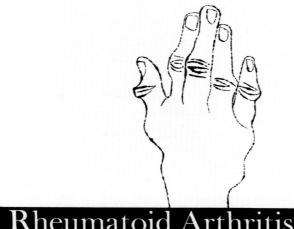

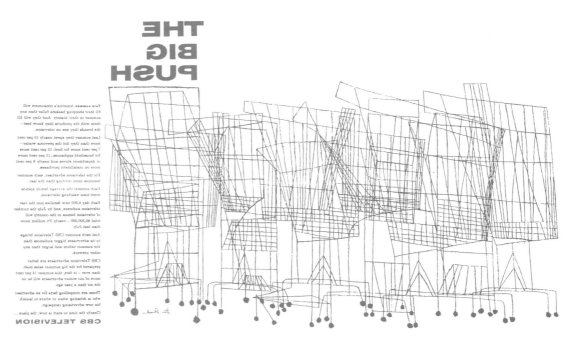

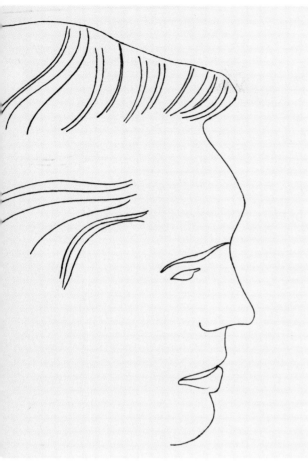

Andy Warhol
Untitled (Male Head), c. 1954
Ink on Strathmore paper
© The Andy Warhol Foundation
This drawing demonstrates the blotting tech-
nique that became Warhol's signature style.
Created by drawing in ink on non-absorbent
paper and then pressing the image onto a
fresh sheet, the process interrupted the
immediacy of drawing with a chance process.

Ben Shahn
The Big Push
Illustration for CBS Television advertisement
Variety, June 12, 1957

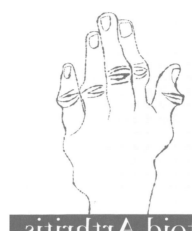

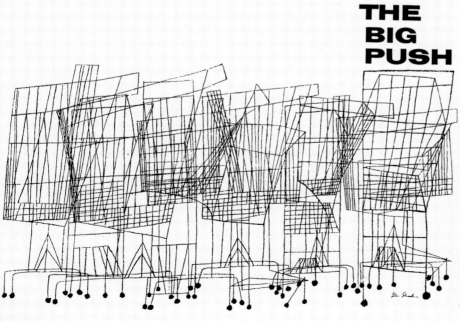

THE BIG PUSH

THIS SUMMER America's consumers will fill their shopping baskets fuller than any summer in their history. And they will fill them with the products they know best — the brands they see on television.

Last summer they spent nearly 10 per cent more than they did the previous winter — 7 per cent more for food; 12 per cent more for household appliances; 15 per cent more in department stores and nearly 8 per cent more on installment purchase.

For the television advertiser, each summer becomes more inviting than the last.

Each summer the average family spends more time watching television.

Each day 8,000 new families join the vast television audience, and by July the number of television homes in the country will total 40,300,000 — nearly 3½ million more than last July.

And each summer CBS Television brings to its advertisers bigger audiences than the summer before and larger than any other network.

CBS Television advertisers are better prepared for the big summer sales push than ever — in fact, this summer 14 per cent more of our winter advertisers will be on the air than a year ago.

These are compelling facts for an advertiser who is debating when or where to launch his new advertising campaign.

Clearly the time to start is now; the place…

CBS TELEVISION

By the 50s, photography had come to dominate the promotion of food, furniture, and housewares, areas where the copious detail provided by the camera was invaluable. Some products, however, benefitted from more interpretive merchandising. Fashion and pharmeceuticals were among those industries that favored illustration. In the case of medical products, drawing was considered more appropriate than photography, for it offered a veiled rather than literal depiction of illness. Pharmaceutical advertising was directed at medical professionals, an upper-middle-class group that the ad industry regarded as receptive to the "cultured" appeal of artistic illustration.[4]

Andy Warhol produced illustrations for several pharmaceutical companies during the 50s, including CIBA-GEIGY and Upjohn, both known for their progressive design.

Warhol provided a drawing for a 1952 Upjohn pamphlet designed by the prominent German-born art director Will Burtin, who advocated tasteful modernist design as a product with social as well as economic value. Burton criticized the graphics that characterized American supermarket advertising as "verbal, printed, and visual assaults on the consumer," which perpetuate the assumption that "the majority of people have 'poor taste.'" In the Upjohn pamphlet, Burtin directed Warhol to make the pain of arthritis palpable through his labored, wavering line.[5]

The fashion industry exploited the stylishness of illustration and its ability to bring drama to small objects such as shoes, which were difficult to photograph and were enhanced by exaggerated, elongated lines. Geraldine Stutz, accessories editor for *Glamour* and later vice-president of I. Miller & Sons Co., recalled in a 1988 interview that the techniques of still-life photography had not been perfected in the 50s.[6] An I. Miller ad campaign, art directed by Peter Palazzo, used Warhol's illustrations to represent products through oblique association rather than literal depiction. A writer for *Printer's Ink* called the campaign "idea art," and quoted Palazzo's assess-

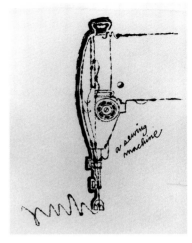

Andy Warhol
Untitled (Sewing Machine Detail), c. 1952
Ink on Strathmore paper
© The Andy Warhol Foundation, Inc.

scarcely perceptible ways."[27] In contrast to such guarded conventionality, the advertising and design that was considered progressive during the early years of Pop Art was inventive; it was derived from a largely urban milieu, and gave expression to an ethnically diverse, culturally sophisticated design community.

The predictable headlines, celebrity endorsements, and slick airbrush illustrations of the immediate postwar period were the creation of an entrenched, homogeneous Madison Avenue ad industry. In the 1920s, ad agencies had sought to create a "science" of advertising by engaging psychological theory; this scientism continued to expand with the rise of marketing and demographic studies, which encouraged conformity and caution.[28] This conservatism was bolstered by a largely upper-middle class, male, Ivy League work force.

In the late 50s the new agency Doyle Dane Bernbach (DDB) began to produce art and copy whose humor and sophistication challenged its consumer audience, exchanging hard-sell tactics for an unprecedented self-consciousness about advertising. DDB's campaign for Volkswagen became the exemplar of the "New Advertising," a style made possible by a closer working relationship between the art director and copywriter. The new advertising strategies also reflected a wider representation of Jewish, Italian, Irish, Greek, and female art directors and copywriters.[29]

In contrast, the realm of communication that served as source material for Pop Art did not come from the vanguard of advertising and design, but from the tried-and-true vocabulary of the "affluent society." Warhol's success as a commercial artist coincided with a gradual shift in the professional standing of illustrators, prompted by the increasing use of photography. While his exuberant, decorative style contributed spontaneity and playfulness to commercial graphics, it also directly exploited the techniques of mechanical reproduction.

24 Glaser asserted his distrust of collage as early as 1960; quoted in Sterling McIlhany, "Milton Glaser," *Graphis*, 16, 92 (November/ December 1960): 508. The same polemic is repeated nearly thirty years later in Milton Glaser, "Some Thoughts on Modernism: Past, Present and Future," *AIGA Journal of Graphic Design*, 5, 2 (1987): 6.

25 Glaser discusses his idea of "vernacular" graphics in Glaser, *Graphic Design*, 14.

26 Interview, Milton Glaser with J. Abbott Miller, December 9, 1988.

27 *Designing a Brand Mark for Today* (New York: Lippincott & Margulies, 1956).

28 Walter Dill Scott, *The Psychology of Advertising* (New York: Dodd, Mead & Company, Inc., 1931). The use of marketing and demographics is descibed in Otis R. Pease, *Responsibilities of American Advertising* (New Haven: Yale University Press, 1958).

29 The influx of urban "ethnics" into the advertising industry is descibed in Larry Dobrow, *When Advertising Tried Harder* (New York: Friendly Press, 1984), 68.

30 Interview, Lou Dorfsman with Donna De Salvo, July 11, 1988.

It is those techniques that bridge the gap between the high-style shoes of his commercial art and the deadpan irony of his Campbell's Soup cans. This continuity is what makes Warhol problematic as a "fine" artist. For example, while Lou Dorfsman admired the artistry of Warhol's illustrations, he remained skeptical of his art-world stardom. For Dorfsman, commercial techniques produce commercial art. He commented in 1988, "Silkscreening Monroe in 12 different color breakdowns is fine, but to me it's a graphic design schtick."[30]

In his transition from the business of illustration to the business of art, Warhol made use of the skills, both manual and social, that he had learned in the commercial art world. While illustration continued to be an important profession within graphic design, Warhol might have sensed photography's encroachment, and surely he sensed its power. The May 1969 cover for *Esquire*,

created by George Lois and Carl Fischer, demonstrated the flexibility and impact of photographic illustration: a "high-concept" image was given the force of realism by a seamlessly crafted photomontage. Warhol is shown sinking in the commercial mire he celebrated. The fact that his descent is depicted photographically indicates the rise of the camera and the diminishing prestige of hand-drawn illustration in a commercial art world that was increasingly self-conscious about the boundaries between art and design.

The authors thank Seymour Chwast, Lou Dorfsman, Milton Glaser, and Barbara Nessim for their comments on illustration and design in the late 1950s. Thanks also to Donna DeSalvo for generously providing access to her interviews with Lou Dorfsman, Steve Frankfurt, Tina Fredericks, Art Kane, Gene Moore, Peter Palazzo, Philip Pearlstein, and Geraldine Stutz.

Cover of *Esquire*, May 1969
Art director: George Lois
Photographer: Carl Fischer

Perhaps Fiore's most unusual project was a collaboration with Jerome Agel and Buckminster Fuller. Echoing the success of *The Medium is the Massage,* the book *I Seem To Be a Verb* (1970) became Fuller's biggest seller. Like *Massage,* it served as a general introduction to a study of the environment, focusing (loosely) on technology rather than media. The first few spreads have a traditional vertical orientation, but the pages soon divide horizontally along a central axis, with the lower half printed upside down in green ink. Across the center of each spread, a quote from Fuller, which continues throughout the entire book, is conveyed in a telegraphic line of large capital letters. When the quote reaches the end of the book, it turns and loops back, continuing in the opposite direction. The pages themselves resemble a scrapbook, crammed with advertisements, newspaper clippings, paintings, camp film stills, lyrics, wire-service photographs, and quotes set in contrasting typefaces. *I Seem To Be a Verb* is even

Book, *I Seem to Be a Verb,* by Buckminster Fuller with Jerome Agel and Quentin Fiore; designed by Quentin Fiore (New York: Bantam, 1970).

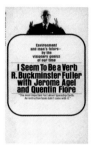
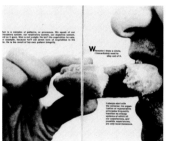
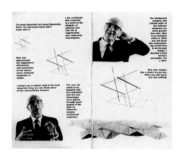
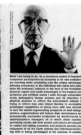
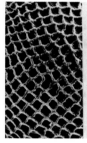

less linear and didactic than *The Medium is the Massage,* and seems to revel in its puzzling discontinuity, mixing the words of Charlie Brown and Charles de Gaulle, images of Hollywood and starving children. The quote from Fuller is the only apparent thread holding things together.

Common to all of Fiore's books is the deliberate repetition of images and text. This technique seems partly inspired by the serial forms of Pop Art; more fundamentally, repetition is an effect of the mass media which McLuhan sought to explain. Throughout his career, McLuhan described his work as a series of "probes." Bruce Powers, one of McLuhan's collaborators, has explained how these "probes" were conducted not through argument, but with "semantic wedges." Phrases like "the medium is the message" allowed McLuhan to shift attention from content to form. Fiore complemented these "semantic wedges" with a design strategy centered on repetition, reinforcing McLuhan's larger premise that America is a culture of reproduction.

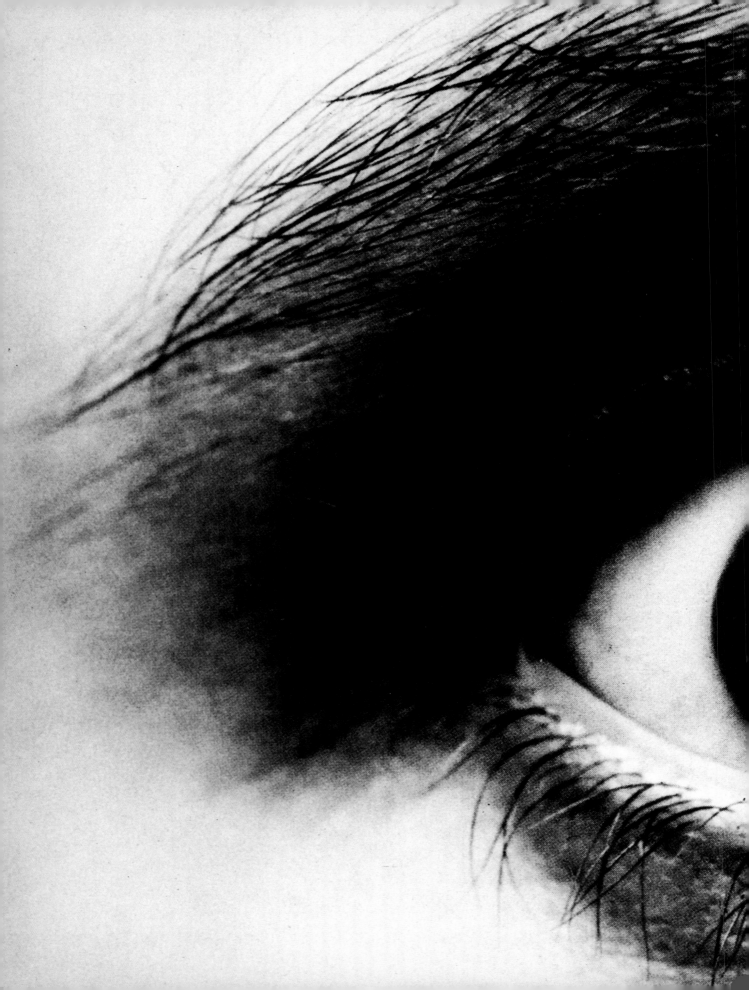

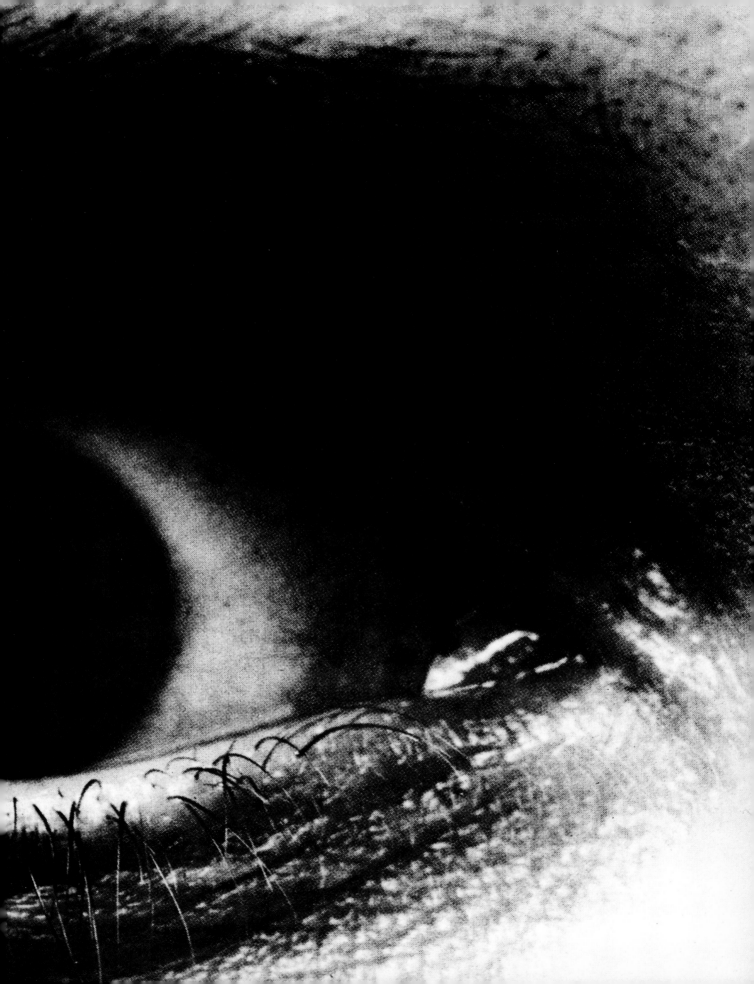

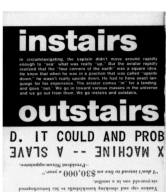
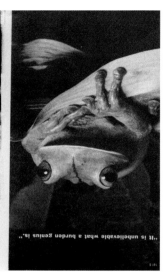

instairs

In circumnavigating, the captain didn't move around rapidly enough to "sea" what was really "up." But the aviator rapidly realized that the "four corners of the earth" was a square idea. He knew that when he was in a position that was called "upside down," he wasn't really upside down. He had to have exact language for his experience. The aviator comes "in" for a landing, and goes "out." We go in toward various masses in the universe and we go out from them. We go instairs and outstairs.

outstairs

D. IT COULD AND PROB
X MACHINE -- A SLAVE

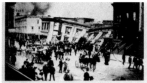
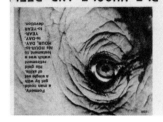
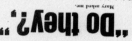

"I'd like to be Vice President."—Julian Bond, on being nominated at Democratic national convention.

The truth of a thing is in the feel of it, not the think of it.

BLY WILL BE PROVIDE
PLE MUSCLE AND REFL

Cities, as we know them, are obsolete in respect to yesterday's function as warehouse and trading post. Trying to rebuild cities to make them accommodate the new needs of World Man is like trying to reconstruct and improve a wrecked ship as it rests upon a surf-pounded reef. The great cities, like New York, Paris, London, Tokyo, will turn into universities as automation replaces the humans who function only as automatons.

The computer is an imitation human brain, but its capacity, speed of operation, and tirelessness, as well as its ability to operate under environmental conditions intolerable to the human anatomy, make it far more effective in performing special tasks than is the human brain minus the computer.

"Any of you who can't SHOUT in a company president's FACE and MAKE him BUY might as well LEAVE now. You WON'T be around LONG anyway."—24-year-old executive.

D BY THE UTTERLY IM
AN THAT OF BEING SIM

I Seem to Be a Verb is conceived as a landscape that could be taken apart and laid out end-to-end to form a panoramic view of American culture. A teletype quotation by

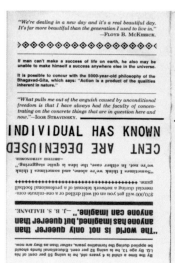
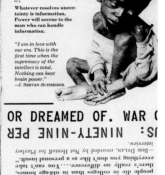
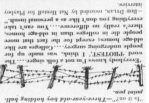

"We're dealing in a new day and it's a real beautiful day. It's far more beautiful than the generation I used to live in."
—Floyd B. McKissick

If man can't make a success of life on earth, he also may be unable to make himself a success anywhere else in the universe.

It is possible to concur with the 5000-year-old philosophy of the Bhagavad-Gita, which says: "Action is a product of the qualities inherent in nature."

"What pulls me out of the anguish caused by unconditional freedom is that I have always had the faculty of concentrating on the concrete things that are in question here and now."—Igor Stravinsky.

INDIVIDUAL HAS KNOWN

Whatever resolves uncertainty is information. Power will accrue to the man who can handle information.

"I am in love with our era. This is the first time when the supremacy of the intellect is total. Nothing can beat brain power."—J. Servan-Schreiber.

OR DREAMED OF. WAR

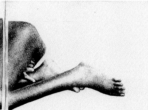
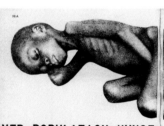
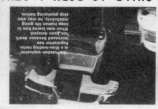
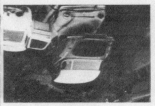

VER POPULATION HUNGE
R DISEASE WOULD CEAS

Jean Baudrillard has noted the relationship between McLuhan's "medium message" and Walter Benjamin's landmark 1936 essay "The Work of Art in the Age of Mechanical Reproduction." As Baudrillard writes, "Benjamin (and later McLuhan) grasped technique not as productive force (where Marxist analysis remains trapped) but as medium, as the form and principle of a whole new generation of meaning."[4] Benjamin and McLuhan both drew attention to reproduction, confronting it as a definitive aspect of modern culture.

The ability to create meaning by recycling, repeating, and reframing images and texts constitutes Fiore's graphic response to McLuhan's assessments of the cultural impact of communication and technology. This McLuhanesque design strategy informed Fiore's work with Rubin and Fuller as well—appropriately, since these authors, too, were concerned with the reproduction of social life, from Fuller's celebration of liberating technologies to Rubin's critique of oppressive institutions.

1 Robert MacMillan, "Marshall McLuhan at the Mercy of his Commentators," *Philosophy of Social Sciences*, 22, 4 (December 1992): 475-91.

2 Marshall McLuhan's most influential books include *Understanding Media: The Extensions of Man* (New York: McGraw-Hill, 1964); and *The Gutenberg Galaxy: The Making of Typographic Man* (Toronto: University of Toronto Press, 1962).

Buckminster Fuller, looping back on itself at the end, holds together a disparate collection of words and images.

Philip Marchand's book *Marshall McLuhan: The Medium and the Messenger* (New York: Ticknor and Fields, 1989) is a critical biography; it includes a complete bibliography of McLuhan's published works.

3 Quotes from Quentin Fiore are from an interview with J. Abbott Miller, Fall 1992.

4 Jean Baudrillard, "Symbolic Exchange and Death," in *Selected Writings*, Mark Poster, ed. (Stanford: University of Stanford Press, 1988), 138.

Fiore finds irony in the fact that his 50-year career is measured by work he produced at the margins of publishing during a span of two and a half years. In retrospect, the late 1960s have emerged as a period of re-evaluation and re-invention in American history, an era whose momentous wave of cultural change carried design along with it. Like the 1920s, the 60s witnessed international upheaval in art and politics, in sexuality and social transgression, and in the theory and practice of media. Fiore's books collapsed together the roles of author, editor, designer, and producer. The fact that this strategy has been so rarely repeated says more about the conservatism of the "industry of the word" than about the success of the projects. The enthusiastic merging of theory and populism, words and pictures, forged by Fiore and his collaborators deliver a formidable challenge and an inspiring model to contemporary graphic designers who are seeking to rethink the normative boundaries of professional practice.

**First of a
seven-part series**

"Black History:
Lost, Stolen or Strayed."

America has camouflaged the black man. For three hundred years the attitudes of white Americans to black and black Americans to white have been subjected to misunderstandings, erasures and distortions damaging to both. The black American's achievements have been misplaced, his contributions obscured. He has been told so often who he is not that he no longer knows who he is. And the frustrations of his search for identity and recognition underlie much of today's crisis of alienation in American society.

Tonight, in the first of a seven-part series broadcast on Tuesdays in the coming weeks, CBS News tries to set the record straight to help close some of the gaps of understanding that separate black and white America.

In tonight's broadcast, Bill Cosby, actor and comedian, guides us through a history of the attitudes that have distorted the image of the Negro in America. He shows how those attitudes were formed and what they have done to us. He shows the black man's need to know who he is and what happens to him when he cannot find the answer.

On succeeding Tuesdays, Of Black America will present a study of the Negro soldier, a conference of black American and African leaders, a public opinion survey of black and white attitudes, a look at what the black American has contributed to sports and music, a history of slavery, and an examination of African life and

civilization through the eyes of three young black Americans.

Sponsored by Xerox Corporation, with Perry Wolff as Executive Producer, Of Black America presents the Negro in a new light, with balance and perspective. If it helps both black and white Americans to understand each other a little better, if it helps to change some of their attitudes toward each other, it will prove to be one of the most rewarding series ever presented on television.

OF
BLACK
AMERICA

10 TONIGHT CBS NEWS ⊙ 2

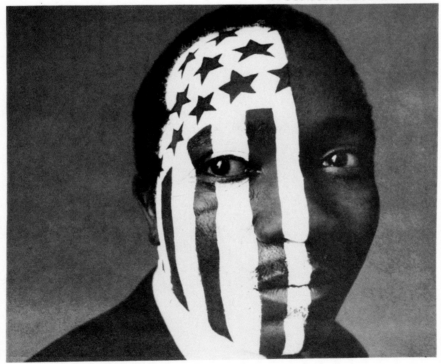

This ad by CBS art director Lou Dorfsman for the program "Of Black America" appeared in the summer of 1968. It ran in several major American newspapers, including *The New York Times* and *The Chicago Tribune*. The photograph, taken by Ron Borowski, was also used for television spots promoting the program. This widely disseminated image continues to circulate as an icon of design history, preserved in professional annuals of design and in textbooks and reference works on graphic design.

White on Black on Gray

Representations of otherness form part of the social construction of reality and the negotiation of the future. Images of others are a form of cultural polemics; they are contested and are themselves forms of contestation.
JAN NEDERVEEN PIETERSE

Following enormous social and political changes in the U.S. in the 1960s, the representation of African-Americans in print and broadcast media changed in both number and character. The history of demeaning and stereotyped representations of African-Americans has been the subject of much recent scholarship; few writers, however, have discussed the impact of the civil rights movement on the nature and scope of advertising imagery.[1] What follows is not a history of stereotypes, but an investigation of representations that negotiated the issue of race in the context of advertising. The essay considers how what we refer to as "mass" media mimicked patterns of cultural and economic segregation, mapping patterns of exclusion onto the terrain of advertising and publishing.

At the forefront of this consideration are two well-known advertisements, each produced by prominent New York art directors. The advertisement, "Of Black America," art directed by Lou Dorfsman, promoted a seven-part CBS television series on the history of African-Americans.[2] The program, sponsored by Xerox Corporation and presented without commercial interruption, examined the distorted representation of African-Americans in history books, movies, and other media. "Of Black America" was one of several network and local programs broadcast in the summer of 1968 that examined the status of African-Americans. Critics at the time noted that this and other consciousness-raising programs were being aired in summer months when audiences were low, and that the programming was a weakly conciliatory gesture. The comedian Godfrey Cambridge ironically remarked: "We burn down three more cities, and I'll be president of CBS."[3] It was also noted that many of these programs were written, produced, and directed by white journalists; among seven producers of the CBS series, none were African-Americans.

1 See Jan Nederveen Pieterse, *White on Black: Images of Africa and Blacks in Western Popular Culture,* (New Haven: Yale University Press, 1992). For an overview that surveys film, television, radio, and advertising, see Jannette L. Dates, William Barlow, eds. *Split Image: African Americans in the Mass Media* (Washington, D.C.: Howard University Press, 1990).

2 The writer-producers of the series were Andrew Rooney and Perry Wolff. The narrator was Bill Cosby.

3 "The Race Race," *Newsweek* (July 15, 1968): 74.

"Some American advertisers are color-blind," designed in 1968 by Herb Lubalin, also appeared as a full-page ad in *The New York Times* and other publications. Its function was to encourage major corporations to advertise in the pages of *Ebony*, then the largest magazine in the U.S. directed at African-Americans. The *Ebony* ad was part of a larger campaign designed and written by Lubalin that featured various messages directed at presumably white executives or senior managers who buy advertising space.

Both ads employ large, closely cropped photographs and an emphatic use of high-contrast black-and-white photography. Both ads derive their impact from face painting: the "design" occurs primarily on the face of the model, rather than in the composition of the page. The CBS ad turns the American flag into a provocatively ambiguous mask, situating the image in a theatrical rather than a documentary context. The *Ebony* ad also invokes the theatrical arena by reversing the "blackface" of the minstrel tradition, popularized by white entertainers since the 1820s.

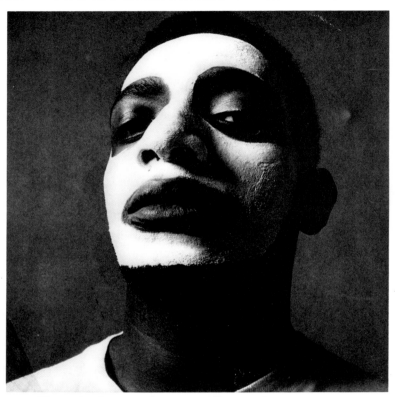

Some American advertisers are color-blind.

Some advertisers see the Negro as a black man in white-face. What a mistake! The Negro doesn't respond to lily-white advertising in mass media. How could he? The Negro thinks black, feels black, and lives black simply because Jim Crow is still the national custom.

If you want to reach the heart of a $30-billion-a-year market, you'll have to recognize that the Negro is nobody's fair-haired boy. You'll have to change the color of your advertising. And you'll have to advertise in a publication of the Negro, by the Negro, and for the Negro.

That's Ebony—a magazine as different from mass media as black is from white.

Ebony.
The magazine
that gets to the heart of
the Negro market.

This 1968 *Ebony* advertisement was part of a series that appeared in *The New York Times* and other major American newspapers. Art director and designer: Herb Lubalin; photographer: Irv Bahrt; copywriters: Byron Barclay, Herb Lubalin; agency: Wyse Advertising. The campaign was included in the *47th Annual of Advertising, Editorial & Television Art & Design* (New York: Watson-Guptill, 1968), 75, 104.

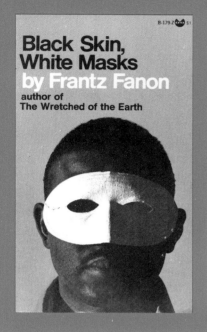

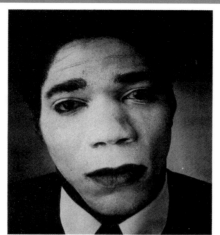

Whiteness as a mask has been a recurrent theme in graphic design dealing with subjects of race. The pathos of the clown, the muteness of the pantomime, the "mystery" of the masked man, and the spectacle of the minstrel are theatrical associations conjured by such imagery.

Frantz Fanon's landmark book *Black Skin, White Masks* was first published in French in 1952, followed by a U.S. edition in 1968. One U.S. edition carried the image of a black model wearing a white eye mask like those worn at masquerade parties.

In a 1984 public service ad for the New York Urban League, created by Doyle Dane Bernbach, the model peers out plaintively in a variation on the sad clown role. Art director: Ervin Jue; copywriter: Chuck Gessner; photographer: Gil Cope.

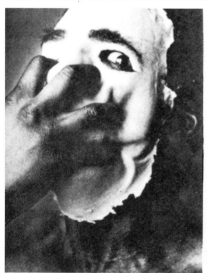

"Black Theatre: The American Tragic Voice," art director/designer: Kenneth R. Deardoff; photographer: Peter Papadopolous; publisher: Grove Press/Evergreen Review. Reproduced in *The 49th Annual of Advertising, Editorial & Television Art & Design* (New York: Watson-Guptill Publications, 1970), 51.

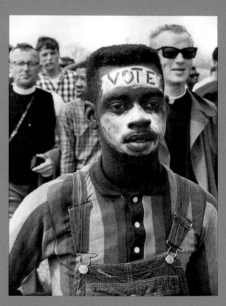

This photograph of the 1965 Selma-to-Montgomery march reverses the victimized imagery evident in many public service ads about race. An unidentified demonstrator has written the message of the march in the zinc oxide used to protect his skin during the fifty-four-mile journey. Photo by Matt Herron.

THE AGE OF THE 'WORD PICTURE'

The CBS and *Ebony* ads were designed by two of the most esteemed art directors of the post-war period. Lubalin's playful, punning, and narrative typography was influential in the fields of advertising and graphic design. Lubalin worked for a number of liberal publications including *Eros*, *Avant-Garde*, and *Fact*, and he worked on the catalogue for the controversial *Harlem on My Mind* exhibition at the Metropolitan Museum of Art in 1968.[4] Dorfsman contributed significantly to advertising and corporate identity. Joining CBS in 1946 as an assistant to William Golden, Dorfsman eventually became vice president and creative director for advertising and design until his departure in 1988.[5]

The CBS and *Ebony* campaigns are products of the larger phenomenon of the New Advertising. This label was retrospectively applied to work which, beginning in the mid-1950s, closely integrated the editorial and visual aspects of an advertisement.[6] The New Advertising produced unexpected, ironic, and humorous relationships between image and text.

Collage, photomontage, "typophoto," and staged photography were consistent visual strageies in the New Advertising. The use of these techniques had been explored in the work of John Heartfield and other Dada, Constructivist, and Bauhaus designers. The New Advertising, like Heartfield's work in the 1930s, favored strong, readily legible concepts over abstract, formally complex compositions.

The appearance of experimental approaches in American mass-media of the 1960s may be linked to the rise of television. The verbal and visual flow of television allows for a rapid layering among image, text, and sound. Because television competed for the time people had formerly spent reading, print graphics were forced to invent new strategies. In 1959, Herb Lubalin remarked on the rising trend towards "word-pictures," which had reversed "the usual advertising procedure of copy dictating the graphic approach."[7]

Another factor which made the New Advertising new was the influx of women and ethnic writers and designers into the advertising industry.[8] Major ad agencies had been dominated by an elite of Ivy League-educated WASP men. The 1960s saw the growth of smaller agencies with a more diverse workforce. Jewish, Greek, Italian, Irish, and female writers and art directors found some newly opened doors; African-Americans, however, were still rarely employed in the industry or represented in advertisements.[9]

A celebrated 1965 campaign by Doyle Dane Bernbach carried the line, "You don't have to be Jewish to love Levy's Jewish Rye." The models included an American Indian, an Irish policeman, an Asian man, and an African-American boy. The humor of the series is revealing in that it depended on the *infrequency* with which ethnicity and racial difference were represented in advertising.

4 Gertrude Snyder and Alan Peckolick, *Herb Lubalin: Art Director, Graphic Designer, and Typographer* (New York: American Showcase, Inc. 1985).

5 Dick Hess and Marion Muller, *Dorfsman and CBS* (New York: American Showcase, Inc. 1987).

6 Robert Glatzer, *The New Advertising* (New York: Citadel Press, 1970); Bob Levenson, *Bill Bernbach's Book: A History of the Advertising that Changed the History of Advertising* (New York: Villard Books, 1987).

7 Herb Lubalin, address to the Art Directors Club of New York, 1959.

8 Larry Dobrow places great importance on the role of "streetwise" graduates from urban art schools and colleges in transforming the advertising profession. Larry Dobrow, *When Advertising Tried Harder* (New York: Friendly Press, 1984), 68.

9 A 1968 article on black graphic designers profiled five individuals, including William Wacasey, who was identified as having opened New York's "first black-owned design studio." The article also reported on the formation of an organization called GAP (Group for Advertising Progress), that acted as an information network for black designers seeking advice and employment. Despite evidence of growing participation, the article warned that "black designers constitute perhaps one or two percent of the total...." Dorothy Jackson, "The Black Experience in Graphic Design," *Print* XXII:VI (November-December, 1968): 48.

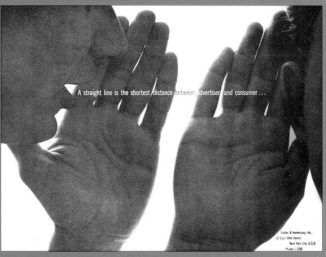

A straight line is the shortest distance between advertiser and consumer...

Sudler & Hennessey, Inc.
130 East 58th Street
New York City, U.S.A.
PLaza 1-7290

break up cough

relax bronchioles, reduce histamine-induced congestion and irritation throughout the respiratory tract, liquefy thick, tenacious mucus.
PYRIBENZAMINE EXPECTORANT with Ephedrine
ALSO AVAILABLE: PYRIBENZAMINE EXPECTORANT WITH CODEINE AND EPHEDRINE (EXEMPT NARCOTICS), PYRIBENZAMINE CITRATE (TRIPELENNAMINE CITRATE CIBA)

THE NEW YORK TIMES, FRIDAY, APRIL 25, 1969

WHITE VS WHITE
WHITE VS BLACK
BLACK VS BLACK
BLACK VS WHITE
WHITE VS YELLOW
YELLOW VS YELLOW
YELLOW VS BROWN
BROWN VS BROWN

WATCH THE WORLDWATCHERS CBS NEWS

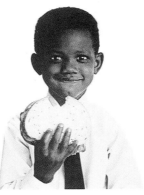

You don't have to be Jewish

to love Levy's
real Jewish Rye

Herb Lubalin's work is characterized by illustrative typography and clever relationships between image and copy. In a 1959 advertisement for a drug manufactured by CIBA, Lubalin illustrated a "cough" by photographically manipulating the typography. Lubalin was vice president, art director and creative director of Sudler & Hennessey from 1945 to 1964. In his 1955 promotional piece for Sudler & Hennessey, above right, Lubalin strikingly visualized an advertising truism. Photograph by Irv Bahrt.

This advertisement for CBS NEWS by Lou Dorfsman ran as a full-page in *The New York Times* on April 25, 1969. The copy states: "Our world seems racked by divisions. Color is only one. The gap between rich and poor, some say, is deeper. Between young and old, more frightening. CBS NEWS has been studying such collision points for a long time. In broadcasts like *Who Speaks for Birmingham?* in 1961; *Black Power—White Backlash* in 1966; the seven-part series *Of Black America* in 1968."

A 1965 campaign by Doyle Dane Bernbach used the slogan "You don't have to be Jewish to love Levy's real Jewish Rye" with images of an Irish-American, an Asian-American, and an African-American. The humor of the series depended on the infrequency with which advertising represented ethnically and racially diverse models. The popularity of the series resulted in its distribution as posters.

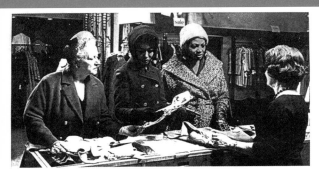
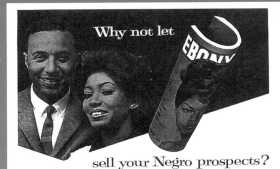

WHITE MEDIA / BLACK MEDIA

Apart from the Levy's campaign, and the increasing use of black celebrity athletes and performers, national advertisers were reluctant to represent racial and ethnic diversity.[10] The inclusion of black models in advertising remained a rarity, even though blacks constituted as much as 20% of the American population in 1966. Within advertising and television programming, there was little indication of this demographic shift, despite the anti-segregationist, anti-discrimination efforts of the civil rights movement.[11]

The unwillingness of advertisers to represent this large segment of their consumer constituency was institutionalized in the advertising and public relations industries through the phrase "white media," which ostensibly referred to white-oriented magazines, newspapers, and television stations. The term "white media" posited the existence of two cleanly separable social spaces, as though one might exist in isolation of the other. Through a terminological maneuver, "white media" sanctioned its exclusion of the cultural Other, and simultaneously installed "black media" as its semantic opposite.

These terms framed two fields in which the advertising industry operated in the 1960s. The "us/them" structure is evident in *Ebony's* campaign in *Advertising Age*, which urged readers to consider that "Negro customers, just like white customers, are interested in media which reflect *their* specific needs, *their* unique interests and *their* distinct desires" (the italics were added).

10 The incorporation of black celebrities in advertising increased throughout the 1960s. In *The 49th Annual of Advertising, Editorial & Television Art & Design,* published in 1970, African-American celebrities appeared in a number of ads: Joe Frazier (Personna Shavers), Ray Charles (Coca-Cola), Mohammed Ali (*Jock* magazine), Sonny Liston (Braniff International Airlines), Duke Ellington (Olivetti Typewriters).

11 A number of surveys on the representation of blacks in the mass-media were conducted in this period. The American Civil Liberties Union conducted a television content analysis in December 1965, concluding that "Negroes were given only .65 percent of the speaking roles on commercials and 1.39 percent of the non-speaking roles." See "TV Ads, Shows Still Lag in Use of Negro, Other Races: ACLU," *Advertising Age,* 37 (April 11, 1966): 128. A 1969 study looked at twelve "mainstream" magazines for the years 1946, 1956, and 1965 to evaluate the nature and frequency of representations of blacks in

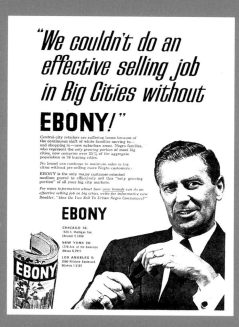

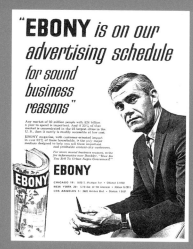

Ebony ads typically used a white male "spokesperson" to address the audience of *Advertising Age*. In instances where *Ebony* did represent black models within the pages of *Advertising Age*, they were not cast as spokespersons for "black media" who directly address the audience; instead they are portrayed as consumers or as the models who might appear inside a fashion spread in a typical issue of *Ebony*. The appearance of black models in these ads is often visually mediated by the presence of white models.

OPPOSITE, LEFT Two black "consumers" are framed by a white "clerk" and a white "consumer," who looks on. *Advertising Age* (March 23, 1964): 56.

OPPOSITE, RIGHT The stylish young couple in this ad are not given any "speaking parts," parallel to tendencies in television of the period. *Advertising Age* (February 24, 1964): 129.

ABOVE, LEFT The model in the ad is not identified as a specific individual, but the suit and tie suggest he is an executive of some type—perhaps he is a "creative" since he is shown holding a pair of scissors. The text describes the "white flight" to the suburbs, and notes that "Negro families…represent the *only growing portion* of most big cities." *Advertising Age* (November 9, 1964): 46.

ABOVE, MIDDLE The text assures us that the motivation for advertising in *Ebony* is based in rational business strategies not bleeding-heart liberalism. The pen prominently held by the model connects him with the world of decision-making and alludes to his responsibility for the "bottom-line." *Advertising Age* (December 7, 1964): 14.

ABOVE, RIGHT In another advertising and design trade journal, *Ebony* ads feature a model in the role of an advertising agent who visits a potential advertiser. Again, the white model frames the scene. *Printer's Ink* (September 16, 1960): 68.

Several *Ebony* ads refer to a set of "Negro Market Facts" that are said to arise from "psychological needs and many spending restrictions in other areas." The ads report such "facts" as "Negroes spend 38% more for personal care items, 50% more for clothing and accessories, and 19% more for appliances and home furnishings."[12] By characterizing markets in racial rather than economic terms, *Ebony* reinforced the notion of a psychologically distinct "black market" reachable solely through "black media."

A series of ads that appeared in 1964 featured a white male model acting as a liaison between the "black media" of *Ebony* and the "white media" of *Advertising Age*. The copy is rendered in quotation marks as a testimonial statement from one representative of white media to another. Text within other ads explains the decision to use "black media" in economic terms: "EBONY is on our advertising schedule for sound business reasons…. *Any* market of 20 million people with $24 billion a year to spend is important."

advertising: "the number of Negro ads comprise less than one third of one percent of the total [ads studied]." See Harold H. Kassajian, "The Negro and American Advertising, 1946-1965," *Journal of Marketing Research*, 6 (February 1969): 32. The historic Kerner Commission report summarized its findings as follows: "By failing to portray the Negro as a matter of routine and in the context of total society, the news media have, we believe, contributed to the black-white schism in this country." (Pieterse, 147, 242).

12 The characterization of blacks as a group that spends more on personal-care products was a consistent feature of *Ebony's* appeal to advertisers. The research director of Johnson Publishing Company, which published *Ebony*, referred to "the Negro's propensity to consume," and stated that "the Negro family… spends a larger percentage of its disposable income for goods yielding immediate or relatively short-run satisfaction." See "Ads Must Enhance Negro's Prestige, *Ebony's* Davis Says," *Advertising Age* 29 (October 6, 1956): 87. W. Leonard Evans, the editor of *Tuesday*, the black-oriented newspaper supplement, astutely noted that the term *Negro market* is a misnomer. He preferred to characterize the market economically rather than racially. See Arnold M. Barban, "The Dilemma of 'Integrated' Advertising," *Journal of Business*, 42, 4 (October 1969): 477.

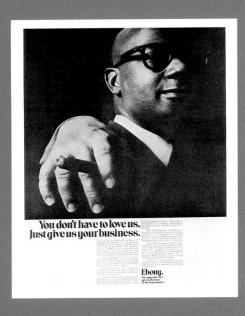

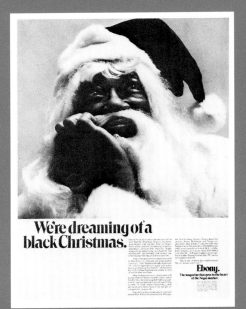

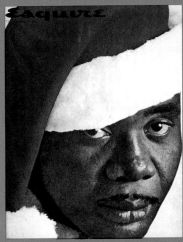

THE FRAME OF 'WHITE MEDIA'

National advertisers such as Pepsi-Cola, Proctor & Gamble, AT&T, and IBM began to produce ads with black models for black-oriented publications as a result of both the pressure exerted by civil rights groups and the commonsense advice offered in some industry trade journals. These gestures, however, were a disturbing echo of the segregationist *Plessy vs. Ferguson* ruling of 1896, which upheld segregation in schools as long as equal accommodations were provided. National advertisers were repeating, in effect, the "separate-but-equal" policy that had served as an alibi for segregation. *Plessy vs. Ferguson* was declared unconstitutional in the *Brown vs. the Board of Education of Alabama* case in 1954, yet the advertising industry, not bound by such regulations, bore few signs of integration in its imagery or in its workforce.

In the mid-1960s, civil rights groups saw that the frame of "black media" supplied by the advertising industry was a strategy of containment. The term

"white media" acted as a substitute for "mainstream media," obscuring the issue of integration *within the mainstream*.[13] The term conferred a marginal status to African-American audiences, suggesting their cultural isolation from "mainstream" media. The terms "white media" and "black media" suggested two distinct realms. Activist groups such as the NAACP and CORE recognized the exclusionary logic of this framing and called for national advertisers to create integrated advertising for mainstream media. Fearing a "white backlash," especially in southern markets, national advertisers were reluctant to integrate their ads. A 1969 article referred to this set of tensions as the "dilemma of integrated advertising."[14] This dilemma was voiced in numerous articles in advertising and marketing journals in the late 60s and early 70s.

From this vantage point, Lubalin's *Ebony* ad may be seen as a variation on earlier campaigns for the magazine. It restates the basic content of previous

"You don't have to love us. Just give us your business," and "We're dreaming of a black Christmas." Art director: Herb Lubalin; photographer: Irv Bahrt; copywriters: Byron Barclay, Herb Lubalin; agency: Wyse Advertising; client: *Ebony* magazine, 1968.

Esquire magazine, December 1963. Art director: Geroge Lois; photographer: Carl Fischer. Heavyweight champion fighter Sonny Liston was cast as Santa Claus. *The Art of Advertising: George Lois on Communications,* George Lois, Bill Pitts (New York: Harry N. Abrams, 1977), 68.

"They aren't your best friends' kids." Art director/designer: Carmen Farese; photographer: Joe Gianetti; copywriter: Jim Cornelius; agency: Marsteller Inc.; client: National Association of Businessmen. Reproduced in *The 49th Annual of Advertising, Editorial & Television Art & Design* (New York: Watson-Guptill Publications, 1970), 104.

"Joey is dying of a skin condition." Art director/designer: David Wiseltier; photographer: Howard Krieger; copywriter: Lew Sherwood; agency: Daniel & Charles; client: MacFadden Bartell Media (for True Story). Reproduced in *The 49th Annual of Advertising, Editorial & Television Art & Design* (New York: Watson-Guptill Publications, 1970), 42.

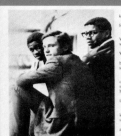

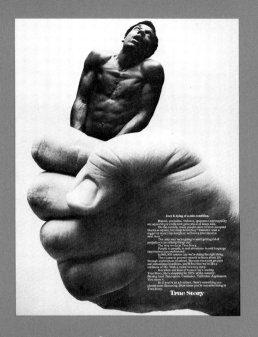

ads, updated with the strategies of the "new advertising." In both the CBS and the *Ebony* ads, the framing effect achieved by the use of the terms "white media" and "black media" is reiterated on a visual and verbal level. Visually, the "frame" of white media is articulated in the earlier ads through the position of white models in relation to black models. Black models are flanked by white models, or the copy speaks in the voice of "white media." The ads present pictorial or textual "evidence" of mediation by and through "white media." This framing is underscored by the recurrence in the copy of pronouns such as "us/them," and "your/their." The frame of white media is thematized in Luablin's ad "You don't have to love us. Just give us your business"—the hand of a white model rests on the shoulder of the black model. Like a frame, the hand sets up the conditions in which one views the scene. *Ebony* magazine drew attention to the hegemonic frame of "white media" by titling

its August 1964 issue "The White Problem in America."

In the advertising and editorial design of this period, African-American men were frequently portrayed in scenarios that referred to the history of racism, slavery, and domination. In the process of making the "invisible man" visible, advertising and editorial design often rehearsed the imagery of oppression. The paradoxical quality of this "becoming visible" through the imagery of oppression is a tendency in colonial discourse.[15] Stuart Hall has written of the "absent" but imperialistic "white eye" as the seemingly neutral position from which representations of the colonized are made: "This is the history of slavery and conquest, written, seen, drawn, and photographed by The Winners. They cannot be read and made sense of from any other position. The 'white eye' is always outside the frame—but seeing and positioning everything within it."[16]

13 In an editorial piece written for *Advertising Age*, John Johnson of *Ebony* wrote: "The Negro market…is not a special market within the white market—it is, on the contrary, a general market defined, precisely, by its exclusion from the white market." *Advertising Age* (September 21, 1964): 119.

14 See Arnold M. Barban, "The Dilemma of 'Integrated' Advertising" *Journal of Business*, 42, 4 (October 1969): 477-496.

15 This phenomenon is remarked upon by Kobena Mercer and Isaac Julien who note that many of Robert Mapplethorpe's photographs of African-American men reiterate "the terms of colonial fantasy, [and thereby] service the expectations of white desire…." "True Confessions," *Black Male: Representations of Masculinity in Contemporary American Art*, Thelma Golden, ed. (New York: Whitney Museum of American Art, 1994), 194.

16 Stuart Hall, "The Whites of their Eyes: Racist Ideologies and the Media," Manuel Alvarado, John O. Thompson, eds., *The Media Reader* (London: BFI, 1990), 14. On the supposed "neutrality" status of whiteness in cinema see Richard Dyer, "White," *Screen*, 29, 4 (Autumn 1988): 44-64.

MYTH TODAY

Dorfsman and Lubalin were part of a liberal urban milieu that was largely sympathetic to the goals of equality sought by protest movements of the 1960s. They were, however, creating messages for powerful media companies that were targets for much of the left and liberal critique of these institutions.

In the academic realm, a culture of criticism had emerged in the 1950s that aggressively attacked social norms from a vantage point informed by Marxism. A key figure in this movement was Roland Barthes. In his 1957 essay "Myth Today," one of Barthes's primary objects of interpretation is a cover of *Paris-Match* magazine that features a photograph of a young black soldier saluting the French flag.[17] For Barthes, this image serves as an example of the way in which "mythic speech" hijacks one sign (a photograph of a soldier saluting the flag) and makes it the material basis for another sign (benevolent French colonialism). According to Barthes, myth operates by liquidating the sign's original "meaning" in order that it may receive the mythic "concept." In the case of the *Paris-Match* cover, the photograph serves to legitimate French imperialism by giving it the appearance of naturalness. As Barthes states, "I see very well what it signifies to me: that France is a great Empire, that all her sons, without any color discrimination, faithfully serve under her flag, and that there is no better answer to the detractors of an alleged colonialism than the zeal shown by this Negro in serving his so-called oppressors" (116).

According to Barthes, the vehicles for myth must not be clichéd or stereotyped: myth takes root in the image of the young man saluting the flag precisely because of its particularity and specificity—the photograph is not a "symbol" of French power, but a form of evidence, imparting a naturalness and inevitability to French rule by connecting it to the vivid history of this particular person.

Barthes compares myth to a virus that needs a carrier in order to spread. What Barthes refers to as the full, original, primary "meaning" of the black man saluting the flag is turned into an "empty, parasitical form" by the consuming appetite of myth: "one must put the biography of the Negro in parentheses if one wants to free the picture, and prepare it to receive its signified" (118).

For Barthes, myth comes in from outside to rob the image of its former truth. His theory suggests that the image possesses a core of *denotation*, which is then corrupted by the *connotational* registers of the image.[18] Barthes locates this core of denotation in the "biography of the Negro," which, he implies, might be told innocently, outside of the corrupting influence of mythic speech. Barthes revised this conception of denotation and connotation in *S/Z*, where he stated that "denotation is not the first meaning, but pretends to be so....it is ultimately no more than the last of the connotations (the one which seems both to establish and close the reading)."[19]

17 Roland Barthes, *Mythologies*, trans. Annette Lavers (New York: Hill and Wang, 1972), 109-159.

18 Steve Baker analyzes the role of denotation and connotation in the work of Barthes, especially in relation to the *Paris-Match* cover. Baker was the first writer to locate and reproduce the *Paris-Match* cover, bringing to light the gaps between Barthes's memory of it and the actual image. "The Hell of Connotation," *Word and Image*, 1, 2 (April-June, 1985): 164-175.

19 Roland Barthes, *S/Z*, trans. Richard Miller (New York: Hill and Wang, 1974), 9.

The *Paris-Match* cover is important to Barthes's analysis because, as a photograph, it is the record of a real (even if staged) event. But the belief in its naturalness would depend on a viewer who accepts it as an uncontrived image. While Barthes accords a critical capacity to the journalist, who constructs such images, and to the mythologist, who deciphers them, he posits a gullible public as the consumers of such myths.

The 1960s witnessed the "creative revolution" of the advertising industry, as well as the social revolutions of the civil rights movement and student protests. Because of an increasingly indifferent, media-saturated public, American advertising and mass-media became more visually and conceptually sophisticated. One of the results of this transformation was that the relationship between senders and receivers of advertising messages was conceived of quite differently from the uncritical reception of myths described by Barthes in 1957. Despite the fact that both the CBS ad and the *Paris-Match* cover featured images of people in positions of subservience to the flags of colonizing nations, the two images anticipated different audiences. The *Paris-Match* cover lent a *naturalized* image to a situation of culturally enforced oppression, whereas the CBS ad (and the *Ebony* ad) produce *ambivalent* messages through deliberately theatrical constructs. Readers would not mistake the CBS and *Ebony* ads for photojournalism, as they might in the case of the *Paris-Match* cover.

For Barthes, the consumption of ideological messages was facilitated by the guise of *naturalness*. It was the job of the critic to decipher and, in doing so, defuse mythic speech. The strategies of the "new advertising," however, were developed in a more critical context: audiences no longer believed the truth claims of advertising and were increasingly immune to its conventions.

An audience can recognize "mythic speech" as ideological, but recognition does not necessarily defuse the power of the myth. We can consume stereotypes and clichés knowingly, but this knowledge does not preclude the ability of such images to shape beliefs.

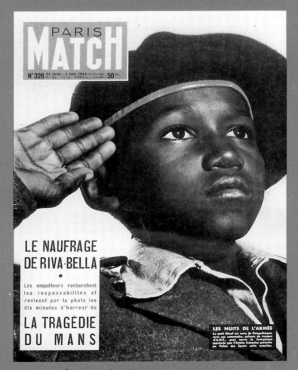

Front cover of *Paris-Match*, 326 (June 25 - July 2, 1955). Although the magazine cover formed the principle subject of Barthes's 1957 essay *Myth Today*, he did not reproduce it in his book. Photograph courtesy *Paris-Match IZIS*.

The CBS and *Ebony* ads appeared in the context of
the "dilemma of integrated advertising."
They existed within the framing effect produced
by the polarization of white and black media: both
ads circulated in the largely unintegrated spaces of
"mainstream" media.
Thus the institutional frame in
which they appeared
was "white." The image of the
Other, historically
represented in ways that
emphasized his or her
marginal status, moved to the
center in these two
advertisements. But this
centering within
the frame of white media
is accompanied by a
simultaneous inscription
of whiteness: white mask,
white stripes.

"The minstrel visage — broad whitened lips in a
blackened face, the caricature of a caricature — has
become the most enduring of black caricatures....
One clue to the everlasting popularity of the minstrel
show is no doubt the principle of role-reversal:
in blackface, whites can play their black alter egos.
It permits identification in the context of segregation"
(Pieterse, 135).

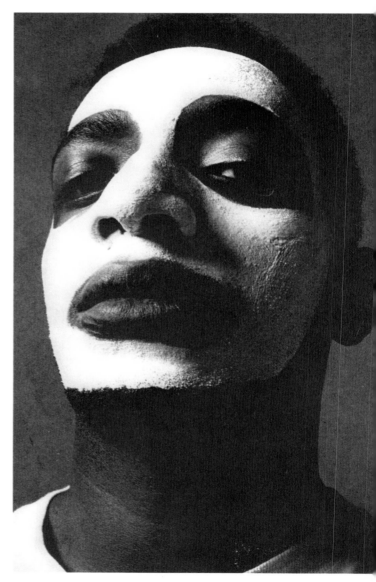

In each ad there are
two texts: the
"facial text" of the
photograph and the
typographic message
that underlines it.
Without being
tethered to these textual foundations, the
photographs are subject to divergent
interpretations. Captions, as Roland Barthes
has described, serve to "anchor" images.

These two advertisements responded to the dilemma of integrated advertising, a situation in which the representation of African-Americans in mainstream media was both imperative and fraught with ambivalence. The CBS and *Ebony* ads resulted in images that could be described as both "black and white," "yes and no," "revealing and concealing." They offered a pictorial reenactment of social contradictions by writing in white on top of black. They offered a self-critical message at the same time that they reasserted the hierarchy of race relations in America.

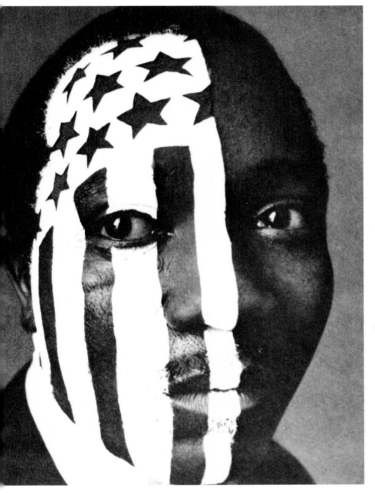

Stuart Hall has argued that representations in contemporary media retain traces of the "base images" of the "grammar of race." He identifies the "slave figure," "the native," and "the clown" as the principle figures in this grammar. "These *particular* versions may have faded. But their traces are still to be observed, reworked in many of the modern and updated images. And though they may appear to carry a different meaning, they are often still constructed on a very ancient grammar" (16).

Both images depend on the documentary status of the photograph for their shock value; a drawing of the same scene would diminish the impact by introducing the marks of a subjective transcription. The "facticity" of the photograph obliges the reader to consider the history implicit in the image: a photographer and a make-up artist have collaborated with a hired model. Thus while there is an overt reference to tribal *self*-adornment in the CBS ad, the model's relationship to the paint on his face is *contractual* rather than *ritual*. The model is in a position of subservience: he is the passive vehicle for someone *else's* statement *about* oppression.

If these kids don't make it, neither do we.

These are big city school children. They are partners of all who try to build and keep our cities alive with hope and promise of personal dignity. If we fail these partners, they will fail, as finally will we all.

To the Bell System, they also are customers and, prospectively, many are fellow employees. Those we hire will bring with them attitudes and skills produced by city life and city schools. Their qualities will help shape the quality of our service. And service is our product.

Bell System companies and people are increasingly engaged to help meet the problems of the cities, especially those concerning education and employability. In these areas our skills and other business resources may have extra value. We shall try to keep our deeds outrunning our words.

AT&T

ACTIVISM AND ADVERTISING

The CBS and *Ebony* ads should be seen against the backdrop of activism *towards* and *within* the advertising industry. These other discourses on "Black America" dealt with the representation of African-Americans in ways which were just as confrontational, but which avoided the paradigm of victimization that characterized many messages. Direct political action by civil rights groups also helped transform advertising. A number of grassroots efforts to integrate advertising were initiated in the 1960s, including a 1961 campaign by the NAACP called "Desegregating Advertising."[20] The NAACP's desire for integration *within the mainstream* was made explicit in a letter to the American Tobacco Company: "We understand that there are some ads located in colored neighborhoods that show colored people but this type of advertising distribution is not satisfactory because it is ghetto advertising."[21] CORE also organized campaigns to put pressure on advertisers "to include Negroes in advertising layouts, to use more Negro actors in television programming, and to hire more Negroes into the advertising industry."[22]

This second goal, to diversify the institutions as well as the products of the advertising industry, was equally difficult. An exceptional figure in this regard was Georg Olden, an African-American who forged a remarkable career at CBS as a broadcast designer. A recent article on Olden described the context in which he worked: "It was a tribute to both CBS's liberalism and Georg Olden's survival skills that he was among the 'less than 200 of the estimated 72,400 full-time television employees in the nation' who were black."[23] Olden directed and produced an award-winning public service announcement that contrasted stereotypes of black entertainers and sports figures with a voice-over describing African-Americans' other roles as accountants, executives, etc.

20 *Split Image: African Americans in the Mass Media*, Dates, Barlow, eds. (Washington, D.C.: Howard University Press, 1990), 425.

21 Sylvia Appelbaum, *The Crisis* (June-July 1962): 315.

22 See "CORE Intensifies Drive for Negroes in Ads; Zeroes in on Pepsi-Cola Co." *Advertising Age* 35 (November 1964): 3; and "CORE Pleased with Advertisers' Attitudes in Latest Meeting," *Advertising Age* 35 (November 30, 1964): 46.

23 Despite his many awards, Olden's contributions have been largely forgotten in the history of design. See Julie Laskey, "The Search for Georg Olden," *Print*, XLVII:II, (March-April 1994): 26.

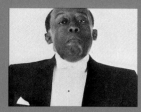

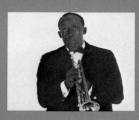

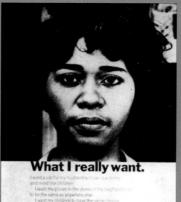

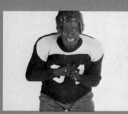

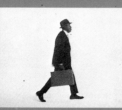

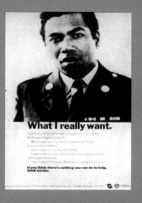

OPPOSITE A 1968 ad for American Telephone and Telegraph Company featuring a multicultural classroom. AT&T's manager of public relations was Ramon S. Scruggs, who was also senior vice president of the National Urban League. Scruggs stated, in a 1967 article, "no segment in America has done so much to make Negro Americans the invisible men as the advertising industry." *Editor and Publisher*, 100, 46 (November 18, 1967). The advertising agency for the AT&T ad was N.W. Ayer & Son, Inc. Art director: Philip Shulman; copywriter: Richard Golden; photographer: I.C. Rapoport.

This ad for the Urban League presents a series of stereotypes about the "natural" talents of African-Americans. The text is as follows: "Not every Negro can sing or dance or play third base. But some are pretty good salesmen, bookkeepers, writers, engineers, secretaries, machinists, nurses—even executives. All they want is an equal chance to prove it. And that plus a lot of other things is what the Urban League is all about." Despite being designed, written, and produced by an African-American, for an equal rights organization, the text is still written in the third person: instead of "all *we* want," the text is rendered as "all they want," inferring that the text is spoken on *behalf* of African-Americans. Art director, designer, director, writer: Georg Olden; producers: Georg Olden, Bonnie Deems; photographers: Burt Greenberg, Tom Hollyman; client: National Urban League.

The Advertising Council initiated a campaign on behalf of civic organizations. The participating advertising agencies worked on a volunteer basis to produce public service messages. In this series for Urban America Inc., the Ketchum, McLeod & Grove agency produced portraits of average people (i.e. not celebrities or athletes) declaring "What I really want." The ads are remarkable for their use of the first person and their head-on documentary style of photography. The texts are also unusually direct. The female version says: "If I wanted less for my family than other mothers want, what kind of mother would I be?" The male version states, "I don't want sympathy. Or charity. I want a decent job. I want to be able to get married and support a family. I don't expect miracles. But I won't settle for a broom." The ads close with the line: "If you think there's nothing you can do to help, think harder." Art director: Joseph H. Phair; copywriter: Arthur X. Tuohy.

Logo for the National Urban League, designed by Georg Olden.

TARGETED MARKETS

The "dilemma of integrated advertising" is a dynamic that continues to shape the imagery of advertising and the practices of marketing. The use of "separate-but-equal" campaigns has carved out distinct territories for advertising. This territorialization has been exploited in many urban areas where liquor and cigarette advertising is concentrated in poor neighborhoods. Recalling the civil

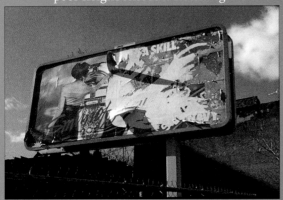

rights campaigns of the 1960s, The Reverend Calvin O. Butts, of the Abyssinian Baptist Church in Harlem, initiated a 1990 campaign of white-washing billboards in the neighborhood surrounding the church. Similar campaigns were undertaken in Chicago, Detroit, and Dallas. These actions ignited a fierce debate about the ability of communities to control outdoor advertising and the rights of manufacturers to "commercial free speech." Butts compared the situation to South Africa: "The prevalence of alcohol and cigarette advertisements in Soweto and America's inner cities manifests the elastic ruthlessness of these companies' greed and proclivity to exploit the poor and disenfranchised people."[24] DeWitt F. Helm Jr., president of the Association of National Advertisers, argued that

such attitudes were condescending and paternalistic. The protests had a dramatic effect on spending for outdoor advertising, and brought national media attention to the issue of marketing targeted toward African-Americans.[25] Many tobacco and alcohol billboards were replaced with public service announcements sponsored by corporate advertisers. Protests in 1990 also derailed attempts by R.J. Reynolds Tobacco Company to introduce Uptown, a new brand of cigarettes aimed at black consumers.

The incorporation of images of African-Americans in advertising runs parallel to the broader history of film, television, music, textbooks, and other media. This perspective is a necessarily partial one, offered from a "white" vantage point that views integration and intercultural representation as an important goal. Critics and activists need to be vigilant about instances of overt racism, and sensitive to traces of the "grammar of race" that are evident everywhere.

24 Stephanie Strom, "Billboard Owners are Switching, Not Fighting," *The New York Times* (April 4, 1990): B1.

25 *Advertising Age* attributed the fifteen percent drop in spending for the first quarter of 1990 to the billboard protests. Alison Fahey, "Outdoor feels drought," *Advertising Age* (August 6, 1990): 3.

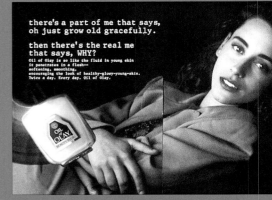

there's a part of me that says, oh just grow old gracefully.

then there's the real me that says, WHY?

Oil of Olay is so like the fluid in young skin it penetrates in a flash--softening, smoothing, encouraging the look of healthy-glowy-young-skin. Twice a day. Every day, Oil of Olay.

LEFT A whitewashed billboard, New York City, September 1990. Spurred by community church leader Rev. Calvin O. Butts, a whitewashing campaign against liquor and cigarette advertising was initiated in Harlem.

ABOVE Like many campaigns today, this Oil of Olay series was produced in "separate-but-equal" versions. The "white" version appeared in *Vogue*, September 1990, while the "black" one ran in *Ebony* the same month.

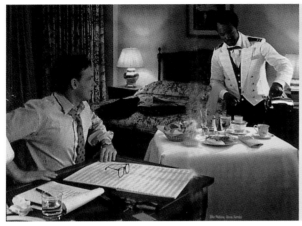

A 1990 ad for Westin Hotels shows a scene of a male African-American attendant serving a white male executive "Mushroom omelette, coffee, and fresh strawberries, 3:30 a.m., The Westin Hotel, Washington, D.C." The ad was part of a series of over 20 related scenes for Westin, produced by HDN, that portrayed hotel guests and employees. Out of the series, only one of the "guests" was an African-American—seen in the background of a hotel lobby. A number of ads in the series identified the employee: for example, "Maria Escobar, Laundry/Valet," helps a white woman in a bathrobe by unwrapping the dress that she pressed for her after replacing the button at "5:22 p.m." In another, "Violet De Silva, Concierge," hands a white male executive his "Urgent eleven-page fax from New York, 11:04 p.m., The Westin Plaza, Singapore." See "Invisible People: The Depiction of Minorities in Magazines and Catalogs," a 1991 study published by the City of New York's Department of Consumer Affairs.

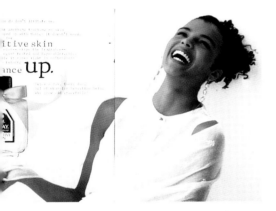

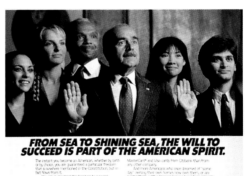

FROM SEA TO SHINING SEA, THE WILL TO SUCCEED IS PART OF THE AMERICAN SPIRIT.

The Prescriptives line of cosmetics includes different shades for women with different skin tones, rather than grouping its products according to skin "color." Unlike Oil of Olay's "separate-but-equal" strategy, the Prescriptives 1995 campaign incorporates diversity within "mainstream" advertising by using one ad for all media.

A 1989 ad for Citicorp presents a multicultural group pledging allegiance to the flag, with a portrait of George Washington visible in the background. The "message" of the ad is that America is an equal-opportunity nation. However, traditional relations of power are apparent in the placement of the models. The older white man holds the center: he is the only figure not obscured by any other. He seems to be leading his colleagues (perhaps his staff) in this midday outburst of patriotic fervor.

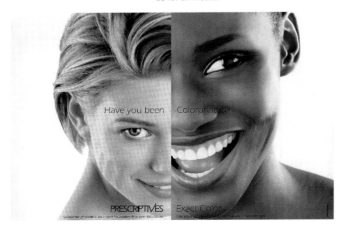

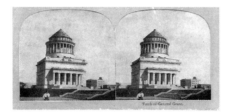

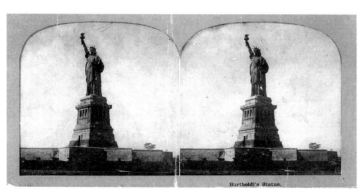

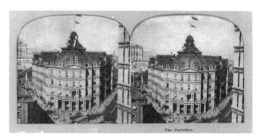

Stereoscope viewing cards,
ca. 1900. Typical tourist scenes
on stereoscope cards offered a
vicarious form of travel. Viewing
cards were called "programs"
by the manufacturers of the
stereopticon viewing devices.

"In the late eighteenth century *stereotype*
was coined as a technical designation for the
casting of multiple papier-mâché copies of
printing type from a papier-mâché mold.
By the mid-nineteenth century the term has
already achieved the level of abstraction we
find in such phrases as 'a stereotyped
expression.' For, just as a series of unvarying
casts could be made from one mold, so too
were commonplaces seen as unchanging.
[D]uring the early twentieth century, social
psychologists adopted stereotype to designate
the images through which we categorize the
world ..." Sander L. Gilman, *Difference and
Pathology: Stereotypes of Sexuality, Race, and
Madness* (Ithaca: Cornell University Press,
1985), 15-16.

Pictures for Rent

From Stereoscope to Stereotype

Photography, like typography, is technically, historically, and aesthetically wedded to graphic design. Yet unlike type, photography is rarely accorded attention as one of graphic design's primary resources. Histories of photography usually focus on inventions, genres, and influential photographers. Such histories ignore the relationship of the medium to graphic design, and they overlook the ubiquitous but unfashionable area of "stock photography," a sub-genre defined by agencies and researchers as "pictures for rent."

Stock photography offers a way of studying images as a form of currency that funds advertising, text books, real-estate pamphlets, greeting cards, magazines, book covers, posters, annual reports, and innumerable other forms of visual communication. It cuts through the genres—and the class distinctions—of graphic design. This kind of photography is not the award-winning sort commissioned by leading art directors, nor is it a heartfelt grass-roots expression. It is, instead, a kind

of corporate vernacular that fuels a vast amount of graphic design practiced in both amateur and professional settings.

The two major sources for stock photos are out-takes from commissioned shoots (often of a documentary nature) and photographs shot specifically as "stock." It is difficult to trace the history of the phenomenon because it is both a border activity—a stepchild of more respected forms—and a transient, commercially driven undertaking. Nor is stock photography a stable, continuous, or discrete entity. The strands that contributed to its development include the nineteenth-century stereoscope business, the formation of picture agencies to serve the magazine and advertising industries in the 1920s, and the formalization of the "stock market" in images during the 1970s. There is no single point of origin for stock photography, which has grown out of the diverse areas of photographic production and consumption.

PICTURE RESEARCH

The stock photography industry's own history is part of its capital. Outdated images can come back into fashion, imbued with values of camp or nostalgia. While quaint, retro images of domestic harmony are offered for their sentimentality or humor, stock agencies are also busy cataloguing new clichés for today's social order and tomorrow's dictionary of received ideas.

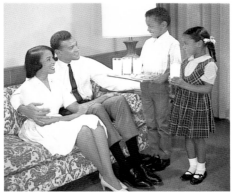

This idealized "milk and cookies" scene has lived several "stock-photo" lives, from its usage as a contemporary shot in the late 50s, to its present status as a nostalgic image. In between, it probably languished in obscurity. There is an unwritten rule in stock photo agencies that images need to be about 20 years old before they can be re-circulated as nostalgia. Campy 1950s images are a mainstay of many agencies that supply clients in advertising and publishing. Photograph by Willinger. © 1994 FPG.

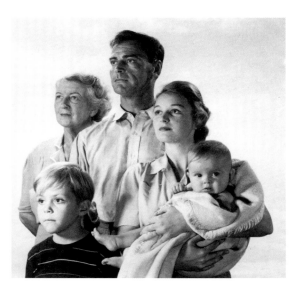

For contemporary viewers it is hard to imagine that this was ever seen as a sincere image. Historian Michael Schudson has called advertising "capitalist realism." The glazed expressions and upward tilt of the heads in this 1940s image echoes the visual tactics of Soviet propaganda from the same period. Photographer unknown. © 1993 FPG.

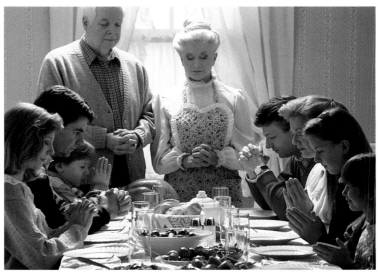

This is only one of several stock photo scenarios offered by different agencies that directly mimic Norman Rockwell's famous painting *Freedom from Want*. Rockwell, Leonardo da Vinci, Magritte, and Michaelangelo are all major sources for stock photographers. Photographer not credited. © 1994 Comstock.

The condition of hyper-clarity in stock photography results in blunt visualizations of cultural stereotypes such as this geisha woman buying American soft-drinks from a vending machine in Kyoto, Japan. Photograph by Paul Chesley. © Tony Stone.

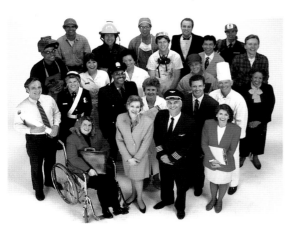

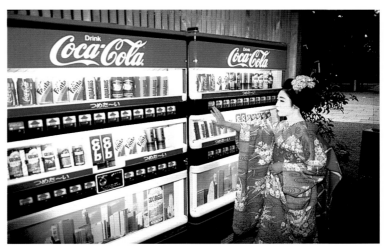

Many stock photo catalogues offer categories of individuals identified as "executives" and "executives off duty," referring to class and income brackets. There are no corresponding categories designated as "working class," or "blue collar," even though there are many photographs of models styled as blue-collar workers. These images can be found under classifications such as "The Diversified Workforce" in scenarios that hyperbolically mix occupations and nationalities. In this "workers of the world" scenario, executives mingle with mechanics, seamstresses, construction workers, teachers, policemen, and bakers. Photographer not credited. © 1995 Comstock.

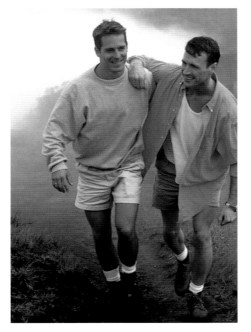

Same-sex relationships have begun to be portrayed in stock catalogues, often under the category of "alternative lifestyles." Mass-market advertising has recently recognized the gay consumer as a significant market, and major advertisers (Ikea, Johnnie Walker Scotch, Banana Republic, Toyota) have begun to incorporate gay and lesbian couples into their ads. This scene of two men hiking is grouped under the "men" category from an FPG catalogue. The physical intimacy, and the ring on the right hand of the model, suggests that they are a couple. Photograph by Rob Lang. © 1994 FPG.

In the U.S. the early market for images was dominated by manufacturers of stereoscopic picture cards. Stereoscopes are viewing devices that create a three-dimensional effect when the eye blends together two photographs of the same scene taken at slightly different angles. Stereoscope viewing soon became a widespread pastime. As early as 1859 Oliver Wendell Holmes speculated that the popularity of the stereoscope would soon generate "such an enormous collection of forms that they will have to be classified and arranged in vast libraries, as books are now."[1]

One of the most successful stereoscope companies was Underwood and Underwood, established in 1880 by Bert and Elmer Underwood, of Ottawa, Kansas. The Underwoods began as distributors of photo cards produced by three of the larger companies at that time—Charles Bierstadt of Niagara Falls, Littleton View Company of Littleton, New Hampshire, and J. F. Jarvis of Washington, D.C.[2] Within two years the brothers became the sole agents for all regions west of the Mississippi, and two years later, sole distributors for the entire country. Branch offices were opened across the U.S., in Canada, and in Great Britain. In 1891 the company made its headquarters in New York and began publishing its own stereoscopic photos.

By 1896 Underwood and Underwood began supplying photographs to newspapers and magazines, marking their first foray into what resembled a "pictures for rent" agency. Their entry into this market coincided with the rise of halftone reproductions in American newspapers. By 1901 the company commissioned and produced 25,000 stereoscopic pictures a day, and is estimated to have sold 300,000 stereopticon viewing devices a year.

Six years after the Underwood brothers retired in 1925, the firm was reorganized as Underwood and Underwood News Photos, a supplier of historical and contemporary news subjects. This trajectory—from a stereoscope factory producing travel and entertainment images to a news photo specialist—was typical of early picture agencies. Three other firms that followed this route were Brown Brothers, B.W. Kilbourn, and H. Armstrong Roberts. Roberts was the first agency to publish a catalogue of its holdings, which was circulated to potential customers in 1920. Previously, agencies conducted picture research in response to requests for a generic subject. The catalogue, which did not reproduce every photograph in the collection but included broad types of imagery, introduced a new paradigm to the business, putting the pictures on display like goods in a department store, in contrast to the more hermetic model of the archive.

Roberts survived the mergers of the internationalized photo agencies and is still in business today, with branches in several U.S. cities. The current owner, Bob Roberts, said that in producing a catalogue of available images, his grandfather invented the notion of "stock photography"—that is, of a speculative market for photographs.[3]

1 Oliver Wendell Holmes, "The Stereoscope and the Stereograph," in Alan Trachtenberg, ed., *Classic Essays on Photography* (New Haven: Leete's Island Books, 1980), 81.

2 Charles Bierstadt's brother Albert Bierstadt, the famous painter, made stereoscopic views of the West as early as 1859.

3 The market H. Armstrong Roberts served was primarily the burgeoning advertising industry, specifically the firms of J. Walter Thompson and N.W. Ayer. The agency's sales records date back to 1913, and are dominated by the sale of images of people, particularly salesmen. Interview, Bob Roberts with J. Abbott Miller, February 1, 1994.

4 On the history of modern German news photo agencies see Diethart Kerbs, "Die Epoch der Bildagenturen," in Kerbs, et. al., eds; *Die Gleichschaltung der Bilder: Pressefotografie 1930-36* (Berlin: Fröhlich und Kaufmann, 1983), 32-76.

5 In her book on the German photomontage artist Hannah Höch, Maud Lavin surveys the illustrated magazines and newspapers of Weimar Germany. *Cut with the Kitchen Knife: The Weimar Photomontages of Hannah Höch* (New Haven: Yale University Press, 1993).

6 For a brief overview of photography in publishing, see John Schultz and Barbara Schultz, *Picture Research: A Practical Guide* (New York: Van Nostrand Reinhold, 1991), 1-31.

7 On the formation of *Life* magazine, see Loudon Wainwright, *The Great American Magazine* (New York: Alfred A. Knopf, 1986).

8 *Bettmann: The Picture Man,* Otto L. Bettmann (Gainesville: University Press of Florida, 1992).

9 On the FSA see William Stott, *Documentary Expression and Thirties America* (Chicago: University of Chicago Press, 1986), and Martha Rosler's "in, around, and afterthoughts (on documentary photography)," in Richard Bolton, ed., *The Contest of Meaning: Critical Histories of Photography* (Cambridge: MIT Press, 1993), 303-340.

SERVING THE MASS MEDIA

The rapidly expanding magazine and advertising industries in America and Europe in the 1920s widened the scope and formalized the practices of photo agencies.[4] In Weimar-era Germany, publishers of photo weeklies such as Ullstein Verlag had in-house photographers but also commissioned freelancers through Dephot (Deutsche Photodienst), Wide World, and other agencies. Photographs were often shot without the assurance of a commission, discouraging political imagery since neutral pictures had more potential to be sold to both liberal and conservative publications.[5] Dephot was among the first and most prominent of the photo agencies and developed largely as an intermediary between mass-media publications and the photographers.[6]

Just as many of America's most influential art directors were European emigrés, so, too, were some of the most important figures in photojournalism. Kurt Szafranski, formerly at Ullstein, emigrated to the U.S. and founded Black Star, one of the first such agencies in the country. Kurt Korff, also formerly at Ullstein, wrote a proposal for an illustrated magazine that was followed closely by publisher Henry Luce in the formation of *Life*, America's main photojournalistic outlet, which was launched in 1936.[7] Otto Bettmann, an antiquarian with a life-long obsession with picture- and book-collecting, fled Nazi Germany for New York in 1935 with suitcases full of pictures from which he built the Bettmann Archive.[8]

Bettmann organized his picture library in a self-consciously academic fashion, with each picture illustrated on an index card and cross-referenced with as many as seven different topics. He had close ties with New York's graphic design community, receiving early encouragement from Dr. Robert Leslie, whose typesetting firm The Composing Room provided a model for Bettmann of a supplier of services to the publishing and design industries. Bettmann's story is characteristic of other European immigrants who set up agencies in New York and other U.S. cities, including the founders of Globe Photo, Three Lion, Camera Press, and Shostall.

A parallel development was the U.S. Government's Farm Security Administration photography project, which employed a group of photographers to document American life. Initiated in 1935, the scheme ran for eight years. Walker Evans, Dorothea Lange, Ben Shahn, Esther Bubley and others compiled a photographic record of the country, which served as a public relations tool for New Deal programs.[9] The FSA dossier was used to illustrate government and inter-governmental publications. The agency also made its images available to newspapers and magazines, from mass-market publications such as *Look* to small-scale journals, and kept a vast file of clippings showing the use made of its photographs. Thus the government founded its own picture agency, which still functions as an historical archive today.

WORKING IN THE ARCHIVES

Stock photography is most often used straightforwardly in consumer contexts, but it has also been used ironically and analytically. The appreciation of stock photography for its camp value is linked to the broader cultural recycling of fashion, music, and television sitcoms. A number of designers have employed stock imagery to convey the peculiar gloss and power of media imagery.

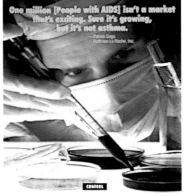

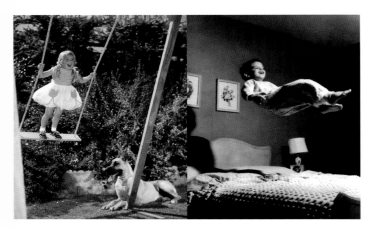

I'm So Happy by Marvin Heifer-man and Carole Kismaric, is a compilation of nostalgic images from stock photo agencies. This book-length visual essay combines texts and photos, frequently juxtaposing photographs to set up an implied dialogue between unrelated images. (New York: Random House, 1990).

Representations of AIDS have only recently, and very tentatively, begun to enter the stock catalogues. In an industry that supplies health-care services and pharmaceutical clients, the lack of powerful and clear imagery is indicative of social responses to the disease. The image at left is from a 1989 project by the collective Gran Fury for *Artforum* magazine. The project used stock photography as a way of emulating the polish and tone of corporate trade advertising. The stock photo heightened the cynicism of the quotation from an executive of Hoffman-La Roche, one of the worlds largest pharmaceutical companies.

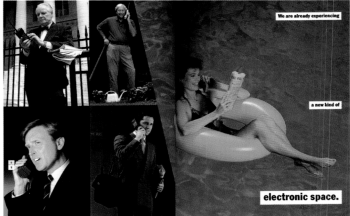

The exhibition catalogues *Post-Human, Cultural Geometry,* and *Artificial Nature,* by the design and editorial team of Jeffrey Deitch and Dan Friedman, offer an amused, sometimes critical response to the image banks of mass media. In all three books, stock photography, celebrity press shots, and mass-market magazines are juxtaposed with works of art that are influenced by mass media imagery of tourism, beauty, and technologies of simulation.

"[*Post-Human*] poses the question of whether our society is creating a new kind of post-human person that replaces previous constructions of the self. Images from the new technological and consumer culture and the new, conceptually oriented figurative art of thirty-six young artists will endeavor to give us a glimpse of the coming post-human world." Jeffrey Deitch, *Post-Human* (Pully/ Lausanne: FAE Musée d'Art Contemporain, 1992).

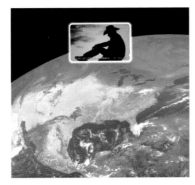

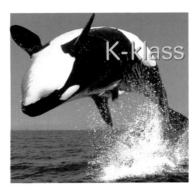

British designer Mark Farrow began using picture-library images in 1990-91 for Deconstruction Records, a major British dance label. In his *Texas Cowboy*'s cover, Farrow used a Japanese phone card, which typically feature arbitrary images, as a point of departure for a sleeve that juxtaposes a lone cowboy and a satellite photograph. In work for a band called K-Klass, he has developed imagery with nautical references because the band's name refers to a type of submarine. The cover for *Let Me Show You* uses an image of a killer whale breaching, obtained from a picture library that specializes in animals.

"The way we use pictures is almost gratuitous. It comes from the logic that record sleeves have pictures, so we provide a picture. Often this has nothing to do with the band, it's just a great image. It's almost a form of generic packaging for records. The bands I'm doing much of this work for don't have a public image or a budget, so it works for economic reasons as well. If anything started our use of picture libraries, it was the financial constraints.... I don't think of this imagery as kitsch: many of these are beautiful, strong photos, and they are not there for their story or for a laugh." Interview, Mark Farrow with J. Abbott Miller, 1994.

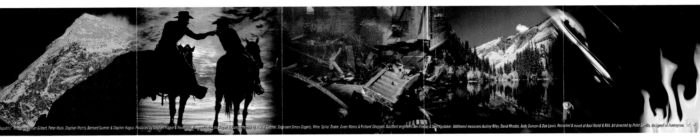

Republic: *Written by Gillian Gilbert, Peter Hook, Stephen Morris, Bernard Sumner & Stephen Hague. Produced by Stephen Hague & New Order. Pre-production on Digital Sound, extended by Pascal Gabriel. Engineers Simon Gogerly, Mike 'Spike' Drake, Owen Morris & Richard Chappell. Assistant engineers Ben Findlay & Steve Hardaker. Additional musicians Audrey Riley, David Rhodes, Andy Duncan & Dee Lewis. Recorded & mixed at Real World & RAK. Art directed by Peter Saville. Designed at Pentagram.*

British designer Peter Saville's work for the band New Order uses stock photography in a metaphorical way. Saville's cover and liner notes for *Republic* skillfully fuse the language of Hollywood and Madison Avenue, movies and cigarettes, nature and culture: "What was evolving in my mind was a post-LA experience: television culture, mass-media overload, the irony and wild juxtapositions of channel-surfing, where you flip from CNN to MTV to the Shopping Channel to something really quite horrific on the news....It's LA, it's a riot, it's Nero fiddling while Rome burns, and the juxtaposition of two images—fire and water—becomes the Los Angeles experience."

"This is a post-design era. It's deliberately embracing the photo library and it's going against all those precious things that were canonized in the 1980s and are now exhausted. This is like plastic clothing. It's a sort of coming to terms with the trashy realities of our time and saying, OK, there is an aesthetic here, let's work with it. Let's stop pretending that our world is antique papers and woodblock type. The real world is a Whoopi Goldberg movie. So what can we find there to talk about and work with?" Peter Saville, interviewed by Rick Poynor, *Eye*, 5, 17 (1995): 15.

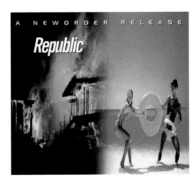

THE STOCK MARKET

In the mid-1970s stock photography began to separate into two fields—photo agencies oriented towards advertising, and news agencies furnishing documentary images. This split formalized a distinction that was already present in most organizations. Photographer Tom Grill and businessman Henry Scanlon, whose agency Comstock is curently among the largest in the field, take credit for "inventing" the contemporary form of stock photography, whereby a photographer shoots prior to any assignment, as a form of speculative image-making.

While Scanlon and others have dated this "invention" to about 1974–75, the same claim was made by H. Armstrong Roberts 50 years earlier. A survey of the work of agencies active in the 30s, 40s, and 50s, reveals that many images were marketed, if not generated, as "generic" in the spirit described by the Comstock agency.[10] A happy family holding hands and gazing at their new home may have been shot to sell real estate, but when it is offered for use in a catalogue it may be used for its symbolic dimension rather than its literal content. The same photo could be used to sell life insurance, government bonds, or aluminum siding.

A difference between Armstrong's and Comstock's claims of invention is that the Comstock approach is more pointedly conceptual, abstract, or metaphorical. Scanlon has stated that he and Grill assigned photographers to shoot for "concept" rather than "content," to think in terms of "word pictures," visual condensations of verbal concepts. Stock catalogues will often group such photographs under categories such as *analogies, business metaphors, symbols,* or *conceptual*. Stock photography was not, and is still not, as respectable as assignment shooting. It is typically seen as a way to make money from photographic leftovers. But as the photography business grew more competitive, stock-market shooting became a significant part of it.

The rapid expansion of the stock market over the last twenty years is the result of many factors. Magazines, which traditionally employed staff photographers whose work was the property of the publisher, gradually eliminated these positions in favor of freelance photographers who could sell their outtakes. This potential was reinforced by the 1978 Copyright Law, which stated that a photograph is the property of the photographer: a client who hires a freelance photographer is paying only for "use" of that property.

Another major change was technological. By the early 1980s nearly all agency photographs were color transparencies, which meant that an original would have to be sent out rather than a print generated from a black and white negative. Most transparencies would be damaged after only five trips to a printer or color house, limiting the lifetime, circulation potential, and profitability of a single image. In 1985 Kodak introduced high-quality duping film (Kodak 50/71), which allowed photographers to make limitless dupes of successful pictures. A typical international agency will now make an average of 125 copies of a single photograph for circulation to sibling agencies in over 15 different countries. Thus the expansion of photographic output is compounded by

10 Professional associations for stock photographers, such as the Picture Agency Council of America and the American Society of Media Photographers, offer only brief histories of their organizations, which were founded in the 50s. PACA and ASMP are trade associations that protect business interests and enforce ethical guidelines; their spokespeople concede the importance of accounting for the history of the field, but do not have the resources or records to begin any formal documentation.

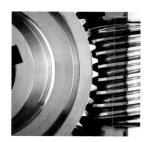

This image of meshing gears, taken by photographer Lester Lefkowitz, has illustrated over 250 different publications, from books on law to journals for accounting, in many different parts of the world. Courtesy of FPG.

11 In October of 1995 the Bettmann Archive was purchased by William H. Gates of Microsoft Corporation. Gates has been acquiring electronic rights to images for use in electronic media. Both Corbis Corporation, Gates's company, and Kraus Organization, the former owner of the Bettmann Archive, are private companies. Corbis had already acquired the electronic rights to 500,000 images from the National Gallery of London, the Barnes Foundation, and the Philadelphia Museum. The Bettmann acquisition will add 16 million images, 11.5 million of which came from Bettmann's 1990 acquisition of the United Press International news service archive. *The New York Times* estimated the worldwide revenue of the photo-archive industry at $500 million a year. The deal foreshadows a consumer market in digital images that may ultimately exceed its current uses in design, publishing, and advertising. The Corbis deal has ignited concern about the monopolization of images in the digital era. Steve Lohr, "Huge Photo Archive Bought by the Chairman of Microsoft," *The New York Times* (October 11, 1995): A1.

duplication. Photographer Lester Lefkowitz has sold one photograph over 250 times; his image of two meshing gears has appeared on posters, books, journals, and other publications all over the world.

Encyclopedic and lavishly produced catalogues are a phenomenon that began in the early 1980s. Unlike earlier catalogues, which merely indicated the type and variety of images available, catalogues now provide a record of the entire archive. Instead of making research requests, clients can ask for a specific picture. Understandably, many photographers demand that pictures accepted for distribution must appear in the catalogue. The volume and waste of the catalogues may shift as they are replaced by photo-CD and on-line services. While these technologies are appealing from an ecological standpoint, they pose a new range of problems for photographers, who will find it difficult to protect their work as it becomes subject to digital manipulation, customization, and disguise.

Photo-CD technology was first exploited by traditional agencies merely as a storage device. It is now used by image-entrepreneurs who load many thematically grouped images onto one photo-CD and charge customers for unlimited use of the images. This mutation of the industry has upset established agencies that base their fees on the size of an image and the scope of its use. Photo-CD publishers, such as PhotoDisc, circumvent the negotiations and complex fees of the traditional stock house, creating a new model for the industry, the impact of which remains to be seen.[11]

Within the stock industry there is a commercial mainstream—Image Bank, Comstock, Tony Stone—and an "avant-garde" wing, best represented by Photonica, established in Tokyo in 1987 and in New York in 1990. The sophisticated color and abstracted forms of Photonica represent a reaction against the "stock photo" look. The imagery is highly specific rather than generic, and the style foregrounds the signature style of individual photographers. The Photonica look uses details to evoke a larger scene, a strategy in marked contrast to the stock photo tendency to encapsulate, summarize, and thoroughly frame its subject. Photonica's success has led other agencies to mimic its approach: FPG now offers an imitative *Photo Haiku* catalogue, and the "want lists" issued by other agencies will often specify a "Photonica" approach.

In another recent shift, FPG has compiled a "Real Life" series that offers images of subjects outside the usual terrain of stock imagery. Along with poverty, drug abuse, aging, and divorce, the catalogue includes working parents, ethnic diversity, day care, and recycling, inadvertently creating a catalogue of modern day ills (is there a causal connection between day care and drug abuse?). The majority of these images are rendered in black-and-white, establishing the appropriate "documentary" overtone for "serious" subjects. It is easy to complain about the new clichés that replace the old ones—"white-collar-executive-snorting-coke," "daddy-on-cell-phone-changing-diaper"—but such attempts *have* broadened the repertoire of stock imagery.

A PATTERN LANGUAGE

The stock industry converts photographic history into the everyday language of commerce, as seen in the numerous echoes of Dr. Harold Edgerton's famous stroboscopic study of a milk droplet. The patterned "phrases" offered in the stock photo vocabulary are related to the repetition of imagery found in mass media, a phenomenon especially evident in the heavily codified merchandising of popular entertainment.

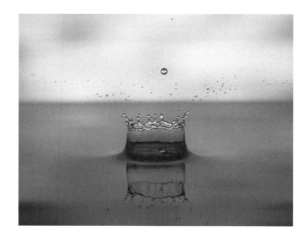

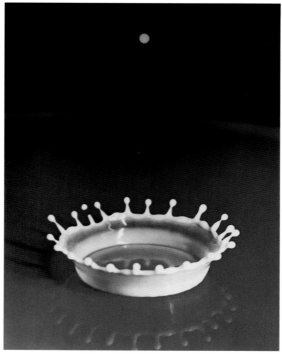

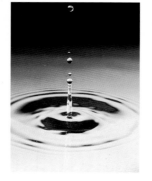

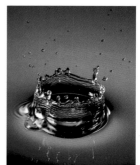

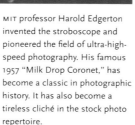

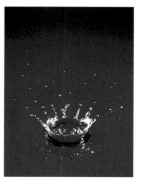

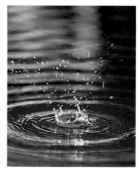

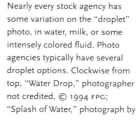

MIT professor Harold Edgerton invented the stroboscope and pioneered the field of ultra-high-speed photography. His famous 1957 "Milk Drop Coronet," has become a classic in photographic history. It has also become a tireless cliché in the stock photo repertoire.

Nearly every stock agency has some variation on the "droplet" photo, in water, milk, or some intensely colored fluid. Photo agencies typically have several droplet options. Clockwise from top, "Water Drop," photographer not credited, © 1994 FPG; "Splash of Water," photograph by

Guy Marche, 1993 © 1994 FPG; untitled, photographer not credited, © 1995 Comstock; "Water Drops," photographer not credited, © 1994 Comstock; "Water Drop," photograph by Jean Paul Nacivet, 1992, courtesy FPG.

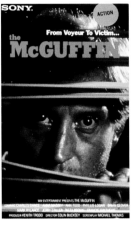

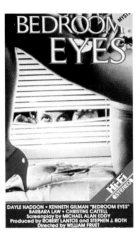

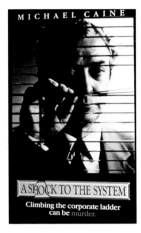

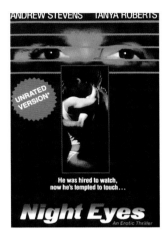

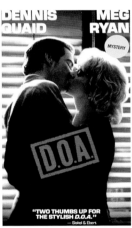

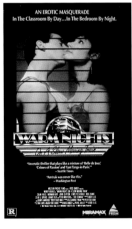

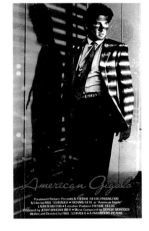

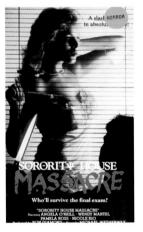

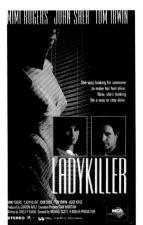

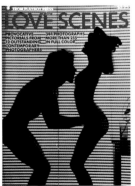

Venetian blinds have become a
signifier for eroticized danger in
the packaging of film and video
thrillers. The viewer is invited
to peer into a half-hidden world
of mystery and sex. Like the
movie screen, venetian blinds
oscillate between an opaque
surface and a transparent
window. The repetition of this
motif on countless film and
video promotions reveals the
legibility of this stock image of
voyeuristic pleasure.

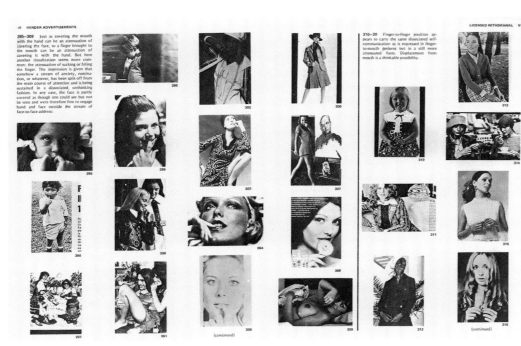

Gender Advertisements by Erving Goffman, a 1976 publication, classified the rhetoric of advertising and mass-market imagery according to recurrent poses and compositional relationships. The book is a compendium of facial expressions and gestures that echo from one image to another. Goffman's work suggests that media imagery operates as a language, and his book is a kind of thesaurus of popular culture. Goffman's work predates the artistic production of post-modern photographers such as Cindy Sherman and Richard Prince, who investigated similar terrain in the 1980s.

A spread from the December 1995 issue of *Colors*, edited by Tibor Kalman and produced by the Benetton Company. *Colors* promotes itself as a magazine "about the rest of the world," echoing the global marketing strategies of Benetton, an Italian clothing manufacturer. In this "wordless" all-photography issue, images from stock photo houses are paired with images from news photo agencies. The "non-design" of the layouts echoes the gridded pages of stock catalogues. Like Goffman's *Gender Advertisements*, Kalman invites a comparative reading of contemporary media imagery, though with a less specific editorial agenda. Art director: Fernando Gutiérrez.

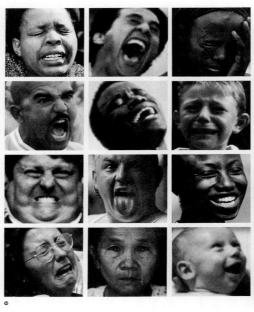

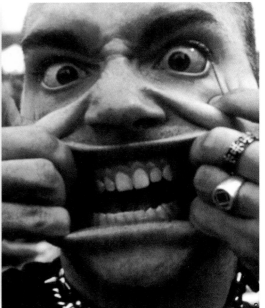

12 "In early modern Europe, alphabetization combined with printing served as a potentially unifying force in many states by imposing a standard form of linguistic communication, which in turn influenced the spoken word by offering high-prestige models." Jack Goody, *The Interface Between the Written and the Oral* (Cambridge: Cambridge University Press, 1988), 283.

13 "[Photography]...has resulted in a kind of progressive eviction of the word by the image." Paul Valéry, "The Centenary of Photography," *Classic Essays on Photography*, Alan Trachtenberg, ed., (New Haven: Leete's Island Books, 1980), 192-193.

14 In his book *The Politics of Pictures*, John Hartley uses the term "popular reality" to refer to the forum of imagery that creates our concepts of the public. John Hartley, *The Politics of Pictures: The Creation of the Public in the Age of Popular Media* (London: Routledge, 1992).

THE AUTHORS WOULD LIKE TO THANK COMSTOCK, TONY STONE AND FPG FOR THEIR SUPPORT.

STOCK PHRASES AND STEREOTYPES

The business of stock photography is predicated on the notion that a single photograph has the potential for multiple applications or, to invert a cliché, a word is worth a thousand pictures. In modern stock photography, the informational richness and depth of the photographic image is at odds with the imperative for the generic, the symbolic, the superficial, and the stereotypical. This striving for clarity and legibility (in both formal and conceptual terms) unites the products of stock photo agencies, whether they are artfully blurred still-lives or sharply focussed portraits.

The catalogues and archives of the stock industry provide an index of how images communicate in the context of mass media. In the process of building and marketing their collections, stock agencies are establishing a visual dictionary of mass media—a visualization of emotions and situations such as leisure, parenthood, friendship, work, power, confusion, love, and aggression.

Historians of writing and printing have shown that the formalization of writing through the medium of typography—which eliminated the inconsistencies of handwriting—affected the development of grammar and vocabulary.[12] While grammatical rules became more narrow and restrictive, the lexicon of words rapidly multiplied. A higher degree of structure yielded an expansion of vocabulary.

The notion that modern culture is characterized by a shift from print-based literacy to picture-based literacy has been discussed since the advent of photography.[13] With the pervasiveness of photographic imagery—in magazines, advertising, newspapers—it could be argued that a formalization is occuring in the realm of images parallel to that which occurred in writing.

Stock photography is an index of how images speak in the public realm. Writers as diverse as Daniel Boorstein, Guy Debord, and Jean Baudrillard have written about the disturbing power of "the image" in contemporary society. Less frequently has this phenomenon been looked upon as the effect of a new kind of literacy.

The growth of stock photography has brought a tremendous increase in the *supply* of pictures available, but this expansion of output has also yielded pictures that look more and more alike. The codification of poses, subjects, settings, and styles in stock photography indicates a *narrowing* of the representational field for this commercially-driven practice.

Designers engage stock imagery in ways that could be described variously as sincere, naïve, pragmatic, ironic, humorous, political, or appropriationist. In some designers' work, stock photos become discursive, reflecting on their own status as a form of "popular reality."[14] Historical and comparative studies of stock photography could yield insights into the often hypothesized domination of the image over the word, and the ways in which the specificity captured by the camera serves to fund a repetitive set of visual phrases describing modern life.

Wilson Bryan Key's 1973 book *Subliminal Seduction* offered readers a guided tour of an advertisement for Gilbey's Gin in which, he asserted, the following images were subliminally embedded:

a face in the top of the ice cube, peering down at the word SEX, subliminally encoded in the ice cubes

another face peering out from behind the letter x

"a man's legs and partially erect genitals" in the reflection of the bottle and cap

a "vaginal opening" between the reflection of the tonic glass and bottle

and a horizontal vaginal image in the tonic glass reflection

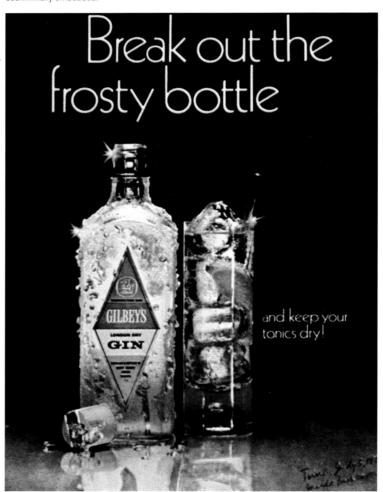

"LET YOUR EYES CONCENTRATE momentarily upon the third ice cube from the top. Without stretching your imagination beyond reasonable limits, can you see an E formed in the cube? Some interpret the letter as an F. But, hypothetically for the moment consider the letter an E. Do not read further until the E is established clearly in your mind. The second ice cube from the top is also interesting. Let your mind relax and consider what letter might be in this cube. Start at the top of the lime slice, letting your eyes move left to the point of the slice, then down and right, following the lime pulp to about the midpoint on the slice where a black line slants diagonally from the slice to the left. Now, briefly retrace the above instructions. You should have outlined on the ice cube, in the silhouette formed by the lime slice, the letter S. Now…let your eyes move from the S to the E and then to the fourth ice cube. If you are relaxed enough, you will perceive a line cutting diagonally across the first diagonal line. Give the perception time to register—and keep relaxed. If the x does not immediately appear, try looking away momentarily, then back quickly at the fourth cube. You have just consciously perceived your first subliminal SEX."

Subliminal Seduction

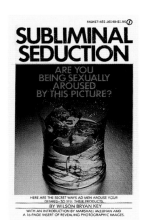

1 Wilson Bryan Key, *Subliminal Seduction: Ad Media's Manipulation of a Not So Innocent America* (New York: Prentice Hall, 1973).

"Are you sexually aroused by this picture?" was the question Wilson Bryan Key posed to readers of his 1973 book *Subliminal Seduction*.[1] This rhetorical question was an invitation to look twice at something that usually is only granted a passing glance. Thus the reader's interest is piqued: *What if something so banal as a whiskey advertisement is having some effect I am unaware of? Could this be why I drink whiskey in the first place?*

The concept of "subliminal seduction" has taken on the dimensions of folklore. Popular wisdom now holds that media images contain hidden words and imagery, including nude bodies, genitalia, skulls, mushroom clouds, and satanic paraphernalia. According to Wilson Bryan Key these were most frequently found in the ice cubes and oozing fluids of alcoholic beverages, but they could also obscenely take root in the folds of a model's shirt sleeve, in reflective surfaces, across a forehead, on a child's tongue, and even in a pat of butter.

The image which forms the central argument of *Subliminal Seduction* is a 1971 Gilbey's gin ad. Key's investigation consisted of interviewing 1,000 people who were "requested not to analyze content, but to just let feelings come to the surface as their eyes moved over the page"—ice cubes instead of ink blots. After taking the reader on a guided tour through the geography of subliminal seduction (at left), Key weaves these various figures into a narrative portraying three women and two men: "the subliminal promise to anyone buying Gilbey's gin is simply a good old-fashioned sexual orgy which developed after 'breaking out the frosty bottle.'"

Key claims that the "s-e-x" he discerns in the ad is the result of a deliberate process of "embedding" provocative words, images, and symbols into advertising photography. Among his 1,000 test subjects, who were also his students, none discovered on their own the subliminal content he reported. This he accounts for by the defense mechanism of *repression,* which disallows the subliminal message into consciousness; subliminal seduction gains its insidious power from the viewer's inability to consciously perceive the embedded information. As Key states, "once the subliminal information becomes apparent to the conscious mind, the persuasive or manipulative potential in the data is destroyed." It's like accidentally erasing your hard-drive. A four-color insert in *Subliminal Seduction* offers numerous examples in support of Key's thesis.

Key's obsessive analyses look for deliberate optical illusions in advertising. Yet Key's detective work is less a critique of advertising than a product of it. His mode of analysis takes its cues from the deliberate gimmickry and novelty of advertising—its use of condensation, puns, wordplay, and visual effects. His choice of the word *seduction* in his title positions the public as a vulnerable, feminized, unprotected victim of the all-knowing media and advertising industries.[2] The back cover copy extends the seduction metaphor, referring to the manipulation of audiences as "media rape." Remarkably, his argument does not explain how subliminally receiving the word SEX leads to making a purchase. The argument rests on the assumption that erotic imagery and naughty words inspire automatic sales. According to Key words such as SEX, FUCK, and DEATH act as "subliminal triggers to motivate purchasing behavior."

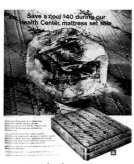

SPRING AIR MATTRESS

An ad for Spring Air Mattresses showing money inside an ice cube appeared in the same issue of *Life* magazine in which Key discovered subliminal messages in the ice cubes of a Bacardi Rum advertisement.

But does subliminal perception actually exist? Subliminal perception *is* a proven phenomenon, referring to the ability to sense impressions that are "below the threshold" of conscious awareness. Historical and contemporary studies support the existence of subliminal perception, yet it is granted an extremely weak and incidental role because of its inability to compete with the stronger impressions of *conscious* perception. The question is not whether subliminal *perception* exists (it does), or even whether subliminal *advertising* exists (it does), but whether it *works*.[3] The effectiveness of exploiting subliminal perception for the purpose of channeling consumer behavior has no empirical support.[4] Lack of evidence, however, has done nothing to weaken the myth that subliminal stimuli are one of the key strategies of persuasion in advertising. Subliminal seduction is a popular conspiracy theory—perhaps the only such "theory" about advertising that is widely known, if not widely believed. Despite its dubious results, the embedding of visual and aural messages in advertising is outlawed by the Federal Communications Commission and the U.S. Bureau of Alcohol, Tobacco, and Firearms.

The myth of subliminal advertising made its debut in 1957 in a movie theatre in Fort Lee, New Jersey. James Vicary of the Subliminal Projection Company flashed fleeting messages every five seconds onto the screening of a motion picture. The messages were: "HUNGRY? EAT POPCORN" and "DRINK COCA-COLA." Vicary claimed that concession sales rose dramatically as a result of his experiment. The event was widely reported in the press as

2 Key's use of the word "seduction" recalls Fredric Wertham's book, *Seduction of the Innocent: The Influence of Comic Books on Today's Youth* (New York: Rinehart & Company, 1953). Wertham's book analyzed comic books for their sexual and masochistic content, arguing their harmful effects on children. Wertham provided examples of "pictures within pictures for children who know how to look." Wertham's book was continuously parodied by comic book artists.

3 The term "subliminal advertising" was first used in a report on Vicary in the September 16, 1957 issue of *Advertising Age*.

4 The literature on subliminal perception is extensive. For a survey of the technical literature on the relationship of subliminal techniques and their effect on perception and motivation, see Timothy E. Moore, "Subliminal Advertising: What You See is What You Get," *Journal of Marketing*, 46 (1982): 38-47. The *Journal of Advertising* has repeatedly taken up the issue of subliminal techniques: "A New Perspective of Subliminal Perception," Ronnie Cuperfain and T.K. Clarke, *Journal of Advertising*, 14, 1, (1985): 36-41; William E. Kilbourne, Scott Painton, Danny Ridley, "The Effect of Sexual Embedding on Responses to Magazine Advertisements," *Journal of Advertising*, 14, 2 (1985): 48-56; Martin P. Block, Bruce G. Vanden Bergh, "Can You Sell Subliminal Messages to Consumers?," *Journal of Advertising*, 14, 3 (1985): 59-62.

5 A 1983 survey found that 81 percent of the public thinks embedding is a standard practice in advertising. See Eric J. Zanot, J. David Pincus, E. Joseph Lamp, "Public Perceptions of Subliminal Advertising" *Journal of Advertising*, 12, 1 (1983): 39-45.

6 Walter Weir, "Another Look at Subliminal 'Facts,'" *Advertising Age* (October 15, 1984).

7 Theodore Schulte, "Getting to the Underlying Truth on Subliminal Ads," *Advertising Age* (April 1, 1985).

a controversial and frightening indication of how evil the advertising profession had become. The event also earned Vicary a great deal of publicity. The story, somewhat transformed, gained wider currency when it was related in Vance Packard's 1957 book *Hidden Persuaders*, an exposé on the incorporation of subliminal tactics and motivation research techniques into advertising and marketing. *Advertising Age* magazine reported on the event, piquing the interest of some readers and inspiring the wrath of others. Challenged by one of his peers, Vicary agreed to repeat his experiment under observation, but there was no increase in sales. He later confessed to inventing the results and to staging the event as a last-ditch attempt to get publicity for his failing business.

The concept of subliminal advertising, enacted by James Vicary's projections, disseminated in *The Hidden Persuaders*, and elaborated by Wilson Bryan Key, constitutes one of the most powerful associations Americans have of advertising and its strategies. Deemed ineffective by the scientific community, and largely ignored by the advertising industry, Vicary and Key's assertions have nonetheless entered the realm of folklore. Like alligators in New York City sewers, the notion of subliminal persuasion has entered a strange arena of popular mythology: whether it happened or not, it serves to unfold beliefs about the manipulation of audiences by advertising. It's a conspiracy theory whose suggestive force outweighs its factual shortcomings.[5]

It's also an idea with endurance. Writing in *Advertising Age* in 1984, an educator stated that "wherever I have lectured, one of the first questions I am asked—by professors and students—is how subliminal advertising is created. While I do my best to explain why it does not exist and could not, the sensationalism of Mr. Key's books leaves a mental impression that is difficult to expunge."[6] In the same publication one year later, a journalism professor complained that "people, especially students, like to think [subliminal advertising] exists. Each year I survey my beginning advertising class to see how many students had any advertising education in high school. Customarily, ten percent answer yes. Their books? Their formal introduction to advertising? Invariably the answer is *Subliminal Seduction, Sexploitation in Advertising, The Hidden Persuaders*. This is where the popular idea gets perpetuated, at the high school level."[7] *Subliminal Seduction* is now nearly 20 years old: one of its largest audiences—both at its debut and since then—has been middle- and high school-age students who delight in the possibility that some of the most visible artifacts of the adult world might be secretly encoded with the same graffiti that covers their desktops, lockers, and bathroom stalls.

META-SUBLIMINAL

The myth of subliminal persuasion has infiltrated American culture thoroughly enough to have become the basis for a series of "meta-subliminal" campaigns in print and broadcast advertising. This is especially prevalent in liquor advertising, which was the most consistent target of Wilson Bryan Key's accusations of "embedded" imagery. This tongue-in-cheek self-reflexivity updates older strategies where the content of an advertisement comments upon the strategy of "selling."

The most literal of the "meta-subliminal" advertisements is the 1990 "Absolut Subliminal" ad which embeds the name of the vodka in the ice cubes, making a direct reference to *Subliminal Seduction.* The 1992 "Absolut Seattle" version, "embeds" the bottle within a puddle of rain, instead of a puddle of vodka.

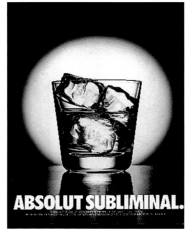

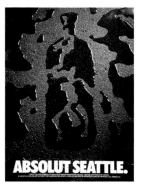

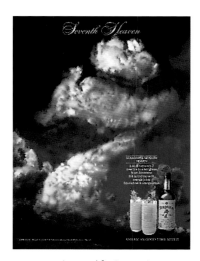

A 1991 ad for Seagram's 7 embeds the logo of the product into a sky full of clouds. Critics of Wilson Bryan Key typically dismiss the images he "discovered" as being no more willful or intentioned than the pictures one can find in cloud formations. The Seagram's campaign, like many liquor campaigns, is a direct take-off from the success of the Absolut campaign.

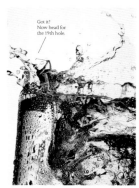

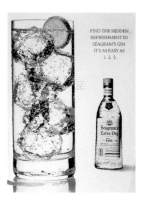

Detail of a 1991 Seagram's ad by Ogilvy & Mather, which photographically embeds a man golfing in the froth of a cocktail. Another ad in the series invites readers to find the hidden message by "connecting the dots" to reveal the form of a woman swimming in a gin and tonic. The Seagram's ads tease readers with the line: "The Hidden Pleasure in Refreshing Seagram's Gin." Advertising critic Leslie Savan has reported that Seagram's conducted a survey prior to launching the ad that found "nearly 62 percent of the public believe that subliminal ads exist, and 56 percent believe that subliminals can get them to buy things they don't want. But, happily, the study found that 54 percent 'liked the idea of subliminal spoof ads!'" See "Burying Messages" in Leslie Savan, *The Sponsored Life: Ads, TV, and American Culture* (Philadelphia: Temple University Press, 1994).

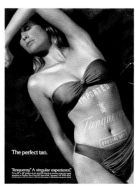

Many of Wilson Bryan Key's examples found bodies hidden within products. In a number of recent meta-subliminal ads, such as this 1990 Tanqueray example, the product is grafted onto the body. What was formerly "taboo" for Key (the sexy woman) comes to the foreground, and the product becomes the shadowy, "hidden persuader." The link with Tanqueray is reinforced by the bathing suit, which repeats the distinctive green and red of the Tanqueray bottle and label.

POST-SUBLIMINAL

The theory of "subliminal seduction" was advanced during a period when the boundaries of acceptability for nudity and sexual innuendo were being tested by advertisers. The "theory" was in itself an effect of this expansion of limits, hypothesizing the saturation of media imagery with veiled sexual content. Many "post-subliminal" campaigns are constructed in anticipation of their audience's readiness to read the sexual content of advertising imagery.

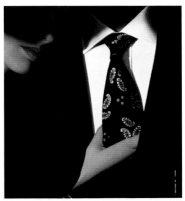

This 1990 Perry Ellis ad is a fresh interpretation of a classic icon. While other ads may dabble with the notion of phallic imagery, this one cuts to the chase and uses it as a towering presence that overshadows the model. More than just a "hidden persuader," this shadowy giant is a scene-stealer. Below, a 1989 ad for Chanel plays upon the tie as another time-honored phallic symbol, but reinforces the message with the promise of sexual gratification. Or is she merely *adjusting* his tie?

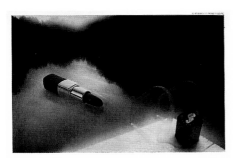

A NEW ERA IN LIPCOLOUR. MOISTURE FORMULA LIPCOLOUR. CHECK IT OUT.

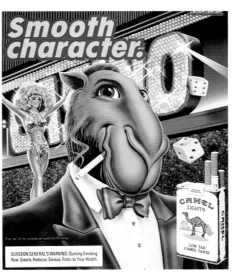

SURGEON GENERAL'S WARNING: Quitting Smoking Now Greatly Reduces Serious Risks to Your Health.

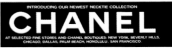

INTRODUCING OUR NEWEST NECKTIE COLLECTION

CHANEL

AT SELECTED FINE STORES AND CHANEL BOUTIQUES: NEW YORK, BEVERLY HILLS, CHICAGO, DALLAS, PALM BEACH, HONOLULU, SAN FRANCISCO.

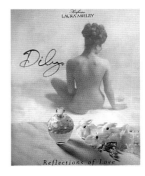

Reflections of Love

This 1979 ad for Ultra-Sheen Cosmetics casts the lipstick container as a male/female dyad, floating towards a blissful reunion. The ad plays upon the phallic association of the lipstick shape, but gives the scene its romantic overtone through the use of hazy, dreamlike photography. The advertisement wears its Freudian imagery on its sleeve, and invites readers to interpret its "message" through an anthropomorphic lens.

Camel's "Smooth Talker" campaign, which debuted in 1987, is a classic post-subliminal ad. Camel manufacturer R.J. Reynolds and Trone, the ad agency that developed the series, have denied Joe Camel's genital references, despite the almost clinical accuracy of detail. Its creators may have been elaborating on the folkloric stories surrounding the supposedly "embedded" imagery of an erect penis on the original "Old Joe" Camel packaging. The new campaign ignited a passionate debate within the advertising community about the use of cartoon-style characters in the promotion of cigarettes. Critics saw it as a transparent lure to encourage smoking among ever-younger audiences. See "Forum: For Old Joe/Against Old Joe," *Advertising Age* (January 27, 1992).

This 1991 ad for "Dily," a parfum by Laura Ashley, rehearses the traditional "woman-at-her-bath" scenario, made popular by art history. But the position of the woman's hand and leg suggests that "Dily" is preoccupied, an interpretation that explains her back-to-the-camera pose.

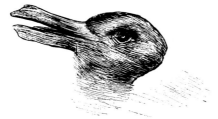

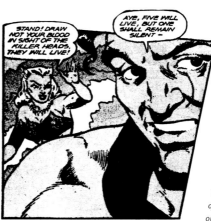

The notion of subliminal seduction may be partly inspired by the phenomenon of single images which yield different interpretations. Images such as the "Duck-Rabbit" and the Necker cube have been termed "multistabile" because they can be perceived in contradictory ways. For a useful discussion of such types of imagery see W.J.T. Mitchell, *Picture Theory: Essays on Verbal and Visual Representation* (Chicago: University of Chicago Press, 1994).

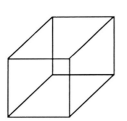

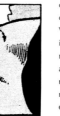

Fredric Wertham's 1953 book, *Seduction of the Innocent: The Influence of Comic Books on Today's Youth* offered examples of "pictures within pictures for children who know how to look." Wertham's example of embedded imagery—the pubic area of a naked woman hidden in the coat and collar of a gangtser—is no more explicit than many of the non-subliminal examples found elsewhere in his book.

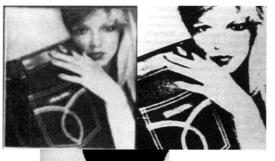

Stuart Ewen's *All Consuming Images: The Politics of Style in Contemporary Culture* (New York: Basic Books, 1988) discusses the role of "sublimated" senses in the jargon of industrial design and marketing in the 1930s and 40s. Using Freudian theory, industrial designers advised that the "sublimated" sense of touch might be exploited by designers and manufacturers to make products more attractive. Ewen also, though less successfully, refers to "subliminal sexual promises" in the context of a Chardón Jeans advertisement. Ewen argues that if one masks the eyes of the female model, a picture emerges of another woman performing fellatio. But isn't that already implied and, in effect, shown through the pose and position of the model?

7 Quoted in Philip Meggs, "*Time* vs. *Newsweek*: Coping and Competing in the Age of CNN," *Print* 42 (September/October 1988): 98-104.

who regard newspapers as a textual medium, that, *when necessary,* may resort to photographs and illustrative graphics. *USA Today* crosses genres freely, incorporating the breezy tone of newscaster speech with the illustrative style of TV weather maps.

Many of the features that make *USA Today* exceptional among newspapers are elements characteristic of other media. The style of the paper's information graphics and typography has been culled from the pages of *Time* and *Newsweek*. Walter Bernard's 1977 redesign of *Time,* which provoked *Newsweek* to change its own graphic style—culminating in Roger Black's 1985 redesign—reshaped the editorial identity of magazines. According to Black, *"USA Today* probably would not be possible without *Time."*[7] Although information graphics had been a standard feature in both *Time* and *Newsweek,* they were usually unimaginative, crude in execution, and limited in number. The pop data graphics for *Time,* begun in 1978 by Nigel Holmes, heavily influenced *USA Today*'s house style.

The *Time* and *Newsweek* redesigns brought visually flamboyant and conceptually elaborate information graphics to the fore of newsweekly journalism, which in turn influenced other print media. A number of publications with a picture-graphic bias attest to an "infotainment" zeitgeist that has influenced design since the early 1980s. Noteworthy examples include Access Press, a publisher of guidebooks established in 1980 by Richard Saul Wurman.

The *Access* series emphasized the role of information graphics in books on travel, medicine, and sports. At the other end of the spectrum were the baroque charts and diagrams of *Spy* magazine, launched in 1986. *Spy*'s techniques of graphic parody reflected a fascination with both naïve and sophisticated modes of information graphics.

While the mass appeal of *Time* and *Newsweek* make them clear predecessors of *USA Today*, the newspaper industry was responding to its own imperative to say less and show more. *USA Today* followed in the footsteps of many newspapers throughout the country— notably the *Morning Call, The Chicago Tribune,* the Orange County *Register,* and *The Miami Herald*—which were increasingly reporting the news through didactic graphics, large photographs, and illustrations arranged in magazine-inspired layouts. Many of the changes that occurred at *The New York Times* in the late 1970s, under art director and assistant managing editor Louis Silverstein, indicated a paradigm shift in American news media. Between 1976 and 1978, Silverstein introduced daily themed sections such as "Science Times," "Home," and "The Living Section." The bold treatment of large illustrations and photographs reinforced the magazine-like quality of the sections and set them apart from the still-sober look of the main section.

USA Today also responded to the expansion of television news, marked by the establishment of CNN in 1980. Programs such as *60 Minutes, 20/20,*

continued on page 148

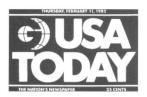

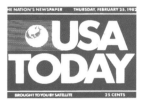

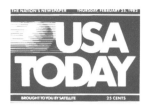

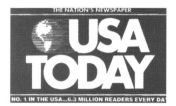

The *USA Today* logo is one of the paper's most important graphic elements. Its sans-serif type punching through a blue field distinguishes it from the black-letter treatments of traditional newspaper logos. Numerous versions, shown above, were developed before arriving at the final one. Another departure from tradition is the use of a circulation tally: "6.3 Million Readers Every Day." While unusual in the world of journalism, it is standard practice in the world of fast-food franchises. Masthead design: Young & Rubicam, New York.

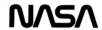

The connecting forms of the letters in the *USA Today* logo are reminiscent of Danne and Blackburn's NASA logo. This subtle link to a space-age theme is bolstered by the presence of the globe. The computer striations featured in many corporate marks of the 1980s, such as the AT&T logo, by Saul Bass, and the corporate trademarks of Sprint and Prudential, are used in the *USA Today* logo to suggest an "upbeat" theme of omnipotence through technology.

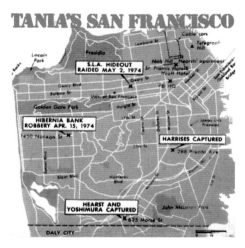

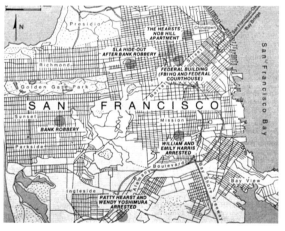

USA Today has eagerly followed a trend, initiated by weekly news magazines, to feature elaborate information graphics. As recently as 1975, the graphics in *Time* and *Newsweek* were executed in one or two colors in a dry, technical style. These two examples from *Newsweek* and *Time*, both dating from September 29, 1975, and both detailing the Patty Hearst saga, reveal how conservatively newsweeklies dealt with information graphics. They are nearly identical in approach.

USA Today's first edition, which appeared on September 15, 1982, indicated the "brighter side" that the paper would consistently emphasize in the news. While most newspaper headlines reported the death toll of 55 people in a major airline crash, *USA Today* saw a glass half full and reported "Miracle: 327 survive, 55 die."

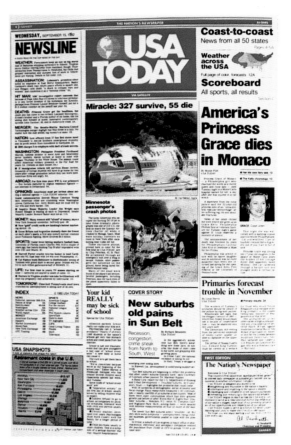

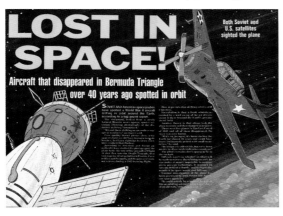

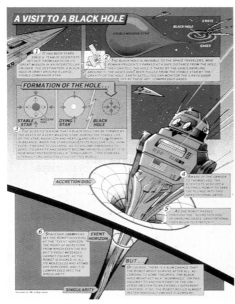

Didactic illustrations, a mainstay in technical and scientific journals, have spilled over into general-interest publications, including *USA Today*. A 1979 *Time* illustration for an article on black holes reveals a stylistic vocabulary that borrows heavily from science-fiction pulp comics. Art director: Walter Bernard; designer: Nigel Holmes. A 1990 article on the "Bermuda Triangle" that appeared in the *Examiner*, a supermarket tabloid, makes a telling comparison. The *Examiner* illustration does not elucidate technical information and is far less sophisticated than *Time*'s; however, both publications mine the same territory of Saturday-morning science-fiction cartoons.

continued from page 145

Nightline, Prime Time Live, and the *MacNeil/Lehrer Newshour* indicated a trend toward "primetiming" the news. Tabloid TV programs, such as *Hard Copy, Rescue 911, Unsolved Mysteries*, and *America's Most Wanted*, provide the same unabashed conflation of news and entertainment as *USA Today*.

USA Today's reporting implicitly equates objectivity with simplicity and brevity. This equation is made clear in *The Making of McPaper*, an in-house history of *USA Today*. Throughout the book, the reader is reminded of the editors' ruthless demands for the simplest presentation of facts. The trademark terseness of *USA Today*'s writing style is partly an effect of production: the news must fit into the 56-page maximum capacity shared by all of the paper's 36 print sites (33 in the U.S., one in Hong Kong, one in Singapore, and one in Switzerland). Thus, *USA Today* is a fixed matrix that the news must be carefully tailored to accommodate. The clipped writing style results from the gap between a small "news-hold" and a broad agenda.

The pursuit of brevity was institutionalized at the paper with monthly "McNugget Awards" for "tight, clear, fact-filled stories." Brevity, clarity, and objectivity are noble goals, but when chosen over other determinants of good journalism, such as comprehensiveness and quality of interpretation, they are incomplete criteria. Moreover, while the writing at *USA Today* is ritually purged of detail and intricacy, the information graphics are complexly rendered and loaded with gratuitous color and illusionistic tonal gradations. This transformation of abstract data into detailed tableaux appears at odds with the brevity of the articles. Yet when asked if the paper had an overall goal in producing its graphics, Richard Curtis cited "simplicity and clarity." He attributed the colorful stylization of the graphics to an effort to provide entertainment and decoration as well as information. This attitude is shared by Nigel Holmes, whose graphics for *Time* familiarize data by converting abstract numbers into iconic forms.[8]

The graphic designer and political scientist Edward Tufte, in his landmark books *The Visual Display of Quantitative Information* and *Envisioning Information*, has argued for data graphics whose visual presentation is the product of a content-based approach to color and form.[9] Color, according to Tufte, should be used to convey concrete distinctions; the amount of ink expended in a chart or diagram should be weighed against the amount of information conveyed. Such criteria play no part in the graphics of *USA Today, Newsweek, Time*, and other newsweeklies. In *Visual Display*, Tufte specifically criticized a *Time* graphic because its pictorial conceit misrepresented the statistic it purported to elucidate.[10] Such pictorial conceits are a staple among *USA Today*'s fifteen full-time graphic journalists.

The design principles outlined by Tufte, with their concern for method and objectivity, recall the rigor and

8 Nigel Holmes, *Designer's Guide to Creating Charts and Diagrams,* and Nigel Holmes with Rose DeNeve, *Designing Pictorial Symbols* (New York: Watson-Guptill, 1985).

9 Edward Tufte, *The Visual Display of Quantitative Information* (Cheshire, CT: Graphics Press, 1983), and *Envisioning Information* (Cheshire, CT: Graphics Press, 1990).

10 Tufte reproduces a *Time* chart of crude-oil exports represented with drawings of barrels and shows that the volumetric amount suggested by the image is at odds with the data. Tufte, *The Visual Display of Quantitative Information.*

purity associated with Swiss modernism. This rigor was also part of Otto Neurath's Isotype movement, which held that information graphics can attain a communicative effect superior —not merely parallel—to the written word. Beginning in the 1920s, Neurath sought a vocabulary of schematic symbols that would operate with alphabetic consistency. Stylistically, Neurath's silhouette forms had a typographic clarity and regularity that aligned them with the reduced imagery of much of modernist graphic design. While the Isotype movement was more narrowly focused than the scope of graphics Tufte is concerned with, both can be located within a Modernist-Rationalist lineage that eschews decorative forms and colors in favor of what could be called "prose graphics."

The graphic journalists at *USA Today* and the mass-circulation news-weeklies, on the other hand, have a more eclectic, Pop-inspired approach, parallel to the sign-based architecture of Robert Venturi, Steven Izenour, and Denise Scott Brown. Their lineage can be traced to the Push Pin Studios, with their distinctly Postmodern approach: pragmatic, anti-systematic, populist, deliberately inconsistent, and playful. The *USA Today* style has much in common with the synthetic blending of cartoon styles and conventions typical of Push Pin illustrator Seymour Chwast's work. The figures that populate many *USA Today* graphics are a kind of hybrid between Otto Neurath's severe "information man" and the more

approachable Elmer Fudd: they are info-toons for the infotainment age. Hollywood's translation of cartoons into the "real life" of cinema—from *Superman* (1978) and *Who Framed Roger Rabbit?* (1988) to *Batman* (1989) and *Dick Tracy* (1990)—has accompanied the incorporation of cartoons into the "real life" of the news. While Neurath and Tufte represent the values of "prose graphics," *USA Today* and its magazine progenitors promote "theatrical

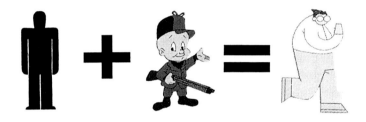

graphics," which spotlight the illustrative, decorative, and emotive potential of data. A serious drawback is that "theatrical graphics" can put an editorial spin on the data being presented. A caricature of an Arab in one of Holmes's graphics for *Time* made the data itself largely irrelevant: the hostility of the image overwhelmed the statistics being presented. Apart from such stylized representations, graphics that are apparently "objective" or straightforward may have complex inflections. For example, in the pictograms in Access Press's book *Medical Access* (1985), the icon that represents "man" is adapted from the 1974 U.S. Department of

continued on page 152

The figures that appear in many *USA Today* graphics are a hybrid between Otto Neurath's severe Information Man of the 1920s and Elmer Fudd. The figure on the right is the 1990 user-friendly Everyman who introduces readers to statistics that "shape the nation." Illustrator: Keith Carter (*USA Today* figure). Elmer Fudd © 1990 Warner Bros.

These stridently "bad" maps from *Spy*
parody the overzealous, confusing quality of
information graphics that try too hard.
Their delight in obfuscation, and their
"serious" approach to humorous content is
an ironic response to the information age.
The "Zoned Commercial" map (January/
February 1987) identifies New York business
districts such as the "Plastic Surgery District,"
and the "Tacky Loungewear District."
Design direction: Drenttel Doyle Partners.

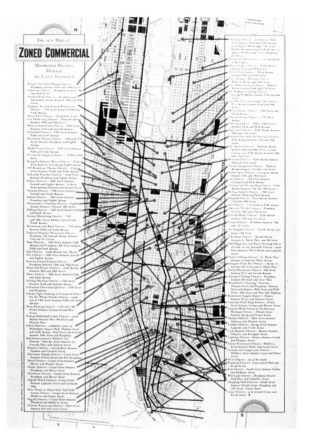

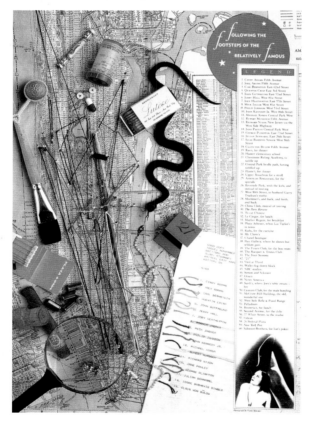

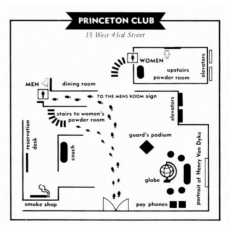

This *Spy* map of the "Relatively Famous"
(November 1986) chronicles the movements
of New York's minor celebrities with string-
and-map-tack, lending a maniacal fervor to
the task of celebrity hunting. The props
evoke the imagery of a pulp detective novel.
Design direction: Drenttel Doyle Partners;
photographer: Victor Shrager.

"Earnest clarity" is another of
the ironic modes of discourse
that were used at *Spy*. This
detail from a series on "Using
the Bathrooms of the Clubs
of the Ivy League" (January-
February 1987) provides
New Yorkers with paths to
relief in a city notorious for
its lack of public restrooms.
Design direction: Drenttel
Doyle Partners; designer:
Sonja Andersson.

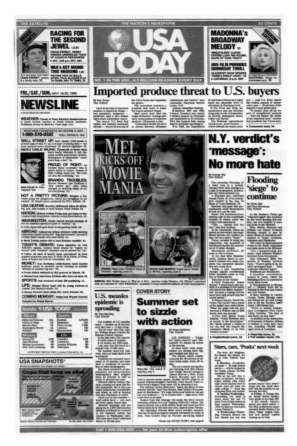

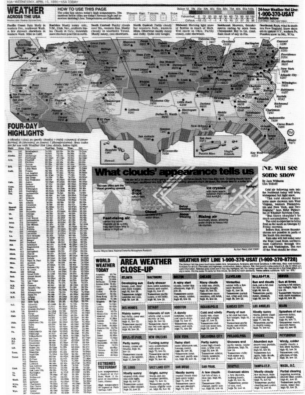

Front-page newsmakers in this May 18-20, 1990, issue include no less than six movie stars: Mel Gibson takes center stage above the fold, flanked by Tom Cruise, Eddie Murphy, and Nick Nolte below the fold. Madonna gets a special Hollywood Square in the upper right-hand corner, while Bruce Willis introduces the cover story. Art director: Richard A. Curtis.

Madonna is a consistent front-page newsmaker. The inset above was followed four weeks later (June 14, 1990) with an identical photo in the same position.

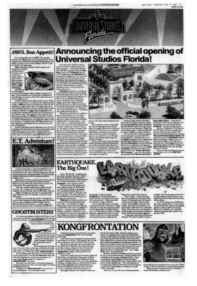

This advertising supplement for Universal Studios Florida, which appeared in USA Today, is difficult to distinguish from the paper itself. The cartoon-style illustrations of sharks and natural disasters looks at home in this context. June 14, 1990.

The colorful weather map is the most widely imitated feature of USA Today. It is a graphic translation of a TV weather anchor's map, without the pulsating suns and encroaching storm fronts. Art director: Richard A. Curtis.

continued from page 149

Transportation symbols that populate airports, restrooms, and lobbies. The symbol for "woman," however, is differentiated from her male counterpart not only by the clichéd curvature of her hips and breasts in silhouette, but also by interior lines that outline her face, indicate her nipples, and suggest her hairstyle. These cartoon-like signs of femininity belie the supposed objectivity of the Access Press style.

Many of *USA Today's* graphics illustrate the tension between journalistic ideals of objectivity and the sometimes conflicting demands for entertainment, "human interest," and decoration. Although statistics are not willfully misrepresented in the information graphics of *USA Today*, the treatment of them as info-toons discourages the sustained analysis this mode of communication can offer. One of the virtues of information graphics is that, unlike narrative forms, they may be read analytically from different vantage points, yielding different insights. Yet in the case of many of *USA Today's* graphics, the multiple content of the data is tied to one simplistic image, which typically indicates only the broadest message of the data, such as *rise/fall, few/many*. The pictorial devices used in the graphics counterproductively anchor the data to one dominant narrative.

While more attention is now given to graphics in news media—with a consequent expansion of opportunity for designers—there is at the same time a narrowing of the kind of information designers and illustrators are called upon to convey. Increasingly, mainstream journalism is exchanging editorial cartoonists, who have traditionally been expected to express their own opinions, for "graphic journalists," whose job is to express the opinions of others, gathered through Gallup polls and reader surveys. Most of the graphics in *USA Today* deal with statistics aimed to show the range of public opinion toward a particular issue — to represent everyone, and yet no one in particular. The historian Warren Susmann has observed that George Gallup's American Institute of Public Opinion, founded in 1935, was pivotal in the culture of the 1930s for "the discovery and molding of dominant cultural patterns...[and] for their reinforcement."[11] The predominance of opinion-survey graphics in *USA Today* is indicative of the paper's vested interest in the theme of national unity, a theme that favors consensus.

USA Today claims that readers buy the paper an average of 3.5 times a week and typically read it in combination with another newspaper. Thus *USA Today* constitutes only one part of a reader's daily intake of news. This fact, frequently offered as a defense in answer to *USA Today's* critics, raises serious questions. Why should the paper attempt to be exhaustive in its coverage when people have all sorts of other news sources? Why should it attempt to be comprehensive in its international reporting when other

continued on page 155

11 Warren I. Susman, "The Culture of the Thirties," *Culture as History: The Transformation of American Society in the Twentieth Century* (New York: Pantheon, 1984), 158.

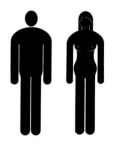

Pictograms used throughout Access Press's 1985 *Medical Access*. Based on the 1974 U.S. Department of Transportation symbols, shown below, the *Medical Access* pictograms reveal a sexist dissymmetry in their representation of gender. A parallel approach would be to outline the male's penis, and vary the silhouette with bulging biceps to indicate virility. Art director: Richard Saul Wurman; designer: Michael Everitt.

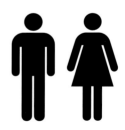

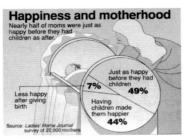

Happiness and motherhood

Nearly half of moms were just as happy before they had children as after.

Just as happy before they had children **49%**

7%

Less happy after giving birth

Having children made them happier **44%**

Source: *Ladies' Home Journal* survey of 22,000 mothers

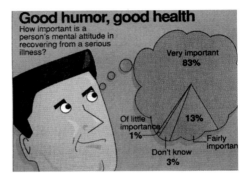

Good humor, good health

How important is a person's mental attitude in recovering from a serious illness?

Very important **83%**

Of little importance **1%**

13%

Fairly importan

Don't know **3%**

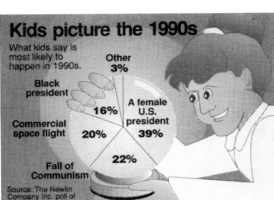

Kids picture the 1990s

What kids say is most likely to happen in 1990s.

Other **3%**

Black president

16%

A female U.S. president **39%**

Commercial space flight **20%**

22%

Fall of Communism

Source: The Newlin Company Inc. poll of 1,000 children ages 5-13

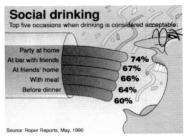

Social drinking

Top five occasions when drinking is considered acceptable:

Party at home
At bar with friends **74%**
At friends' home **67%**
With meal **66%**
Before dinner **64%**
60%

Source: Roper Reports, May, 1990

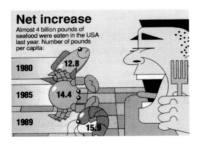

Net increase

Almost 4 billion pounds of seafood were eaten in the USA last year. Number of pounds per capita:

1980   12.8
1985   14.4
1989   15.9

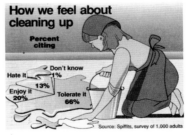

How we feel about cleaning up

Percent citing

Don't know **1%**

Hate it

13%

Enjoy it **20%**

Tolerate it **66%**

Source: Spiffits, survey of 1,000 adults

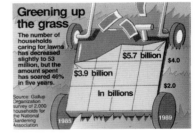

Greening up the grass

The number of households caring for lawns has decreased slightly to 53 million, but the amount spent has soared 46% in five years.

$5.7 billion $4.0

$3.9 billion $2.0

In billions

Source: Gallup Organization survey of 2,000 households for the National Gardening Association

1985   1989

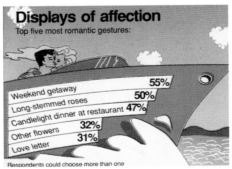

Displays of affection

Top five most romantic gestures:

Weekend getaway **55%**
Long-stemmed roses **50%**
Candlelight dinner at restaurant **47%**
Other flowers **32%**
Love letter **31%**

Respondents could choose more than one

The pie chart, an already metaphor-laden graphic, has undergone countless variations at *USA Today*. Some examples from 1990 are shown, clockwise from top left: Sam Ward (happiness), Michele D. Thorne (good humor), Sam Ward (drinking), Elys McLean Ibrahim (grass), Marcy E. Mullins (cleaning up), Melton E. Castro (affection), Keith Carter (food), Marcy E. Mullins (kids' future).

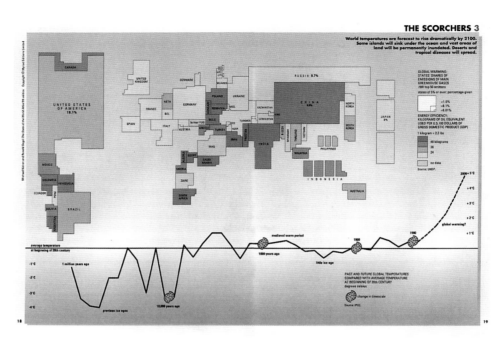

THE SCORCHERS 3

World temperatures are forecast to rise dramatically by 2100. Some islands will sink under the ocean and vast areas of land will be permanently inundated. Deserts and tropical diseases will spread.

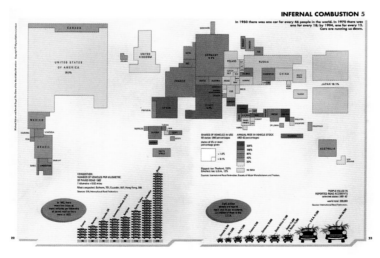

INFERNAL COMBUSTION 5

In 1950 there was one car for every 46 people in the world. In 1970 there was one for every 18; by 1994, one for every 12. Cars are running us down.

The State of the World Atlas by Michael Kidron and Ronald Segal represents a middle-road on the spectrum of information graphics. A *USA Today* palette is employed, but with a more sober use of icons, and a more sophisticated approach to content. The series is published annually by Penguin Books. Graphic design: Corinne Perlman. Text design: Pentagram Design Ltd. Maps created by Angela Wilson for Line + Line.

12 Neuharth, quoted in *The Making of McPaper*, 293-96.

13 Despite enormous strides in circulation, Rock and Hovland state that *USA Today* has reported losses at 850 million dollars to date. "Colored Lenses: The Rise of Color in the Media," in *The News Aesthetic* (New York: The Herb Lubalin Study Center, 1995), 17.

continued from page 152

papers do that better? Why shouldn't it emphasize good news when other newspapers are filled with bad news? *USA Today* defines and positions itself in *opposition* to mainstream journalism. It is stridently *not* comprehensive; instead, it is eager to provide what founder Al Neuharth calls a "journalism of hope."[12] In doing so it positions its competitors as overly serious, argumentative, gloomy, and gray.

"Positioning" is, of course, a marketing term, and *USA Today* has found a large and profitable market by differentiating itself, visually and editorially, from goods that fall into the same category. Curtis succinctly explained the paper's source of distinction: "We use graphics a lot, they use graphics a little. We write short stories, they write long stories. We think of ourselves as lively, upbeat, positive." This incorporation of marketing strategies into the paper's editorial stance raises a number of questions: What happens when a newspaper embraces, not merely accepts, that it is not a primary, or even comprehensive, news source? How does this affect what is deemed newsworthy or what constitutes balanced coverage? What happens to a newspaper (a textual medium) when it is modeled after television (a visual medium)?

The high circulation numbers of *USA Today*, particularly among young readers, indicate that *USA Today* will survive.[13] Its popularity proves that graphic journalists have an increasingly large role to play in the visually saturated contexts of contemporary journalism. Serious magazines and newspapers that fail to take heed of *USA Today*'s popularity, and are even scornful of its emphasis on the visual, will find themselves cast as retrograde and even reactionary. The challenge for designers, publishers, and editors is how to wed state-of-the-art information graphics to a progressive, critical editorial agenda, rather than to the all-purpose marketing opportunity that is *USA Today*.

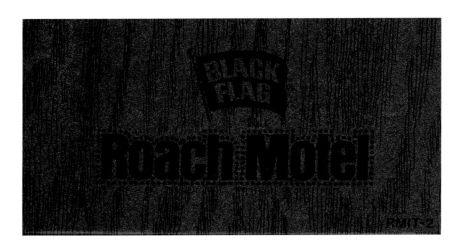

We cannot simply draw a line between low and high, or between the inside and the outside of culture, or between public and private experiences of mass media.

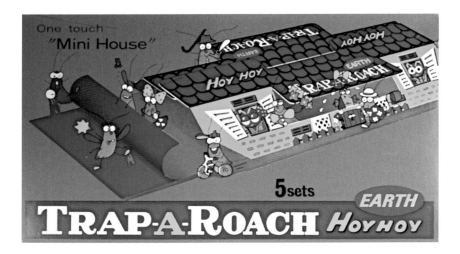

The categories of low and high are relative. Even at the level of the kitchen baseboard, one can find distinctions of low and high, formal and vernacular. The roach motels above recall Robert Venturi's and Denise Scott Brown's opposition between the modernist monolith and the decorated shed. The tasteful, International Style wood-grain model on top is designed to tastefully disappear, while the Trap-a-Roach below joyfully promotes the bugs' final vacation.

Low and High

Design in Everyday Life

In 1990 the Museum of Modern Art organized the exhibition *High and Low: Modern Art and Popular Culture,* which showed how modern artists incorporated elements of low culture into their work. The curators presented newspapers, advertising, comic books, and graffiti as raw material for the hermetic experiments of the avant-garde. In each instance, the "low" was transformed into a higher form, its crude energy diverted to fuel new aesthetic value.

Graphic designers engaged in their own transformations of low into high during the 1980s. Many appropriations of the so-called "vernacular" worked from the top down, viewing ordinary commercial artifacts as external sources to be studied with detached admiration. Yet the question of low and high can also be viewed from the bottom up—from the worm's eye view of everyday life rather than the bird's eye view of the critic. While the bird looks down at the world from above, the worm looks up at the world from below. This essay argues that in order to renew their critical view of contemporary life, designers could find a place to speak from *within* culture, and not position themselves outside and above it.

The line must also be drawn across them, through them: linking the two sides of the divide while separating them, cancelling the opposition while marking it.

The opposition between low and high art parallels oppositions found in language, where the pair low/high describes a spatial relation—as do under/over, down/up, fall/rise, and bottom/top. These spatial conditions can be mapped onto a series of value judgments loaded with cultural connotations: lower class/upper class, downstairs/upstairs, elevate/denigrate, and hell/heaven, to name just a few. Again and again, the English language classifies features of social and spiritual life in terms of proximity to the earth.

The conflict between low and high is not a matter of content but of *structure.* Low and high is a pattern, a conceptual shell, whose value shifts from situation to situation. What is high in one setting is low in another. In the space of a few years, a style can cycle from current chic to dated convention to camp nostalgia to neo-conservative revival. The term "vernacular," like the high/low pair, is relative: it positions a standard language against a lesser dialect, a dominant culture against a secondary subculture. The vernacular is the Other, and any discourse has its Other.

The recent attraction to vernacular styles represents a search for spontaneous, unpretentious voices—voices that belong to the idealized aura of a romanticized past (the roaring 20s, the flamboyant 50s) or to the noble savagery of a visual underclass (folksy signage, campy clip art). Nostalgia, a key ingredient in raising the market value of a vernacular style, is not a return to history but a repackaging of history. It treats the past not as the roots of the present, but as a distanced Other. Appropriations of contemporary vernaculars often project a barrier between a sophisticated "us" and a naïve, spontaneous "them"—the ordinary commercial artifact is an innocent object that fails to comprehend its own genius. Such nostalgic borrowings relegate the vernacular to a space removed from the aesthetic world of the designer.

Setting a distance between design and everyday life was one of the founding acts of modernism, which posed a divide between the consumer culture and a critical avant-garde. Thus William Morris's designed objects stood against the machine ethic of the day: he opposed naturalism with abstraction, artifice with honesty, and the illusion of depth with the honesty of surface. Morris created a conscience for design, and also a consciousness—a sense of opposition between a reform-minded minority and a commercial majority governed by the appetites of the marketplace.

Morris initiated the modernist ideal of the designer as critic, a figure who stands aside from the mainstream and presents alternative visions. The designer-as-critic is not simply an obedient extension of marketing, but aspires to go beyond what people already want, and teach them to want something better. The lofty mission of the designer/critic carries with it an elitist attitude toward the public. The designer is a cultural expert occupying a view from above. Hovering beyond the teaming crowds, the designer hands down master plans for reform.

As modernism became an academic credo in the 1950s and 60s, museums and university design programs became critics of the junk products and street graphics of everyday life. This paternalistic view was attacked by Pop movements in London, New York, and Milan. For American designers, the post-modern rebellion was crystallized in *Learning from Las Vegas* in 1972, which rejected high-minded reformism in favor of embracing the existing landscape of capital. Yet the distanced stance of the critic returns in the voice of Venturi, Scott Brown, and Izenour, whose edict to "learn from Las Vegas" was directed at the late inheritors of modernism, not at the makers of roadside architecture. *Learning from Las Vegas* viewed its subject as an ethnographic specimen, an innocent sample of popular life to be studied by the knowing specialists of high culture.

Robert Venturi, Denise Scott Brown, and Steven Izenour celebrated architecture-as-sign in *Learning from Las Vegas*. They used a road-side egg store store shaped like a duck as an icon for modernist architecture: building and meaning are collapsed into a single, monolithic structure. In contrast, the typical diner or "decorated shed" is a box with a sign attached to it. *Learning from Las Vegas* made the Long Island duck—once considered a trashy eyesore—into a cult object which is now protected as a historical landmark.

The line must also be drawn across them, through them: linking the two sides of the divide while separating them, cancelling the opposition while marking it.

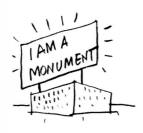
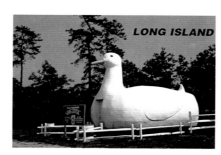
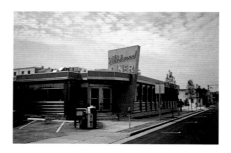

Parallel to the Pop urbanism of Venturi and Scott Brown was the eclectic style of the Push Pin Studio, which recombined elements of avant-garde art, historic ornament, and popular media in the 1960s and 70s. The Push Pin artists favored America's permissive marketing ethos over the normative theories of European modernism—they treated modernism itself as a kind of vernacular, one dialect among many rather than a standard grammar. Milton Glaser transformed his sources—from comic books to Constructivism—into his own signature style, sifting his borrowed material through the filter of a personal "touch." Reflecting the logic of "learning" from Las Vegas, Glaser turned low forms into something higher, refashioning them through his distinctive artistic style.

A similar alchemy of the ordinary appears in the post-Push Pin eclecticism of Charles Anderson, who has tapped the archive of outdated commerical ephemera as a source of familiar codes, ready to be updated into old-yet-new styles. Anderson's appropriation of "naïve" typography and illustration from the 1940s and 50s has capitalized on the nostalgia epidemic which gripped middle-class America in the 1980s and has yet to loosen its hold. Anderson has described the commercial art of 30 years ago with phrases like "naïve, simple, in your face, not intellectual, not slick, bone-head." Beneath his admiration, however, is a sense of distance from the culture he quotes. Anderson's nostalgia marks a divide between "us" in the design-savvy present and "them" in the bone-head past.

The New York design studio M&Co championed the vernacular in the 1980s as a source of clean, honest inspiration—a cold, invigorating shower to cleanse the conscience of style-happy, client-rich designers. Alexander Isley, Marlene McCarty, Emily Oberman and other designers employed at M&Co in the 1980s converted

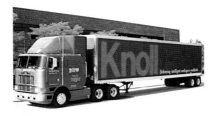

The signage below for a motel in Wildwood, New Jersey was borrowed from Massimo Vignelli's identity for Knoll, designed in the 1970s. The cultural position of a given style along the axis of high and low is not fixed; nor does it move in only one direction. Here, modernism itself serves as a vernacular idiom ripe for quotation—"clean, courteous, convenient."

We cannot simply draw a line between low and high, or between the inside and the outside of culture, or between public and private experiences of mass media.

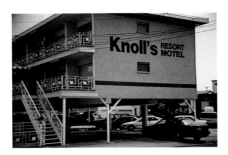
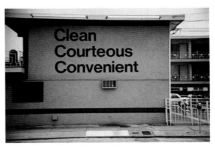

Seed packets, old and new. Adobe's nostalgic package, designed as a promotion for illustration software, shows the capacity of computer-aided design for retro styling. The real seed packets below range from the appealing collectible to the artlessly ordinary.

Study of Heinz ketchup label, designed by Robert Nakata, 1984, Cranbrook Academy of Art. The supposedly naïve "vernacular" of the Heinz label was the subject of a formal experiment. The Heinz label is not truly naïve, but is part of a sophisticated corporate identity program.

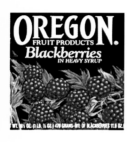
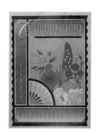
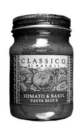
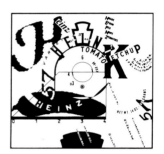

The line must also be drawn across them, through them: linking the two sides of the divide while separating them, cancelling the opposition while marking it.

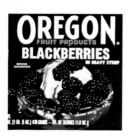
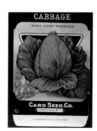
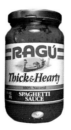
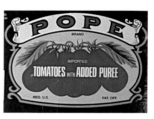

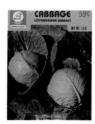
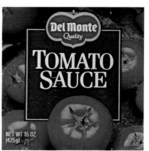

Label redesign, Oregon canned fruit, 1991. In a wave of nostalgia, this fruit packer eliminated the bluntly industrial elements from its old package—sans serif type, photographic illustration—in favor of a quaint retro style reminiscent of collectible fruit crate labels. Two vernaculars clash—a strangely outmoded modernism is supplanted by a sentimental revival.

Within the semiotic landscape of tomato sauce, there are numerous "vernaculars," from a national brand name like Heinz, whose look is deliberately bland and familiar, to an Italian export product whose image is jubilantly inventive, to the psuedo-ethnic identity of Ragu, which draws upon a stock of standard clichés about Italy, to the deluxe graphics of the Duffy Group's Classico label, which appeals to nostalgia for the traditional craft of home cooking. Each of these labels is "vernacular," in so far as each gives voice to a distinct product world, aimed at a distinct market.

the everyday lingo of quick-print wedding typography, felt-board lobby signage, and phone-book iconography into a new urban chic. M&Co's ironic use of over-the-counter graphics suggested the absence of art, the erasure of ego, and the disappearance of the designer. Yet while creative director Tibor Kalman publicly promoted non-design, he built his career on the mystique of the artist-as-witch-doctor, the impresario of taste who turns lead into gold, low into high.

Working in the same New York milieu, Drenttel Doyle Partners incorporated mundane commercial sources into the studio's distinctive use of mixed fonts, graduated type sizes, and literary conventions. Most of Drenttel Doyle's appropriations transformed their low sources beyond recognition. As Stephen Doyle has explained, he adopted tabloid typography and commercial catalogue layouts for "civilized use"—he was interested in the structural ideas, not the surface appearance, of such crude artifacts as the *World Weekly News*.

The commercial vernacular became part of a distinctly modernist experiment at Cranbrook Academy beginning in the mid-70s. Students were asked to submit an ordinary typographic object—such as a Yellow Pages ad or a ketchup label—to a series of formal operations, from rational grid studies to free-form compositions.

We cannot simply draw a line between low and high, or between the inside and the outside of culture, or between public and private experiences of mass media.

The exercise was an object lesson in discovering the distance between "us" and "them," between the esoteric laboratory experiments of graduate students and the specimens they skillfully dissected. What these studies appeared to overlook is the fact that the seemingly naïve "commercial vernacular" often belonged to a sophisticated marketing strategy. The Heinz Company, for example, helped invent corporate identity in the late nineteenth century, by pioneering modern packaging, advertising, and image management.

These quotations of the everyday perform acts of transformation—the Pop makeovers of Milton Glaser, the quirky nostalgia of Charles Anderson, the visual slumming of M&Co. In each instance, the low redeems itself by turning into something better, by offering a source of energy to the higher life form which feeds upon it. Various critics—from Walter Benjamin in the 1930s to writers in "cultural studies"—have argued that mass culture changed the very structure of art, both high and low. Because mass media and mass production altered the conduct of public and private life, "low" culture cannot be treated merely as an innocent source of subject matter, imagery, or style. We cannot simply draw a line between the inside and the outside of culture, or between public and private experiences of mass media, or between low and high forms of expression. The line must also be drawn across them, through them: linking the two sides of the divide as well as separating them, cancelling the opposition as well as defining it.[1]

1 See Meaghan Morris, "Banality in Cultural Studies," *Discourse* 10, 2 (Spring/Summer 1988): 3-28; and Stuart Hall, "Notes on Deconstructing the 'Popular,'" in Raphael Samuel, ed., *People's History and Socialist Theory* (London: Routledge and Kegan Paul, 1981), 227-239.

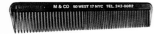

Promotional comb, designed by M&Co, mid-1980s. M&Co became notorious for its surprisingly ordinary gifts.

Film poster, *True Stories*, designed by M&Co, mid-1980s. Tabloid typography is used to promote David Byrne's gothic depiction of Middle America.

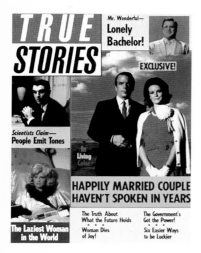

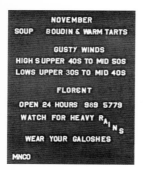

Menu board, Restaurant Florent, designed by M&Co, mid-1980s. M&Co used off-the-shelf typography for this hip down-town diner.

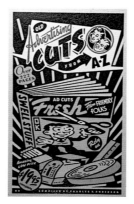

Book cover, *Advertising Cuts from A to Z*, designed by Charles Anderson, 1989. Anderson's book of clip art is a visual dictionary of 1950s nostalgia.

Advertisement, World Financial Center, designed by Drenttel Doyle Partners. The designers based their layout on an industrial catalogue.

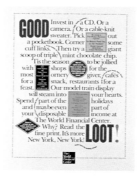

Magazine spread, "Family Ties," designed by Alexander Isley. *Spy*, 1988. Isley's absurd yet rigorously archival graphics explored the messy subconscious of the Information Age.

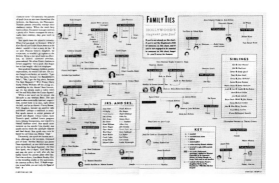

Logo, Drenttel Doyle Partners, mid-1980s. The studio's own graphic identity incorporates vernacular elements, but here—unlike the examples at left—the source is adopted openly, its identity left unobscured. This vernacular source comes not from the visual underclass of clay-coated catalogues and supermarket tabloids, but arrives instead from the genteel world of engraved financial ephemera. The designers have allowed the vernacular to show its face in a situation where the social class involved is high rather than low.

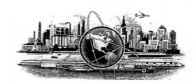

We cannot simply draw a line between low and high, or between the inside and the outside of culture, or between public and private experiences of mass media.

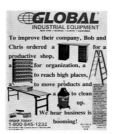

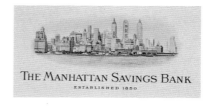

The line must also be drawn across them, through them: linking the two sides of the divide while separating them, cancelling the opposition while marking it.

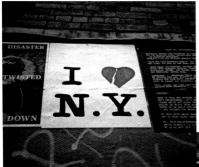

Poster, *Homelessness at Work*, designed by Day Gleeson and Dennis Thomas. Published by Bullet Space, New York, 1991. This series of posters included adaptations of corporate and bureaucratic information styles.

Poster, *Enjoy AZT*, designed by Vincent Gagliostro and Avram Finkelstein. Published by Bullet Space, New York, 1991. This appropriation of the Coca-Cola logo compares the makers of AZT to manufacturers of other products-for-profit.

Poster, designed by Tom McGlynn and Emily Carter. Published by Bullet Space, New York, 1991. This symbol for a broken-hearted city is based on Milton Glaser's famous rebus.

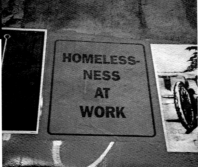

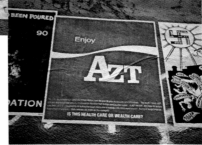

Rave flyer, *Cream of the Crop*, designer unknown, New York, 1995.

The maker of this sign attempted to imitate the "vernacular" of mass-produced typography.

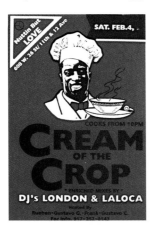

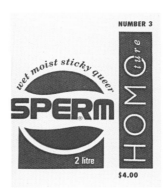

Magazine cover, *Homoture*, 1991/92. The Pepsi generation comes out.

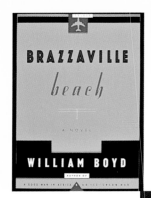

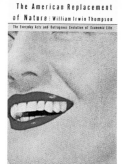

Book cover, *Low Life*, designed by Barbara de Wilde, Alfred A. Knopf, early 1990s. Art director: Carol Devine Carson. Insistently horizontal bands have been used to express the condition of "lowness."

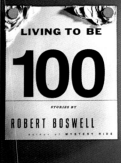

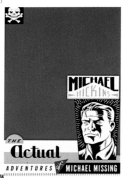

Book covers, designed by Chip Kidd and Barbara de Wilde, Alfred A. Knopf, early 1990s. Art director: Carol Devine Carson. Kidd and de Wilde use cigarette packages, pieces of old magazines, and other scraps of daily life in their book covers. These covers changed the familiar language of design for publishing, precipitating a new "vernacular" out of old ones.

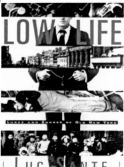

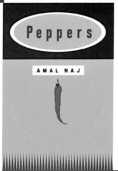

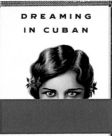

We cannot simply draw a line between low and high, or between the inside and the outside of cult... vate experiences of mass media.

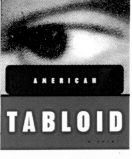

It is this contradictory break between the low and the high—at once there and not there, dividing and connecting—on which modernism was founded. The vanguard opposition to middle-class society, the search for a place above and beyond the mainstream, the need to transform the ordinary into something new: these are features of the modernist vision. The desire to find a space outside of culture was inspired by the very omnipresence of products and media, a socializing force from which no one is exempt.

Many contemporary uses of so-called "vernacular" styles assume a distance between the civilized designer and the raw material to be transformed, while other work acknowledges the position of the designer as someone who is both inside *and* outside of culture: the designer is a spectator of his or her own world, rather than the conoisseur of a nostalgic past, an exotic other, or a visual underclass.

A common strategy among urban subcultures is to remake national trademarks into emblems for alternative ideas and institutions. Appropriations like these are made not from *above* mass culture but from *within* it: a view from the street rather than from the laboratory of the specialist or the studio of the artist. Such designs represent vernacular codes as the visible traces of power. By taking back and rewriting the hieroglyphics of the everyday, these designers are making a language of the ordinary that borrows time from the dominant corporate monologue.

Critical refashionings of a vernacular code include the information graphics of *Spy* magazine. *Spy*'s format was initiated by Drenttel Doyle Partners in 1986 and crafted by Alexander Isley into a ruthlessly funny, rigorously archival typographic language. The vernacular model for *Spy*'s charts, maps, and diagrams is the authoritative lingo of newspapers and science textbooks. *Spy*'s infographics parodied the typographic style of Objectivity, Facts, and Information. They appropriate not a visual underclass but the vocabulary of "knowledge" itself.

CALL AGAIN

The line must also be drawn across   CALL AGAIN   two sides of the divide while separating them, cancelling the opposition while marking it.

Cigar box, designer unknown.
Chip Kidd used cigar box graphics
to express an explicitly consumerist,
American vision of "Cuba" in his
design for the cover of *Dreaming in
Cuban*.

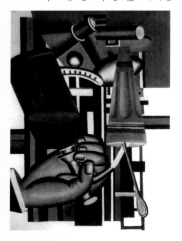

A transformation from the mundane to the
magical was the subject of MoMA's *High and
Low* exhibition, which presented commercial art
as raw nourishment for the hermetic visions of
modern artists. Throughout the exhibition and
catalogue, curators Kirk Varnedoe and Adam
Gopnik reiterated the transformation from the
public to the private, from the external artifact
to the internal vision, from the low to the high.
Newspapers, advertising, and comic books were
treated as modern-day equivalents to the
landscapes, bowls of fruit, and naked women
which have traditionally offered subject matter

The line must also be drawn across them, through them: linking the two sides of the divide while separating them, cancelling the opposition while marking it.

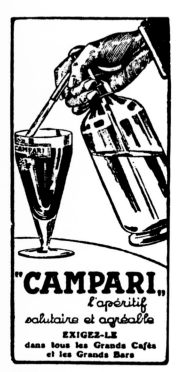

Advertisement, Campari, from
Le Matin, September 12, 1924.
Featured in the exhibition *High
and Low*, Museum of Modern
Art, 1990.

to secular artists. Yet mass media and modern
art are not worlds apart. The modern museum
has itself become a form of entertainment and a
vehicle for corporate image—the *High and Low*
exhibition was, among other things, a promotion
for AT&T, the project's sponsor.

Because designers are taught to focus on
visual style over social function, we often overlook the relation of design to institutions of
power. The tendency to see styles as working in
a free space encourages a romantic view of the
"commercial vernacular" as an innocent Other
rather than an active player in the politics of
daily life. The heroism of the avant-garde lay in
its vision of design as a liberating social force.
The current crisis of modernism lies in the
contradictory desire to occupy a place outside of
society while at the same time transforming it.
The critical stance of modern design can be
relocated as an analysis from *within* culture,
rather than a critique from above and beyond.

HISTORY

Graphic Design in America

Time Line, 1829-1993

As a genre of graphic design, the time line combines pictorial and textual composition. Typically written in a terse, telegraphic style, the time line substitutes the rhythm of chronological order for the flow of traditional narrative. The time line visualizes history in a way that conventional prose does not, distributing words across a grid that regulates their placement.[1]

Often what the time line visualizes is merely the temporal proximity of one event to another. Time becomes an organizing principle that overwhelms other criteria of interpretation. The time line adopts chronology as an explanatory model, conceiving of history as a ribbon whose sequence reveals the significance of events.

In the interest of brevity and clarity, the time line masks the interpretive character of historical narrative—hence its emphasis on "facts" and "information." The objective tone commonly used in time lines and the exclusion of critical commentary obscure the presence of an active author. Time lines are rarely "written" but are more often compiled, researched, and designed. By masking the subjectivity that is part of all writing and research, time lines tend to foster the notion that history is a matter of fact but not a question of values. Time lines de-politicize the writing of history. The linear model of the time line promotes a view of history as an organic "progression" toward contemporary values.

The following series of essays adopts the discontinuous, fragmentary character of the time line. But instead of trying to present a schematic diagram of discrete events, we have tried to show how the history of graphic design is diffused across various institutions and discourses. Rather than construct a spatial field for charting the "most important" events and names, we have used the time line format to create a flexible framework for a set of independent texts.

Whereas many time lines divide a historical span abstractly according to decades, we have used the four-year cycle of the American Presidential term as our unit of measure. While a few of the case studies directly consider the Presidency, we have used the "Presidential grid" primarily for its link to the texture of public life. Some of our essays are broken into two parts, reflecting an opposition within the text. The change in typography marks a shift in content. Each break indicates a polarity such as theory/practice, production/consumption, dominant/marginal, or artistic/anonymous. These divisions have allowed us to indicate contradictions, to bring together isolated discourses, or to present a topic from two different vantages. We have thus tried to use the time line as a critical matrix for representing history.

1 For an expanded discussion of the time line as a way of representing history, see J. Abbott Miller, "Tracking the Elusive Time Line," *AIGA Journal of Graphic Design* 6, 2 (1988): 7.

V_{quo} P_{li} V_{tlu} $+_{so}$ H_{mi} J_{tsu} Λ_{do} ω_{ya} ϑ_{wu} $+_{tlo}$ P_{qui} G_{yu} K_{tso}

Creating National Culture(s): Old Hickory and Sequoyah

Andrew Jackson's fierce campaign in 1828 against John Quincy Adams initiated the modern American system of political campaigning.[1] Because of revisions in state voting laws, the election of 1828 was the first in which nearly all white male adults could vote. Candidates now had to appeal to a mass electorate. The decorum of earlier Presidential contests gave way to an aggressive use of slogans and electioneering, supported by an array of posters, pamphlets, bandanas, buttons, mugs, plates, and snuff-boxes. Jackson's campaign workers distributed sprigs, sticks, and brooms made of hickory, playing upon the "Old Hickory" nickname that Jackson earned when he gave his horse to an injured soldier and journeyed back to camp with a walking stick made from a hickory branch. Much of Jackson's promotional material capitalized on his image as a hero in the 1815 Battle of New Orleans. His war record included the massacre of many Indian populations, earning him a reputation as a ruthless military leader.

While white Americans were forging a "national" culture aided by the military and political campaigns of Andrew Jackson, so too were the Cherokee Indians constructing a formal "nation" with written laws and elected leaders. Although many Cherokees could read English, the native Cherokee language had no written form until, between 1809 and 1828, an Indian named Sequoyah designed an alphabet that would transform his native culture.[2]

Although Sequoyah could neither speak nor read English, during his contact with white Americans he became curious about their books, or "talking leaves." Some Cherokees believed that writing was a gift mystically bestowed on Europeans. But Sequoyah believed that writing was a human invention, and he set out to design a similar system for the Cherokee language. He began by trying to match every word with a separate character, but when this proved cumbersome he began to break the language into syllables, which could be recombined into words. Initially he represented each of his eighty-five syllables with a picture but later turned to arbitrary signs. Many of these, borrowed from the Roman alphabet, were given new meanings; the rest were designed with flourishes, geometric shapes, and fragments of other letters.

The Cherokee Phoenix, established in 1828 as the first Indian newspaper, was printed in English and Cherokee, with castings of Sequoyah's alphabet. The new alphabet became an important tool for the dynamic Cherokee society of the nineteenth century, helping to spread political news and link communities in eastern and western America. At the same time, it participated in the destruction of old ways of life—missionaries used it to teach Christianity and European customs, while members of the Cherokee middle and ruling classes used it to promote the "civilization" of "savages."

1 Roger A. Fischer, *Tippecanoe and Trinkets Too: The Material Culture of American Presidential Campaigns, 1828-1984* (Urbana: University Illinois Press, 1988). The material culture of Presidential campaigns dates back to the founding of the Presidency, when objects generally served as commemorative tokens. The campaign of 1828 marks a turning point in the use of objects and images for persuasive or propagandistic purposes.

2 On Sequoyah, see Althea Bass, "Talking Stones: John Howard Payne's Story of Sequoyah," *The Colophon* (1932); reprint of an 1835 account of the life of Sequoyah. *Cherokee Editor: The Writings of Elias Boudinot*, Theda Perdue, ed. (Knoxville: University of Tennessee Press, 1983) includes an essay on Sequoyah by Elias Boudinot, "Invention of a New Alphabet," originally published in 1832. On American Indian presses, see Daniel F. Littlefield, Jr., and James W. Parins, *American Indian and Alaska Native Newspapers and Periodicals, 1826-1924* (Westport, CT: Greenwood Press, 1984).

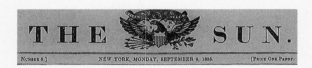

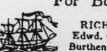

Newspapers Become a Mass Medium

1833 ANDREW JACKSON

Although printed news sheets and handwritten "news letters" were circulated in colonial America, the newspaper did not become a mass medium until the 1830s with the emergence of the penny press. The first penny paper was founded by Ben Day in Manhattan, in 1833. The penny papers, hawked on the street, challenged the established "six-penny" papers, sold by subscription to an elite business class. Whereas most six-penny papers were backed by political parties, the new cheap press was run by independent entrepreneurs; politicians were now represented through an aggressive medium that chose its own candidates. The "news" as we know it today emerged in this period: an ongoing, immediate narrative with no beginning or end, serving as both disposable entertainment and historical record.

As the historian Michael Schudson has pointed out, the names of most six-penny papers included terms such as "advertiser," "mercantile," or "commercial," which referred to the interests of business, while the titles of the new popular papers employed words such as "critic," "herald," "tribune," "star," or "sun," which suggest prophetic sources of enlightenment.[1]

Although the penny press was progressive as an economic and literary institution, it was conservative visually: text ran in densely set columns of tiny type with minimal headlines. The need for a cheap, fast production routine discouraged editors from designing new typographic formats; newspaper production became a rigid trade, changing only incrementally before the rise of illustrated newspapers in the 1880s.[2]

1 Michael Schudson, *Discovering the News: A Social History of American Newspapers* (New York: Basic Books, 1967, 1973).

2 Allen Hutt, *The Changing Newspaper: Typographic Trends in Britain and America, 1622-1972* (London: Gordon Fraser, 1973).

Newspaper Advertising

1837 MARTIN VAN BUREN

Unlike the established six-penny papers that were supported largely by subscription, the popular penny press depended on advertising revenues. The subservience of advertisers to the newspapers they patronized was reflected in the restriction of ads to small "agate" type in a want-ad style, sometimes including a larger initial capital or a generic illustration. Such restrictions did not, however, carry over into editorial matters: for example, the penny press was the primary vehicle for the spurious claims of patent medicine advertising.[1]

The shift in the newspaper-advertiser hierarchy is registered in the increase in size, imagery, and typographic variety of ads during the nineteenth century. When the *New York Herald* allowed advertisers to exceed the traditional one-column width in 1836, the severe reaction among competing advertisers forced the paper to ban display typography and to enforce size restrictions. Techniques for circumventing the "agate only" rule signaled the gradual erosion of these restrictions in the face of the powerful and profitable advertising industry.[2]

1 For the relationship between advertising in the "establishment" press and the penny press, see Schudson, *Discovering the News*.

2 On the early development of advertising typography, see Frank Presbrey, *The History and Development of Advertising* (New York: Doubleday, Doran, 1929).

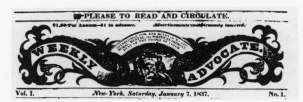

The Ad Man

1841

WILLIAM HENRY HARRISON, JOHN TYLER

In 1841 John L. Hooper was working as an advertising solicitor for the *New York Tribune*. Advertisers who submitted copy to Hooper often requested that he place their copy in other newspapers as well. Realizing that he could work in this capacity for a number of newspapers and advertisers simultaneously, Hooper left the *Tribune* to form his own advertising office. Around the same time, Volney Palmer announced that his Philadelphia real estate office would procure and administer space in newspapers on behalf of advertisers who wished to avoid the "trouble of perplexing and fruitless inquiries, the expense and labour of letter writing, the risk of making enclosures of money &c, &c."[1] Palmer and Hooper did not write or design ads but negotiated the complicated terrain of the newspaper trade.

Newspapers paid a commission to the new agents, who acted as space salesmen, simplifying a process that would otherwise have involved hundreds of individual requests. By the end of the 1840s Palmer had offices in Baltimore, Boston, Philadelphia, and New York and claimed to represent thirteen-hundred newspapers.

Abolition: Idealism and Realism

1845

JAMES POLK

A movement to abolish slavery in the U.S. had gathered force by 1840. Organized by white reformers in the North, the movement spoke through newspapers, pamphlets, posters, books, and almanacs, with the aim of instilling moral outrage among whites. The publications of the American Anti-Slavery Society in New York, for example, included a magazine for children called *The Slave's Friend*, and an illustrated *Almanac* documenting Southern atrocities. The practice of branding slaves was a violent typographic act signalling the conversion of human beings into private property.[1] The white-led abolition movement identified slavery as a self-contained evil that could be cleanly cut away from America's moral conscience; black activists, on the other hand, saw slavery as only one aspect of a culture structured by racism. As the historians Jane and William Pease have noted, white abolitionists had little concern for the civil rights of free blacks in the North or the political and economic future of freed slaves.[2] White abolitionist William Lloyd Garrison transformed the movement by including blacks among the writers, speakers, and audience of his crusade; his journal *The Liberator*, founded in 1831, was largely supported by blacks. Garrison remained dedicated, however, to purging sin from white society: "freedom" served as an abstract ideal. *The New York Weekly Advocate*, a black newspaper, wrote in 1837, "'Free indeed!...when almost every honorable incentive to the pursuit of happiness, so largely and freely held by his fairer brother, is withheld from [the black man]'" (Pease, 9).

1 On the development of the ad agency, see Daniel Pope, *The Making of Modern Advertising* (New York: Basic Books, 1983), 119-129; and Presbrey, *The History and Development of Advertising*.

1 Dwight Lowell Dumond's book *Antislavery: The Crusade for Freedom in America* (Ann Arbor: University of Michigan Press, 1961) includes reproductions of anti-slavery propaganda.

2 Jane H. Pease and William H. Pease, *They Who Would Be Free: Blacks' Search for Freedom, 1830-1861* (New York: Atheneum, 1974). The illustration above was taken from Langston Hughes and Milton Meltzer's book *A Pictorial History of the Negro in America* (New York: Crown, 1969).

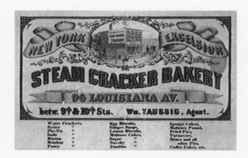

Chromolithography

ZACHARY TAYLOR, MILLARD FILLMORE

1849 In the process of lithography, an image is drawn with a grease crayon onto a stone or a metal plate. When the surface of the stone is bathed in water, ink adheres only to the crayoned areas. A chromolithograph combines several different stones, each carrying a separate color. The first American chromolithograph was printed in Boston in 1840. Printing companies marketed reproductions of oil paintings, bringing art to the middle classes. The technique was also used for advertisements, book illustrations, calendars, and other commercial ephemera. The industry peaked and then began to decline in the 1890s with the improvement of photomechanical reproduction.[1]

1 For an extensive history of chromolithographs, see Peter C. Marzio, *The Democratic Art: Chromolithography, 1840-1900*, exh. cat. (Fort Worth: Amon Carter Museum of Western Art, 1979).

Photography and the Graphic Arts

FRANKLIN PIERCE

1853 Processes for recording an image on a light-sensitive surface—what we now call photography—were announced independently by several inventors in the 1830s and 1840s.[1] Whereas Louis-Jacques-Mande Daguerre's daguerreotype was a unique image imprinted on a heavy plate, the English scientist William Henry Fox Talbot employed a paper negative, which had the potential to generate an infinite series of positive prints. Talbot's book *The Pencil of Nature* (1844-1846) consisted of individually printed and mounted photographs: portraits, architectural views, reproductions of engravings, and cameraless silhouetted prints made by laying botanical specimens directly on light-sensitive paper.

One of the first photographic books published in the U.S. was Nathaniel Hawthorne's *Transformations; or, The Romance of Monte Beni*.[2] Hawthorne's novel was illustrated with actual photographic prints, pasted in by hand. When it was reissued in 1890 it was illustrated by photogravure, a process in which a layer of fine powder is exposed to a photographic negative, and the resulting image is etched into a metal printing plate.

Photogravure offers richer, finer-grained images than process halftone engraving, invented by Frederick Ives in 1881 and commercially viable by 1893, which remains the standard method for reproducing photographs today. In this technique a screen translates tonal gradations into a fine pattern of black dots, perceived by the eye as continuous shades of gray. The halftone can be printed on the same paper, with the same ink, and at the same time as metal type. The halftone revolutionized the graphic arts, allowing photographic images to be cheaply integrated into mass-media publishing.

1 Estelle Jussim, *Visual Communication and the Graphic Arts: Photographic Technologies in the Nineteenth Century* (New York: R.R. Bowker, 1974).

2 Nathaniel Hawthorne, *Transformations; or The Romance of Monte Beni* (Boston: Houghton Mifflin, 1860).

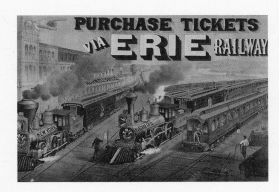

Railroads: Managing Nature and Business

1857 JAMES BUCHANAN

During the nineteenth century the railroad transformed America's landscape, economy, and imagination: it was a vehicle for colonizing the unsettled wilderness and distributing industry, natural resources, and information across the continent; its rails were often the first permanent human path to be cut into a stretch of land.[1]

Although painters such as Thomas Cole and John Kensett often included railroads in their paintings during the 1850s, they usually showed the train as a tiny machine engulfed by its natural setting—the critic Leo Marx contends that because landscape painting in America had an almost religious status, to monumentalize the details of the train would have debased the seriousness of the art.[2] Popular chromolithographs, in contrast, often celebrated the smoke, speed, and mechanical details of the locomotive.

Behind the heroic image of the train as civilizer of the American wilderness lay a revolution of a different sort: a revolution in management. Unprecedented quantities of capital were needed to finance a vast range of enterprises, from the laying of tracks and the construction of engines to the control of traffic and the scheduling of trains. A new form of business emerged to direct these projects: the modern corporation.[3]

In a large corporation, ownership is separate from management—there can be thousands of owners, most of whom have minimal influence on policy. The New York Stock Exchange, where shares in businesses are speculatively bought and sold, was born in the 1840s to finance the railroads. A large corporation consists of independent units controlled by a hierarchy of salaried managers—those at the top of a given unit report to officials at the next level, who may have little knowledge of the operations below. This division of labor was necessitated by the technical and geographic diversity of the railroads. No single individual could control—or even understand—every level of the system.

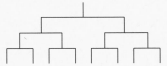

David McCallum, an executive of the Erie Railroad, designed one of the first "corporate management charts" in 1856, made available for one dollar per copy by the *American Railroad Journal*. Today, similar management charts remain an important form of internal—rather than public—imagery, visualizing the position of each employee within a network of varying levels of accountability.

1 On American railroad culture, see Susan Danly, "Introduction, " Susan Danly and Leo Marx, eds., *The Railroad in American Art: Representations of Technological Change* (Cambridge, Mass.: MIT Press, 1988), 1-50.

2 On the meaning of small trains in big paintings, see Leo Marx, "The Railroad-in-the-Landscape: An Iconological Reading of a Theme in American Art," *The Railroad in American Art*, 183-206.

3 On the history of the railroad corporation, see Alfred D. Chandler, *The Visible Hand: The Managerial Revolution in American Business* (Cambridge: Belknap Press of Harvard University Press, 1977). Chandler details the growing independence and professionalization of the "managerial class" in nineteenth- and twentieth-century America.

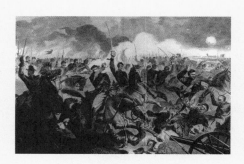

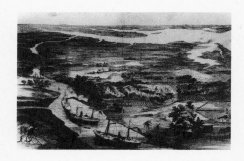

Picturing the Civil War: Art and Documentation

1861 ABRAHAM LINCOLN

The Civil War destroyed many American magazines by starving the Northern-focused press of its Southern readership and by cutting off supplies from the South. (Confederate papers were sometimes printed on wallpaper.)[1] Yet two magazines flourished as never before: *Harper's Weekly* (founded 1857) and *Frank Leslie's Illustrated Newspaper* (founded 1855), which represented the war from the vantage of the Union, with news reports and wood engravings.[2] Although photographs were extensively documenting war for the first time, they could not yet be mechanically translated into a type-compatible medium but had to be interpreted by hand into the linear codes of wood-engraving. Photography had other limitations as well: because the exposure time for film was very slow, photographs could not depict battle scenes but only landscapes, architecture, stiffly posed figures, and corpses.[3]

Winslow Homer had become popular before the Civil War as an illustrator of fashionable urban life for *Harper's Weekly* and other magzines. In the early 1860s he gained a reputation as a painter as well, which raised the prestige of his illustrations.[4] Most of Homer's war engravings represent "genre" scenes (such as *Cavalry Charge*, above, published in *Harper's*, 1862) rather than concrete historical events. Other well-known "signature" illustrators, including Thomas Nast and A.R. Waud, produced similar centerfold designs. Printed at the middle of the journal, such pictures could be removed easily in one piece and framed like paintings. Homer's *Cavalry Charge*, detachable both from the physical binding of the magazine and from the verbal context of news reports, acts as a self-contained aesthetic object that transcends its immediate context.

While the work of well-known artists such as Homer and Nast maintained aspects of painting in the context of journalism, many engravings emulated the documentary functions associated with photography, mapmaking, and newspaper prose. An engraving called *Birds-Eye View of the City of Charleston, South Carolina, Showing the Approaches of Our Gun-Boats and Our Army*, ran in the same issue of *Harper's* as Homer's *Cavalry Charge*. Whereas Homer dramatized the violence of war, the maker of *Birds-Eye View* dispassionately reported the positions of land, water, boats, and army camps. The magazine credits neither the artist nor the source of the image—it could have been reconstructed in the engraver's studio from a map, or from a photograph of a landscape, or from a written report. Thus while *Birds-Eye View* appears more concretely "factual" than Homer's illustration, it may be many steps removed from observation.

The rise of fast film and halftone reproduction at the end of the century forced hand-drawn pictorial journalism to surrender its dual function as art and information. Photojournalism made the ambiguity between hard fact and interpretation unacceptable, and magazine illustration was quarantined, for the most part, to the realm of fiction and editorial commentary.[5]

3 Paul Hogarth, *The Artist as Reporter* (London: Gordon Fraser, 1986). Estelle Jussim discusses the technical relationship between wood-engraving and photography in *Visual Communication and the Graphic Arts*.

4 Phillip C. Bream, *Winslow Homer's Magazine Engravings* (New York: Harper and Row, 1979). John Wilmerding's *Winslow Homer* (New York: Praeger, 1972). The author relates Homer's illustrations to his painting career, arguing that he was influenced by the monumentality and flatness of photography. Texts on Homer tend to devalue qualities typical of illustration, such as anecdotal detail, in favor of modernist values.

5 Neil Harris discusses the importance of halftone reproduction in "Iconography and Intellectual History: The Half-Tone Effect," John Higham and Paul K. Conkin, eds., *New Directions in American Intellectual History* (Baltimore: Johns Hopkins University Press, 1979).

1 An edition of *The Daily Citizen*, Vicksburg, Mississippi, 1863, printed on wallpaper is preserved at the National Museum of American History, Washington, D.C.

2 Frank Luther Mott, *A History of American Magazines* (Cambridge: Belknap Press of Harvard University Press, 1967).

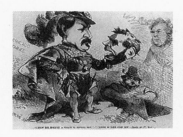
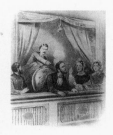
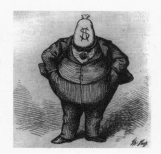

The Election and Assassination of Abraham Lincoln

1865 ABRAHAM LINCOLN, ANDREW JOHNSON

At the beginning of his first campaign for the Presidency, in 1860, Abraham Lincoln's face was virtually unknown to the American public, creating an enormous demand for cheap likenesses. Yet as the historian Harold Holzer has documented, the face of Lincoln was not considered pretty: Abraham Lincoln was seen as almost comically unattractive, even by his supporters. Walt Whitman wrote that Lincoln's face was "so awful ugly it becomes beautiful."[1]

Lincoln was legendary for his humble frontier origins but also for his cultured love of Shakespeare. An anti-Lincoln cartoon published during his second campaign, in 1864, evokes the grave-digging scene in Hamlet, subtitled with the line "I knew him, Horatio: A fellow of infinite jest....Where be your gibes now?" The cartoon makes fun of Lincoln's sense of humor, which his critics believed he exercised inappropriately. On Good Friday, 14 April 1865, Abraham Lincoln was mortally wounded by a well-known Shakespearean actor, John Wilkes Booth, a pro-South Northerner, while attending Ford's Theatre in Washington. The caption for the image above right depicting the assassination adapts lines from Shakespeare, positioning Lincoln as the good king murdered by the evil Macbeth.

The Civil War had ended the week before with the surrender of Robert E. Lee at Appomattox Courthouse in Virginia. Lincoln had professed a conciliatory stance toward the restoration of the South, but his assassination resulted in renewed feelings of hatred toward the fallen Confederacy, which was wrongly blamed for plotting the assassination.[2]

Lincoln's death turned him into a political martyr, converting many of his former critics into regretful admirers. This murder, the first assassination of an American President, shocked the nation, and the face that had once been almost too ugly to elect entered the idealizing realm of myth, taking a place second only to that of George Washington.

1 See Harold Holzer, Gabor S. Boritt, and Mark E. Neely, Jr., *The Lincoln Image: Abraham Lincoln and the Popular Print* (New York: Scribner's, 1984), 89.

2 On public reaction to Lincoln's death, see Thomas Reed Turner, *Beware the People Weeping: Public Opinion and the Assassination of Abraham Lincoln* (Baton Rouge: Louisiana State University Press, 1982).

Visual Muckraking

1869 ULYSSES S. GRANT

Thomas Nast contributed to the tradition of political cartooning in America with his visual campaign against the infamous Tweed Ring in New York City.[1] The series was published in *Harper's Weekly* from 1867 to 1876, concurrent with a journalistic exposé in *The New York Times*. The cartoons vividly publicized the situation, and J. Henry Harper later recalled that Tweed said, "Let's stop those damned pictures. I don't care much what the papers write about me—my constituents can't read; but damn it, they can see pictures!"[2] Tweed was so distressed by the cartoons that he offered Nast $200,000 to "study art abroad." Nast declined.

1 Sources on Thomas Nast include Morton Keller, *The Art and Politics of Thomas Nast* (New York: Oxford University Press, 1968); and Albert Bigelow Paine, *Thomas Nast: His Period and His Pictures* (New York: Macmilan, 1904).

2 Quoted in J. Henry Harper, *The House of Harper: A Century of Publishing in Franklin Square* (New York: Harper and Brothers, 1912), 292.

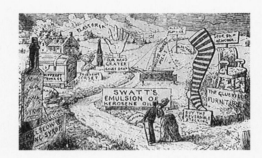

The Public Landscape

ULYSSES S. GRANT

1873 Before the 1870s, outdoor posters and painted signs were a popular, although unorganized, advertising medium: spaces were not formally leased but aggressively taken by bill-posters. By the end of the Civil War there were 275 bill-posting companies with varying rates and business practices. The proliferation of signs accelerated with the perfection of web-fed printing presses in 1870 and the increasing flexibility of lithography. The anarchy of "guerrilla" bill-posting was a visible intrusion of advertising onto the American landscape: temporary fences, lampposts, and facades were buried in layers of typography. A formalization of the profession began in the early 1870s, when companies began to lease temporary fences on a standardized weekly or monthly basis, followed by the formation of professional associations of bill-posters, and billboard regulation.[1] Today, legally and illegally posted messages constitute a collage of commercial images in urban areas. The strength of the billboard industry is expressed in the current slogan of the Outdoor Advertising Association: *"We're not a medium, we're a large."*

1 John W. Houck, ed., *Outdoor Advertising: History and Regulation* (South Bend, IN: University of Notre Dame Press, 1969); and Presbrey, *The History and Development of Advertising*, 490-511.

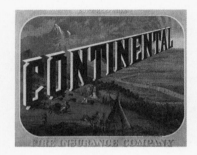

Lettering: Typographic and Lithographic

RUTHERFORD B. HAYES

1877 The growth of advertising during the nineteenth century encouraged the proliferation of new "display" letter styles for use in posters and other ephemera. A technique was invented in 1828 in America for mass-producing typefaces from wood, a material cheaper and more durable than lead. The process involved tracing over the lines of a drawing with a device linked to a mechanical wood-engraver. Whereas the molds for lead type ("punches") were laboriously crafted in metal, the pattern for wood type was simply a drawing.[1]

The wood-type industry reached its creative and economic peak in the 1860s and 1870s, when it was in dynamic competition with the more graphically malleable technique of lithography. Whereas the material constraints of wood or metal typography encourage grouping separate elements into parallel rows, lithography allows letters to be freely arranged in overlapping, interlacing, curving, and perspective patterns. And, unlike typography, lithographic lettering could be easily integrated with illustrations drawn on the same surface.

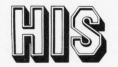

Compare the perspectival illusion of a wood-type design with the chromo-lithograph above. Only by fighting the natural logic of the medium could the letter-press printer compete with the lithographer—by cutting the blocks of type to make them touch, for example, or by setting them into plaster beds to make them follow a curve. The typographic poster remained more economical than the lithograph, however, because the printer could reuse its elements again and again.

1 Rob Roy Kelly, *American Wood Type, 1828-1900* (New York: Van Nostrand Reinhold, 1969). For a more condensed essay by the same author, see "American Wood Type," *Design Quarterly* 56 (1963).

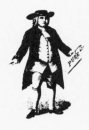 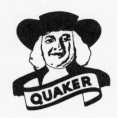 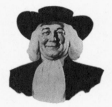 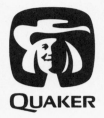

Selling with Pictures and People

JAMES GARFIELD, CHESTER A. ARTHUR

1881

During the 1880s, new production and distribution methods transformed American food culture. Advanced technology made some goods, including flour and beef, more widely available, while it flooded the market with new products, such as cigarettes and oatmeal, for which there was minimal demand. As historian Alfred Chandler has noted, the automatic factory for milling oatmeal forced the leading processors to "invent the modern breakfast-cereal industry" (253).

When Henry P. Crowell opened the first automatic oatmeal factory in 1882, the product had a tiny U.S. market. Breaking the custom of distributing grain in bulk, Crowell decided to ship his product in convenient, graphically appealing containers; he wrapped the oatmeal in its own advertising, enticing the consumer with contests and boxtop premiums and enforcing brandname recognition in store and pantry. Other companies, such as Procter & Gamble, Borden, Campbell Soup, and H.J. Heinz, employed packaging and brand names to create new habits of consumption in the 1880s and 1890s (Chandler, 295).

In 1888 Crowell and his competitors merged into a giant oatmeal conglomerate, the American Cereal Company. One of the businesses the company absorbed had used a picture of a Quaker as its trademark.[1] The conglomerate adopted the symbol and in 1901 changed its name to The Quaker Oats Company.

The symbol of the Quaker has remained constant throughout the product's history, but its graphic form has changed. The logo used in 1946, designed by Jim Nash, replaced the older full-figure Quaker. Nash's Quaker was an established

"household face" when graphic designer Saul Bass was asked to design a corporate mark for The Quaker Oats Company in 1970. Bass, who has designed symbols for Bell Telephone, United Airlines, Minolta, and other companies, created a schematic, shorthand, corporate Quaker in a TV-shaped frame. The modernized mark appears on contemporary packages with the company's address, while the cereal's main image remains a realistic, full-color portrait. Familiar personalities such as Dr. Brown, Uncle Ben, Aunt Jemima, and Old Grand-Dad came to replace the shopkeeper, who was traditionally responsible for measuring bulk foods for customers and acting as an advocate for products. Particularly after the rise of mass-distribution food chains such as the Great Atlantic and Pacific Tea Company (A&P) in the early twentieth century, a nationwide vocabulary of brand names replaced the small local shopkeeper as the interface between consumer and product.[2]

1   Hal Morgan's book *Symbols of America* (New York: Viking, 1986) provides brief illustrated histories of many trademarks, including that of Quaker Oats, 130.

2   On supermarkets, see Chester H. Liebs, *Main Street to Miracle Mile: American Roadside Architecture* (Boston: Little Brown, 1985), 117-135.

THE PRACTICAL HOUSEKEEPER
~EDITED ~AND~ CONDUCTED~
BY MRS. LOUISA KNAPP

SOME RELIABLE RECIPES.   SOME PRACTICAL DISHES.

Modern Advertising

1885

GROVER CLEVELAND

The first advertising agencies of the 1840s acted as liaisons between advertiser and newspaper. Through the efforts of such agencies, the placing of ads was simplified and rates became more uniform. In 1869 the advertising agent George Rowell published his *American Newspaper Directory*, which made circulation and publication data—the guarded expertise of competing advertising agents—commercially available. The function of the agency as a "space-broker" was challenged by advertising's own professionalization and by the growing force of national media, which, sure of their power, could set and maintain rates without the help of intermediaries. Brand-name manufacturers developing national marketing strategies also needed advertising services that could maintain a consistent image across national and local media. The 1880s saw the development of the "full-service" ad agency, which, in addition to securing space and facilitating transactions, offered writing, design, illustration, and production to its clientele.[1]

1 On the full-service ad agency and Rowell's role in its development, see Pope, *The Making of Modern Advertising*, 117-140.

Women as Consumers, Women as Producers

1889

BENJAMIN HARRISON

By the time *The Ladies' Journal* (which later became *The Ladies' Home Journal*) was founded in 1883, innumerable goods previously manufactured at home were being mass produced, making shopping a central part of American life.[1] Under the direction of editor Edward W. Bok and publisher Cyrus H. K. Curtis, *The Journal* became a profitable medium for advertising consumer goods. By 1900 *The Journal*'s back cover was the most expensive advertising position in American magazines.[2]

The Journal built up the trust of its readers by refusing to mention brand names in articles. Yet while forbidding direct links between editorial and advertising, *The Journal* recognized the fruitfulness of juxtaposing relevant ideas; ads for seeds appeared beside the gardening column, and ads for buttons and lace showed up in the fashion section. The ad (opposite page) for Extract of Beef strongly resembles the illustrated logo for the monthly "Practical Housekeeper" column (above right), which appeared on the same page. While both women wear white aprons, dark dresses, and pinned-up hair, the Extract of Beef cook is far more elegant than the Practical Housekeeper. Her apron is pleated rather than plain, her dress is tailored, her hair is ornamented, and her utensils are not homely pots and pans but a decorated tureen and some richly labeled tins of Extract of Beef. The advertiser used the Practical Housekeeper, an image familiar to *Journal* readers, as a modest counterpoint to a glamorous life enhanced by modern packaged goods.

1 On women and work, see Christopher Clark, "Household Economy, Market Exchange and the Rise of Capitalism in the Connecticut Valley, 1800-1860," *Journal of Social History* 13, 2 (Winter 1979): 169-189.

2 Salme Harju Stienberg, *Reformer in the Marketplace: Edward W. Bok and The Ladies' Home Journal* (Baton Rouge: Louisiana State University Press, 1979).

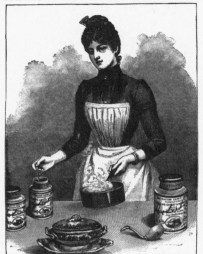

USE LIEBIG COMPANY'S EXTRACT OF BEEF.

The audience of *The Ladies' Home Journal* was presumed to be white, Anglo-Saxon, and middle class; its female readers were assumed to be mothers working in the home. Whereas this audience provided a mass of consumers for advertising, another group of women was engaged in graphic arts *production.* Many working-class women held wage-earning jobs, especially during early adulthood, and in the middle classes, a woman who was unmarried, widowed, or abandoned had to choose between work and dependency on family members.[3]

In response to the growing number of women in need of employment, some reformers promoted the decorative arts as appropriate work for females. While traditional academies taught painting, sculpture, and crafts as genteel avocations for middle-class "ladies," the Woman's Art School in New York, founded by Peter Cooper in 1852, aimed to give working-class women respectable professions in illustration, textile design, and teaching. One of the main skills taught at Peter Cooper's school was wood-engraving, a painstaking and usually anonymous task, in which the engraver translates a design produced by an illustrator into the codes of woodblock printing.[4]

Women by no means dominated the graphic arts work force, however. According to an 1883 account, women in the design industries were paid much less than men, and they would usually do piecework at home rather than earn regular salaries (Tentler, 79). A study conducted forty years later found that among 276 designers surveyed in advertising agencies, only five were women; out of 324 designers employed by independent studios, only eighteen were women.[5]

In 1986 roughly half the students enrolled in college-level art programs were women.[6] More women are represented today in trade annuals than there were thirty years ago, indicating an increased interest in, and perhaps opportunity for, professional self-promotion. Yet there has been little feminist activism within the field.[7]

3 See Leslie Woodcock Tentler, *Wage-Earning Women: Industrial Work and Family Life in the United States, 1900-1930* (New York: Oxford University Press, 1979).

4 On women's education and the industrial arts, see Thomas B. Woody, *A History of Women's Education in the United States,* vol. 2. (New York: Science Press, 1929), 75-80. Peter Cooper's Woman's Art School later became part of The Cooper Union for the Advancement of Science and Art. Although The Cooper Union had a coeducational night school, the day art school did not admit men until 1933. See *The Cooper Pioneer,* 8 March 1933.

5 Charles R. Richards, *Art in Industry: Being the Report of an Industrial Art Survey Conducted under the Auspices of the National Society for Vocational Education and the Department of Education of the State of New York* (New York: Macmillan, 1929).

6 *Peterson's Guide to Four-Year Colleges* (Princeton, NJ: Peterson Guides, 1988).

7 In 1960 the *Annual of the Art Directors Club of New York* listed approximately 380 "art directors and designers," including about a dozen women, or 3.2 percent (New York: Farrar, Straus and Giroux, 1960). In 1982 the *Annual* listed about 1,120 "art directors," including about 240 women, or 26 percent.

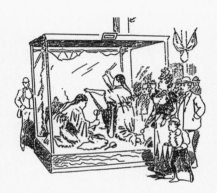

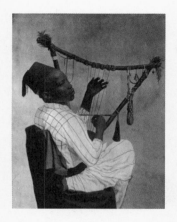

White City, Whited Sepulcher

The World's Columbian Exposition of 1893, held in Chicago, was housed in bright white neoclassical palaces dedicated to art, industry, and agriculture. This architectural setting, dubbed the "White City," was the fair's most spectacular exhibit. It helped make Beaux-Arts neoclassicism the favored style for major civic projects at the turn of the century.[1]

In addition to nourishing an architectural style, the World's Columbian Exposition helped change the role of museums in American culture. Whereas early collections of artifacts were assembled primarily for scholarly study, scientific museums at the end of the nineteenth century turned to the education of the general public. As one historian proclaimed in 1888, "An efficient educational museum may be described as a collection of instructive labels, each illustrated with a well-selected specimen."[2]

The Smithsonian Institution in Washington, D.C., prepared displays on American Indians that elucidated artifacts with charts, diagrams, photographs, and explanatory texts. Historian Robert Rydell has argued that the Columbian Exposition presented Indian life as a "primitive" culture doomed to extinction.[3] A newspaper illustration from the period depicts wax Indians encased in glass; an exhibit on "physical anthropology" described the differences between racial types with charts and diagrams.

A book by anthropologist F. W. Putnam, a lush photographic folio of ethnic "types" in costume, combines the conventions of artistic portraiture with the scientific realism of photography.[4] The publications of the Columbian Exposition were distinguished from those of previous fairs by the preponderance of halftone photographs. The fair marked the death knell of chromolithography and birth of the photographic book. American Indians were not given the opportunity to produce their own exhibits for the exposition; they were treated only as objects of study. Petitions by black Americans to participate were denied, leading Frederick Douglass to write that "to the colored people of America...the World's Fair...[is] a whited sepulcher."[5] Nonwhite Americans, whether black, Indian, or Asian, appeared in the fair as anthropological specimens or menial servants but not as creative participants—a black woman dressed as Aunt Jemima brought graphic design to life, serving pancakes in the food pavilion.[6]

1 On the style and influence of the "White City" see Mario Manieri, "Toward an 'Imperial City': Daniel H. Burnham and the City Beautiful Movement," *The American City: From the Civil War to the New Deal*, Giogi Ciucci et al., eds., Barbara Luigi La Penta, trans. (London: Granada, 1980), 1-142; and Richard Guy Wilson, "Architecture, Landscape and City Planning," *The American Renaissance, 1876-1917*, exh. cat. (New York: Brooklyn Museum, 1979), 74-109.

2 Kenneth Hudson, *A Social History of Museums: What the Visitors Thought* (Atlantic Highlands, NJ: Humanities Press, 1975).

3 On the racial message of the 1893 exposition, see Robert W. Rydell, *All the World's a Fair: Visions of Empire at American International Expositions, 1876-1916* (Chicago and London: University of Chicago Press, 1984).

4 F. W. Putnam, *Oriental and Occidental Northern and Southern Types of the Midway Plaisance* (St. Louis, Mo.: N.D. Thompson, 1894).

5 Reid Badger, *The Great American Fair: The World's Columbian Exposition and American Culture* (Chicago: Nelson Hall, 1979): 106.

6 The presence of Aunt Jemima at the exposition is noted in Morgan, *Symbols of America*, 55.

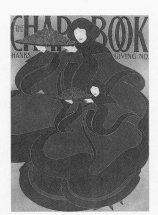

The Modern Poster: Artistic and Anonymous

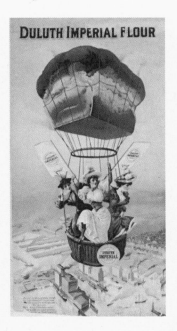

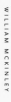

A new kind of advertising emerged in America in the 1890s: the "artistic poster." The genre had originated in France, where posters for books and cultural events incorporated styles such as Art Nouveau and Post-Impressionism. The new French posters functioned both as advertising and as art. During the 1880s books, magazines, and exhibitions established the poster as a legitimate child of painting and inspired the interest of art collectors in Europe and New York.

The first American business to extensively use the artistic poster was *Harper's Monthly,* which assigned its in-house illustrator Edward Penfield to design placards in 1893. Other magazines quickly followed *Harper's,* commissioning posters from Will Bradley, Maxfield Parrish, Ethel Read, and others. By the mid-1890s there was a collecting "craze" in American cities. Booksellers sometimes chose to sell the posters rather than display them—the prints proved more valuable as art than advertising.

As historian Victor Margolin has noted, the artistic poster helped establish graphic design as a respected profession by bringing American illustrators into contact with the European avant-garde, encouraging them to develop distinctive artistic styles and to compete in the international art community.[1] Will Bradley, one of the most influential American poster artists, was also one of the first designers to be called an "art director." His work included typefaces, books, ads, and magazines as well as posters and illustrations.[2] In 1894-1896 Bradley worked for *The Chap-Book,* a progressive magazine that published European avant-garde literature and graphics by Toulouse-Lautrec, Aubrey Beardsley, and others.

The first American book devoted to the poster genre, entitled *The Modern Poster,* was published in 1895. In 1988, nearly a hundred years later, The Museum of Modern Art, New York, published an exhibition catalogue with the same title; despite the historical span dividing the two books, they are remarkably similar. Both describe a history of "the modern poster" that begins with the French lithographer Jules Cheret and progresses toward the work of Toulouse-Lautrec and other avant-garde painters whom he influenced. Although some art historians consider Cheret stylistically frivolous, they refer to him as the "father" of the modern poster because his work, featured in books, magazines, and art galleries, transcended its mundane advertising function to serve as a new kind of fine art.[3] Such genealogies of the poster value graphic design for its relevance to museums and collectors rather than for its role in commercial life. These histories omit "nonartistic" or anonymous posters, which constituted a powerful advertising medium by the 1890s and would continue to flourish after the poster craze ended at the turn of the century.[4] Most advertising graphics were produced by anonymous artists less interested in developing personal styles or in challenging artistic conventions than in depicting products in a clear and dramatic way. The visual impact of the flour poster above comes from delivering a clever concept in a direct, descriptive style.

1 Victor Margolin, *American Poster Renaissance* (New York: Watson-Guptill, 1975).

2 Roberta Wong, *Bradley: American Artist and Craftsman,* exh. cat. (New York: Metropolitan Museum of Art, 1972).

3 Arsene Alexandre et al., *The Modern Poster* (New York: Scribner's, 1895); and Stuart Wrede, *The Modern Poster* (Museum of Modern Art, 1988).

4 Victor Margolin, *The Promise and the Product: 200 Years of American Advertising Posters* (New York: Macmillan, 1979).

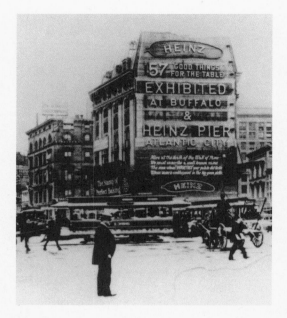

Public Pickles, Private Enterprise

1901 ₹

W I L L I A M   M C K I N L E Y ,   T H E O D O R E   R O O S E V E L T

In 1869 Henry John Heinz began to sell processed horseradish in rural western Pennsylvania, and by 1890 he was manufacturing a nationally distributed line of preserved, packaged, ready-to-serve foods.[1] Heinz's advertising included ten-foot-high, cast-concrete renditions of the number 57, the symbol of the company's range of products, installed on a dozen hillsides across the country. Heinz built one of the first large electric signs in New York, a six-story billboard at the corner of Fifth Avenue and 23rd Street, where huge letters made of light bulbs flashed below a forty-foot pickle.[2]

Environmental graphics like these promoted Heinz products; at the same time, the company worked to advertise the industrial process that made the pickles possible: the factory production of food. A pioneer of the corporate image, Heinz used fine art and feminine beauty to proclaim the benefits of modern industry to his consumers and employees.

Beneath the six-story electric sign in New York was a display window where attractive young women packed vegetables in clear glass jars; one could see hundreds more such workers when touring Heinz's plant in Pittsburgh. The centerpiece of the factory complex was the Time Office, a freestanding Beaux-Arts monument to wage labor. Paintings and drawings were displayed in public spaces, an early use of fine art as a public relations tool.

Heinz provided his all-female labor force with sunroofs, classrooms, and a swimming pool, bringing contentment to his workers and goodwill from the community. Young women commonly worked in factories for several years before marrying, and they routinely were paid less than men for comparable labor—it was assumed that women did not need wages for survival. Heinz used this business custom not only for its obvious economic advantages but also for the image it gave his factory. As period photographs indicate, the women Heinz employed were not only young but also white and well groomed; each wore a freshly laundered uniform that she made from fabric purchased from Heinz, and every week she received a manicure. Heinz's model factory used labor itself as a form of advertising.

1 Robert C. Alberts, *The Good Provider: H.J. Heinz and His 57 Varieties* (Boston: Houghton Mifflin, 1973).

2 For a cultural history of the electric light bulb, see Carolyn Marvin, "Dazzling the Multitude: Imagining the Electric Light as a Communications Medium," *Imagining Tomorrow: History, Technology, and the American Future,* Joseph J. Corn, ed., (Cambridge: MIT Press, 1987), 202-217.

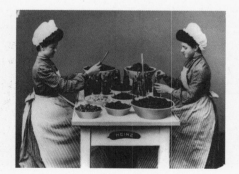

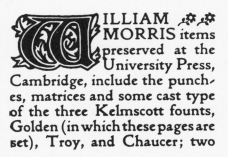

WILLIAM ✿✿ MORRIS items preserved at the University Press, Cambridge, include the punches, matrices and some cast type of the three Kelmscott founts, Golden (in which these pages are set), Troy, and Chaucer; two

Machines and Craft

1905 THEODORE ROOSEVELT

The American type designer Frederic W. Goudy designed the font Village in 1903. By the end of his life, in 1947, he had designed more than one hundred typefaces, an achievement that would have been nearly impossible without the invention in 1884 of the pantographic punch-cutter, which produced molds for metal type. The new technology enabled any letterer to make designs for a typeface; in contrast, typographers traditionally had carved metal punches by hand—a slow, painstaking craft.[1]

❧IT WAS THE TERRACE OF
God's house
That she was standing on,—
By God built over the sheer depth
In which Space is begun;
So high, that looking downward

Although Goudy depended on modern technology, much of his work reflected a medievalizing trend in American design that emerged in the 1890s and continued through the 1920s and beyond.[2] Goudy, Will Bradley, Bruce Rogers, and others were inspired by the English socialist reformer William Morris, a founder of the Arts and Crafts movement.[3]

Morris, reacting against the debased products and working conditions brought on by the Industrial Revolution, rejected contemporary styles and techniques and called for the unification of aesthetics and production that he believed had existed in the Middle Ages. The cost of his labor-intensive products, however, made them inaccessible to most consumers.

Morris modeled his typeface Golden (1891) after the fifteenth-century Venetian font Jenson; his dark letters, with thick slab serifs and a relatively uniform line weight, were a visual critique of the spiky, airy, book faces that dominated Victorian printing. Morris's dense pages fueled a generation of American designers.

Arts and Crafts-inspired typographers such as Goudy, Bradley, and Rogers were moved by the idea of joining aesthetics and technique, yet they worked in a period when devices like the pantographic punch-cutter and Linotype and Monotype machines were widening the gap between design and production. Bradley and Goudy both designed faces for Monotype; the longevity of their influence lies not in reuniting art and craft but in acting as modern "designers," whose plans are executed by technicians and machines.

1 A useful primary text on early twentieth-century typography is Frederic W. Goudy, *A Half-Century of Type Design and Typography, 1895-1945* (New York: The Typophiles, 1946). Secondary sources include Sebastian Carter, *Twentieth Century Type Designers* (New York: Taplinger, 1987).

2 Numerous "literary" and "private" presses were founded in the 1890s, but many failed economically by the turn of the century. Several enlightened trade publishers in the early twentieth century sustained the movement by opening fine-press subdivisions. Bruce Rogers, for example, designed sixty limited-edition books for Houghton Mifflin Company's Riverside Press between 1900 and 1912. In the 1920s Alfred A. Knopf commissioned innovative book designs from William Addison Dwiggins and Merle Armitage. See Joseph Blumenthal, *The Printed Book in America* (Boston: David R. Godine, 1977).

3 On the Arts and Crafts movement, see William Morris, *The Ideal Book: Essays and Lectures on the Arts of the Book*, William S. Peterson, ed. (Berkeley: University of California Press, 1982).

Analyzing the Market

1909 WILLIAM HOWARD TAFT

"Legitimate advertising is simply calling people's attention to a good thing, and describing it."[1] This statement from an 1890 article called "Advertising from a Religious Standpoint" indicates how advertising professionals understood their practice. By 1900 the notion of advertising as a benevolent information service gave way to more aggressive and sophisticated strategies. Pamphlets, lectures, and articles on "advertising psychology" appeared as early as 1896; the first book-length study, Walter Dill Scott's *The Theory of Advertising*, appeared in 1903, followed in 1908 by *The Psychology of Advertising*.[2]

Advertising psychology questioned the dominant understanding of the consumer as rationally motivated, and devalued "objective" or "reason why" approaches to advertising.[3] Scott's theory was based on the concept of suggestion: "Every idea of a function tends to call that function into activity, and will do so, unless hindered by a competing idea or physical impediment" (195). Because purchases are made impulsively, suggestion must be pleasurable and directed, yet not strong enough to "lead the reader into a critical or questioning state of mind"(190). According to Scott, ads should describe not the product itself but its pleasurable *effects*. He also advocated the use of the direct command ("Use Pears Soap") and the return coupon.[4]

1 Quoted in Merle Curti, "The Changing Concept of 'Human Nature' in the Literature of American Advertising," *The Business History Review*, 41, 4 (Winter 1967): 339.

2 Walter Dill Scott, *The Theory of Advertising* (Boston: Small, Maynard, 1903); and *The Psychology of Advertising* (Boston: Small, Maynard, 1908). The references here are to the 1931 edition of *The Psychology of Advertising* (New York: Dodd, Mead).

3 "Reason-why" advertising is credited to John E. Powers, who advocated telling the truth rather than exaggerating in the manner of patent medicine advertising. See Presbrey, *The History and Development of Advertising*, 302-309.

4 David P. Kuna, "The Concept of Suggestion in the Early History of Advertising in Psychology," *Journal of the History of the Behavioral Sciences* 12 (1976): 347-353.

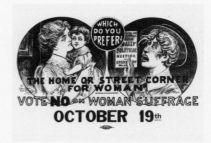

The Suffragette and the Suffragist

1913 WOODROW WILSON

The struggle for women's voting rights entered a new phase in 1910 when the National American Woman Suffrage Association, having successfully campaigned in a number of states, began a concerted effort toward federal legislation. One of the tactics employed by suffrage activists was the picture poster. As historian Paula Hays Harper observes, these images mark some of the earliest uses of the political picture poster, predating its extensive use in World War I, when posters and publicity helped consolidate and legitimize the advertising industry.[1] Prior to the war, suffragists had established the picture poster as a political forum, using commercial imagery for a political struggle. The suffragist's use of commercial imagery was not, however, parodistic or subversive. Instead it used images of women as wives and mothers to assure the continuity of roles in spite of political change. One such poster features a row of marching toddlers, stylistically reminiscent of figures from children's books, who plead for daddies to "GIVE MOTHER THE VOTE." These posters affirmed traditional roles for women and thus acted as a buffer to anti-suffrage posters that represented suffragists as enraged, homely spinsters.

1 Paula Hays Harper, "Votes for Women?: A Graphic Episode in the Battle of the Sexes," Henry A. Millon and Linda Nochlin, eds., *Art and Architecture in the Service of Politics* (Cambridge: MIT Press, 1978), 150-161.

2 Aileen Kraditor, *Ideas of the Women's Suffrage Movement, 1890-1920* (New York: Columbia University Press, 1965).

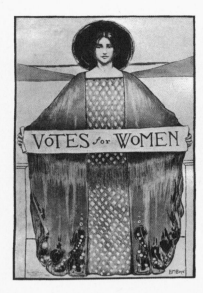

Some of the posters invoke the high-culture tradition of artistic design, using the decorative style and Pre-Raphaelite imagery of the Art Nouveau posters that advertised cultural events and publications. As Harper notes when discussing this pictorial tradition, "They are 'feminine' styles not created by women but carrying connotations of what constitutes femininity from a masculine point of view." As women's enfranchisement rested in the hands of a male legal system, so, too, did their imagery: "They had no tradition of image making to draw upon except the masculine one in which they were embedded as second-class citizens" (156-7).

Thus the projection of positive, traditional imagery maintained politically useful notions of the feminine. Perhaps this conservative strategy was a response to the ridicule, hostility, and violence that had confronted the earlier suffrage movement of the nineteenth century. Historian Aileen Kraditor has noted that the early suffrage movement, shaped by its abolitionist origins, waged its campaign on the moral issue of equality.[2] Early leaders, notably Elizabeth Cady Stanton, Lucy Stone, and Susan B. Anthony, encouraged a fundamental reevaluation of social roles and familial traditions, questioning values considered sacred to the middle class. When these pioneer activists died or retired in the 1890s, their posts were filled by younger, more conservative women who, in response to the intensified anti-suffrage movement, based their appeals on the political expediency and social benefits of suffrage rather than on the more incendiary issues of equality and justice. The broad critique initiated by the early women's movement was narrowed into a contest for the ballot: marching toddlers proved more effective than appeals to equality.

The War and *The Masses*

1917 WOODROW WILSON

Many Americans opposed United States entry into World War I because of commitments to pacifism, cultural ties to Europe, or belief in America's former policy of neutrality. President Wilson's statement that "It is not an army we must shape and train for war, it is a nation," aptly summarizes the government's interest in securing unified national support for the war. The principal means of mobilizing public sentiment was the Committee on Public Information (CPI), founded in 1917, which served as information clearinghouse, publicity organ, and censor.

George Creel, a journalist who chaired the CPI, was an early critic of any form of blatant, unreflective censorship.[1] The information and public relations aspects of the CPI were intended, as Creel noted, to overshadow its repressive, undemocratic role as censor: "suppressive features [will be] so overlaid by the publicity policy that they will go unregarded and unresented" (17-8).

The committee's twenty divisions each concentrated on particular forms of propaganda. Press releases, pamphlets, radio programs, photographs, films, books, cartoons, lectures, store displays, English classes, exhibitions, and posters were disseminated in America and in more than thirty countries. Described as a "war emergency national university," the CPI gave America and the rest of the world a crash course in "Americanism" (37-9). Creel conceived of the committee as an educational agency that would provide a "simple, straightforward presentation of facts" (20).

Conflicts between the educative aims and manipulative tactics of the CPI are visible in the posters and graphics produced by the Division of Advertising and the Division of Pictorial Publicity. The Division of Advertising engaged the ad industry in the creation of

1 Stephen Vaughn, *Holding Fast the Inner Lines: Democracy, Nationalism and the Committee on Public Information* (Chapel Hill: University of North Carolina Press, 1980), 251. Quotations from the makers of the CPI come from this text.

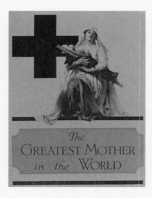

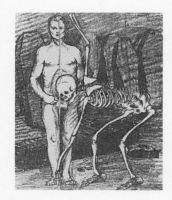

campaigns and the contribution of space in service of the war effort. The Division of Pictorial Publicity, headed by the prominent illustrator Charles Dana Gibson, worked to promote enlistment, volunteer work, war bonds, and other interests. Creel's ideals of "objectivity" and "facticity" were not shared by Gibson, whose belief that people are essentially irrational echoed contemporary advertising theory. The posters commonly make an emotional appeal by connecting domestic comfort and intimacy to the specter of modern war: "Every bond you buy fires point blank at Prussian Terrorism," "Don't Waste Bread! Save Two Slices Every Day and Defeat the U Boat." Less subtle threats to the sanctity of the home were horrific illustrations of atrocities in Belgium, which portrayed women being choked and children having their hands cut off.[3]

Despite the propaganda efforts of the CPI, many people discerned in the war the corrupt interests of big business. Among the voices of antimilitarism and dissent was the socialist press, which was a growing vehicle for progressive and reform issues.[4] "A Revolutionary and not a Reform Magazine" called The Masses, founded in 1911, rejected the "official" left-wing imagery of the period, which consisted of romanticized allegorical figures symbolizing the class struggle.[5] Irreverent and inconsistent, The Masses was a forum for radical writers and artists.

Collectively owned, and edited through group meetings, the magazine rejected traditional editorial hierarchies. Writers and artists received no pay and were not commissioned; thus the topic and editorial angle of a given piece were not predetermined. This was especially liberating to artists, who, when working for the commercial press, were expected to "illustrate" someone else's article. The Masses considered illustration equal, rather than subservient, to text. This parity was reinforced by the design of the magazine, whose generous margins and high production values accorded an autonomy and importance to images.[6]

Writers and artists attracted to The Masses—Max Eastman, Emma Goldman, John Reed, John Sloan, Art Young, Stuart Davis, and others—were part of the larger bohemian community of Greenwich Village. The magazine's effectiveness in reaching "the masses" remains dubious, since the range of issues it covered—free love, Freud, contraception, feminism, homosexuality—placed it outside mainstream America.[7]

In 1917 Congress passed the Espionage Act, allowing the government to suppress activities and messages considered injurious to the U. S. When an issue of The Masses was declared "unmailable," the editors brought the case to court. The government was forced to specify the treasonable items, which included a drawing by Henry Glintenkamp entitled Physically Fit. The drawing darkly alludes to a contemporary newspaper account of the Army's plans to order coffins in bulk quantities. The court eventually ruled against the magazine. Drained of funds and without access to the postal service, The Masses closed in December 1917.

2 Creel Report: Complete Report of the Chairman of the Committee on Public Information, 1917; 1918; 1919 (New York: Da Capo Press, 1972), 43. Reprint of first edition, published in 1920.

3 Creel stated that atrocity materials were used in instances not under his supervision. The poster referred to is This is Kultur, reproduced in Vaughn, 165. For Creel's statements on atrocity images, see Vaughn, 156-158.

4 Rebecca Zurier, Art for The Masses: A Radical Magazine and Its Graphics, 1911-1917 (Philadelphia: Temple University Press, 1988), 85-91. An indication of the importance and range of socialist positions on the war is the fact that the CPI organized lecture tours for "patriotic American socialists" to represent our positions on the war to foreign leftists. Emily S. Rosenberg, Spreading the American Dream: American Economic and Cultural Expansion, 1890-1945 (New York: Hill and Wang, 1982): 79.

5 The Masses began with a traditional socialist look and agenda but departed from those conventions in 1912.

6 The Masses was modeled after visually sophisticated European satiric journals such as Le Rire, Simplicissimus, and Jugend.

7 The magazine was distributed through Socialist Party offices in a number of states. All records have been lost, thus it is impossible to know if The Masses reached its namesake (Zurier 66).

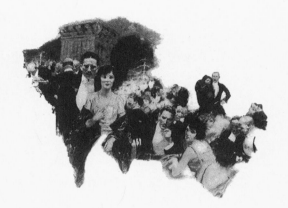

Artistry and Industry

1921 WARREN G. HARDING, CALVIN COOLIDGE

The Art Directors Club was formed in 1920. An annual exhibition and catalogue of "advertising art" were the club's chief means of publicity. The first exhibition, held in the prestigious galleries of the National Arts Club in New York, displayed paintings and drawings that had been commissioned for advertisements—the ads themselves were not shown, however. This blurring of the distinction between fine art and mass media was reinforced by the catalogue: paintings and drawings appeared as large-format reproductions at the front of the catalogue, while their "application" in actual advertisements appeared in an appendix of small images at the back.

The exclusion of actual advertisements—which represent an art director's use of the artist's work—was not repeated in the second exhibit, a decision considered "valuable" by the exhibition committee, even though a reviewer felt it "detract[ed] a bit from the neat and orderly arrangement."[1] The second exhibition also included photography, a medium pervasive in advertising yet relatively new to the art gallery. Throughout the early catalogues the work is described as not merely equal to fine art but more significant, since it is an art for the masses, able to "create a new state of mind in a nation" (13).

The artistic status of advertising art and the professionalization of the art director were part of a larger expansion of advertising in the 1920s. As manufacturers increased in number and output, market research became an important agency service.[2] J. Walter Thompson, then one of the largest firms in the country, added, in 1919, a statistical and investigation department and two planning departments—one for male and one for female consumers. Such bureaucratic complexity had a twofold appeal: it mirrored the structure of the corporations that such agencies served, and it helped build the image of advertising as a science.

Stanley Resor, president of J. Walter Thompson, hoped to create a "university of advertising" at the firm, instituting a two-year course for incoming employees and hiring John B. Watson, a former Ivy League professor, who was well known for his controversial books on behavioral psychology. Watson believed that three instincts guide human behavior: fear, rage, and love. These result from, respectively, a loss of support, constraints on bodily movement, and stroking of the skin. For Watson, all other emotional responses emerge from this original trio; advertising could learn to guide consumers by triggering such sensations. Fear was frequently turned to the advantage of business through advertisements that played upon the insecurities of women as inadequate dates, wives, mothers, or housekeepers. Behaviorism lent to advertising the rhetoric of science, serving to legitimize an increasingly irrational conception of human nature.[3]

1 *The Second Annual of Illustrations for Advertisements in the United States* (New York: Art Directors Club, 1922), 14.

2 On the expansion of advertising agency services see Pope, *The Making of Modern Advertising*. The expansion of agency services has continued into the present: the JWT Group, a holding company for J. Walter Thompson, has subsidiaries specializing in recruitment and medical advertising, two public relations firms, and a market research company.

3 For information on Watson's career in advertising, see David Cohen, *J.B. Watson: The Founder of Behaviorism. A Biography* (London: Routledge and Kegan Paul, 1979): 168-194. For the cultural context in which behaviorism came to fruition, see Lucille Birnbaum, "Behaviorism in the 1920s," *American Quarterly* 7, 1 (Spring 1955): 15-30.

ABCD

M. F. Benton, Broadway, 1929

abcde

Josef Albers, stencil, 1925

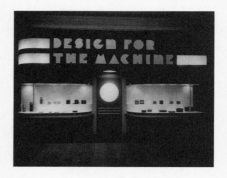

Modernistic vs. Modern

1925 CALVIN COOLIDGE

The term "Art Deco" was derived from the title of the 1925 Paris Exposition Internationale des Arts Decoratifs et Industriels Modernes. Historian Rosemarie Haag Bletter has called the Art Deco architect "an avant-garde traditionalist," a term that suggests the way elements of Futurism, Cubism, and Constructivism were used to construct an appealing, uncontroversial, and often luxurious interpretation of modernism.[1] In the 1920s Art Deco styling was applied to numerous department stores, corporate headquarters, restaurants, and hotels in New York and other cities. In graphic design and illustration, Art Deco encompassed a loose set of ideas and motifs, ranging from reductive geometry, elongated figures, and mannered angularity to the repetition and regularity associated with the machine, as seen in M. F. Benton's typeface Broadway.

The opulence of Art Deco was curbed by the 1929 stock market crash. During the Depression, the availability of new materials—aluminum, plastic, black Vitrolite glass, Masonite, linoleum—encouraged industrial designers to develop a simple vocabulary that made Art Deco appear fussy and anachronistic. Many designers began looking to the machine as both a functional and aesthetic model. The American interpretation of the machine amended austere European precedents with complex curves and tapering forms borrowed from the aerodynamic streamlining developed for airplanes and automobiles. Parallel stripes and "speed whiskers" were employed as graphic expressions of speed, progress, and modernity.[2]

Walter Dorwin Teague's streamlined facade for a 1932 exhibition, *Design for the Machine,* in Philadelphia, uses continuous, flush surfaces and spare detail. The customized lettering combines the step-motifs of Art Deco with an "ascetic" modern interest in the elementary forms of the circle, square, and triangle.[3] Art Deco and streamlining have been devalued by proponents of the supposedly more pure and functional modernism exemplified by the Bauhaus and Le Corbusier. The Museum of Modern Art, New York, presented exhibitions such as *Modern Architecture: International Exhibition* in 1932 and the first American survey of the Bauhaus in 1938. MoMA positioned itself as an arbiter of good design and an opponent of "modernistic" streamlining.[4]

The effort to separate "modern" from "modernistic" betrays the links between popular and elite design. Benton's typeface Broadway and Teague's facade lettering share with Josef Albers's stencil alphabet an interest in standardized, geometric elements. Albers's typeface, designed in 1925 at the Bauhaus, is composed from an armature of geometric shapes. Like Benton and Teague, Albers adopted an assembly-line logic of interchangeable parts. The work of Albers issues from the vanguard heritage of the Bauhaus, while the American designs embrace a more decorative, consumer-oriented tradition. The unquestioned separation of these discourses, however, obscures the interconnections between mass culture and the "progressive," critical heritage of modernism.

1 Rosemarie Haag Bletter, "The Art Deco Style," *Skyscraper Style,* Cervin Robinson and Rosemarie Haag Bletter, eds. (New York: Oxford University Press, 1975), 41. See also Patricia Frantz Kery, *Art Deco Graphics* (New York: Harry N. Abrams, 1986).

2 On streamlining, see Donald J. Bush, *The Streamlined Decade* (New York: George Braziller, 1975); and Jeffrey L. Meikle, *Twentieth Century Limited: Industrial Design in America, 1925-1939* (Philadelphia: Temple University Press, 1979).

3 Teague refers to the "ascetic manner" of Le Corbusier and Mies van der Rohe in *Design This Day* (New York: Harcourt Brace, 1940), 172.

4 See John McAndrew, "Modernistic and Streamlined," *Bulletin of The Museum of Modern Art* 5, 6 (December 1938): unpaginated. Today, Art Deco is still barred from MoMA's canon. In the words of the late curator Arthur Drexler, "The department's definition of quality excludes unsuccessful or ephemeral styles....Even such popular manifestations as Art Deco and other 'modernistic' furniture which, in the 20s and 30s, initiated the stepped contours of skyscrapers, are not eligible for inclusion." *The Museum of Modern Art, New York: The History and the Collection* (New York: Harry N. Abrams, 1984).

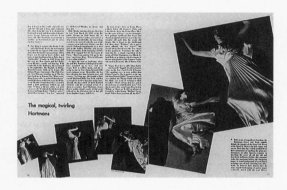

Fashion Plates

1929 European modernism was filtered to American audiences through fashion and interior design magazines.[1] These transient media deployed modernism as a range of stylistic options, freed from the weighty dogmas that characterized the historical avant-garde movements. In the 1920s *Vogue* and *Vanity Fair* brought European illustration and industrial and graphic design to an American audience. This tradition was pursued more actively in the 1930s by Alexey Brodovitch at *Harper's Bazaar* and Mehemed Fehmy Agha at *Vogue, Vanity Fair,* and *House and Garden.*[2]

While Agha preceded Brodovitch and provided a model for his work at *Harper's Bazaar,* the two designers worked in a situation of mutual influence, bringing similar backgrounds to similar tasks. Agha came to America from Berlin in 1929 at the invitation of the publisher Condé Nast; Brodovitch, who had come from Paris to teach in Philadelphia, was invited to New York by *Harper's Bazaar* editor Carmel Snow in 1934. Thus both men were "imported" and then empowered to bring a specifically European quality to American magazine design. Their pluralistic approach to European art and design is evident in the range of artists they employed: A.M. Cassandre, Man Ray, Cartier-Bresson, Salvador Dali, Lisette Model, Brassaï, Jean Cocteau, Isamu Noguchi, and others.

Prior to the work of Brodovitch and Agha, magazines such as *Harper's* and *Vogue* used traditional layouts and conventional framing techniques—circular insets, overlapping corners—which treated photographs and illustrations as discrete compositional units. Spreads designed by Brodovitch (top) and Agha (bottom) often let images cross the binding and bleed off the page, bringing an unprecedented centrality and force to photography in publication design. By considering the coherence of each spread and the sequential rhythm of the entire magazine, Brodovitch and Agha transformed the role of the art director in publication design.[3]

1   Frank Crowninshield, the editor of Condé Nast's fashionable arts and letters magazine *Vanity Fair,* was a key member of the organizing committee for the Museum of Modern Art, New York. Russell Lynes, *Good Old Modern* (New York: Atheneum, 1973), 11-18.

2   On Brodovitch, see Andy Grundberg, *Brodovitch/Masters of American Design* (New York: Documents of American Design, Harry N. Abrams, 1989). For information on Agha's contribution to magazine design, see Sarah Bodine and Michael Dunas, "Dr. M.F. Agha, Art Director;" and M.F. Agha, "Reprise: On Magazines," *AIGA Journal of Graphic Design* 3, 3 (March 1985): 3. Brodovitch and Agha are profiled in R. Roger Remington and Barbara J. Hodik, *Nine Pioneers in American Graphic Design* (Cambridge: MIT Press, 1989).

3   In addition to his impact on the profession as a practitioner, Brodovitch taught classes and seminars at a number of schools, influencing a generation of art directors and photographers, including Irving Penn, Richard Avedon, Art Kane, Henry Wolf, Otto Storch, Bob Gage, Sam Antupit, Steve Frankfurt, and Helmut Krone. See Allen Hurlburt, "Alexey Brodovitch: The Revolution in Magazine Design," *Print* 23, 1 (January-February 1969): 55.

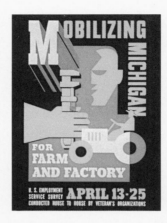
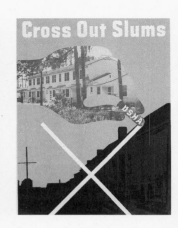

Representing the New Deal:
Stylization and Documentation

The Works Progress Administration (WPA), instituted by President Roosevelt in 1935, employed millions of workers left jobless by the Great Depression.[1] Although most WPA programs utilized unskilled labor, the Federal Art Project (FAP) employed professional writers, painters, actors, and musicians. At the height of the New Deal these artists constituted only two percent of WPA employees, and the arts projects received less than seven percent of the total budget.[2]

Divisions within the FAP ranged from easel painting and community art centers to film and stained glass. The poster division, which publicized health-care issues, cultural events, and WPA programs, began as a primitive atelier in New York City, where artists hand painted individual posters, often producing several copies from a model. Through the efforts of artist Anthony Velonis, New York's poster division moved into the age of mechanical reproduction, and its output increased to six hundred posters a day.[3]

The reduced, bold shapes typically employed in the posters reflected the influence of such vanguard designers as A. M. Cassandre, Stuart Davis, and Joseph Binder. The posters' reductive style also exploited the qualities of silkscreen printing, an inexpensive technique used for short-run commercial printing. The silkscreen process favors the use of simple, stenciled forms, bold expanses of opaque color, and hard-edged silhouettes, as seen in the poster shown above left by the Detroit designer Merlin.

Anti-New Deal sentiment was, from the very beginning, intense. The FAP was especially contentious, since the arts were viewed as elitist and urban. Much of the overtly political work produced under the WPA, such as the Federal Theater Project's "Living Newspapers" and the documentary photographs of the Farm Security Administration, garnered the hostility of conservatives, who claimed the project's membership was comprised of left-wing radicals. The words and pictures of poverty and decay reported by writers and photographers compose an image of the era quite different from that conveyed by the bright compositions of the poster division. Neither the textual conventions of "documentary expression"—techniques such as quotation, statistical evidence, and direct address—nor the photographic "evidence" that inspired so many of the photo-texts in magazines and books, seems to have influenced the poster units.[4]

Most WPA designers avoided the use of photography. A notable exception is Lester Beall, who designed the poster shown above right for the United States Housing Authority in 1941.[5] Beall's design combines the flat colors and schematic shapes characteristic of the poster projects with a documentary photo sensibility. Perhaps influenced by the political photomontages of John Heartfield and Hannah Höch, Beall's work conveys a feeling of urgency and contemporaneity that is absent from the more painterly posters.

1 On the FAP, see Francis V. O'Connor, *Federal Art Patronage: 1933 to 1943*, exh. cat. (College Park:University of Maryland Art Gallery, 1966). See also *The New Deal Art Projects: An Anthology of Memoirs*, Francis V. O'Connor, ed. (Washington, DC: Smithsonian Institution Press, 1972).

2 Basil Rauch, *The History of the New Deal, 1933-38* (New York: Capricorn Books, 1944, 1963).

3 Christopher DeNoon, *Posters of the WPA* (Los Angeles: Wheatley, 1987).

4 On documentary and the WPA, see William Stott, *Documentary Expression in America* (University of Chicago Press, 1973, 1986); and John Rogers Puckett, *Five Photo-Textual Documentaries from the Great Depression* (Ann Arbor: UMI Research Press, 1984).

5 Beall, who emerged as a major corporate designer after the war, earlier had produced a series of strikingly simple and forceful posters for the Rural Electrification Administration that have become icons of vanguard American design of the 1930s. Beall is profiled in Remington and Hodik, *Nine Pioneers of American Graphic Design*.

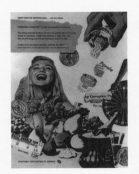
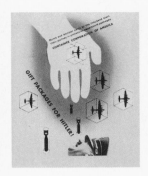
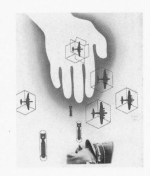

Corporate Design, Corporate Art

1937

FRANKLIN DELANO ROOSEVELT

In 1934 Walter Paepcke, founder and chairman of the Container Corporation of America, hired the Chicago designer Egbert Jacobson to redesign nearly every surface of his company: factories, offices, trucks, stationery, and advertising.[1] This kind of commercial "packaging," which encases not the product but the company that manufactures it, is known today as "corporate identity" or "corporate image."[2]

CCA's most influential contribution to business culture was its advertising program. At the advice of the agency N.W. Ayer & Son, Paepcke commissioned designs from European modernists, including A. M. Cassandre, Herbert Bayer, and Gyorgy Kepes. The first ad ran in the luxurious, design-conscious business journal *Fortune* in 1937. Some of these early images incorporated photomontage, and would have been considered aesthetically radical at the time, departing from the more established Art Deco and streamlining modes of modernism.

After World War II CCA advertising shifted away from avant-garde design toward contemporary "fine art." Two 1940s campaigns featured tentatively cubist, expressionist, or pseudo-primitive illustrations. In these ads, typography ceased to be integral to the design and served instead as discrete captions for autonomous paintings. CCA's most celebrated ad campaign was *Great Ideas of Western Man*, in which artists and designers interpreted quotations from the Western tradition, from Aristotle to John F. Kennedy. The 1959 collage by Herbert Bayer, shown above, was a commentary on American consumer culture; the ad makes no reference to packaging and instead aspires to be a work of art with an oblique advertising function.[3]

Such acts of patronage promoted CCA as a benevolent sponsor of the arts. As artist Hans Haacke has pointed out, corporate patronage buys respect for the corporation from a public that might be suspicious of business while admiring high culture.[4] The CCA collection was eventually donated to the National Museum of American Art at the Smithsonian Institution, an event celebrated with a major exhibition in 1985. The catalogue for that exhibit chose to represent *all* the works from the CCA collection as if they were fine art, even those conceived as applied design. Thus the early ads, which had actively integrated word and image, are presented in the museum's catalogue without typography. The ad above is shown as it originally appeared and as it was reproduced by the museum. Like CCA's later advertising programs, the museum's presentation favored fine art over applied design.[5]

1 On the cultural projects of Walter Paepcke and CCA, see James Sloan Allen, *The Romance of Commerce and Culture: Capitalism, Modernism, and the Chicago-Aspen Crusade for Cultural Reform* (University of Chicago Press, 1983). See also Neil Harris, "Designs on Demand: Art Nouveau and the Modern Corporation," *Art, Design, and the Modern Corporation: The Collection of the Container Corporation of America, A Gift to the National Museum of American Art* (Washington, D.C.: Smithsonian Institution, 1985), 8-30.

2 See *Container Corporation of America, Modern Art in Advertising: Designs for Container Corporation of America,* exh. cat. (Chicago: Paul Theobald, 1946).

3 Trade articles dealing with CCA's *Great Ideas* campaign include Walter J. Johnson, "The Case for Management's Advertising," *Public Relations Journal* 19, 10 (October 1963): 10-12; and Andrew J. Lazarus, "Corporate Advertising—A Fad or Fundamental?" *Public Relations Journal* 20, 10 (October 1964): 35-37.

4 On Haacke, see Brian Wallis, ed., *Hans Haacke: Unfinished Business* (New York: The New Museum and Cambridge: MIT Press, 1987).

5 The book *Art, Design, and the Modern Corporation,* cited above, is the catalogue for this exhibition. Other corporate patrons of the fine arts have included the Johnson Wax Company, which commissioned its corporate headquarters, in Racine, Wisconsin, from Frank Lloyd Wright in the 1930s. The company also sponsored the fine arts. "Art: USA: Now Thanks to a Wax Company," *Fortune* 66, 3 (September 1962): 133-139.

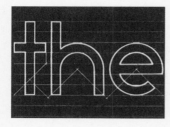

abcdefghi
jklmnopqr
stuvwxyz

The New Bauhaus: Function and Intuition

The New Bauhaus was founded in 1937 by a group of citizens seeking to revitalize Chicago manufacturing.[1] The school was directed by the Hungarian artist and designer Laszlo Moholy-Nagy, who had taught at the Bauhaus in Germany. After a year the association withdrew its support, unprepared for the radicalism of the school. Moholy-Nagy reopened the institution as the School of Design in 1939; it became the Institute of Design in 1944 and is now part of the Illinois Institute of Technology.

The name Bauhaus is commonly associated today with "functionalism," the theory that an object's use, materials, and means of production should dictate its form.[2] The lettering shown above left was designed in 1938 by Hin Bredendieck, a student at the New Bauhaus. All angles are drawn with a T-square and a right triangle, and all curves are made with a compass. Thus the letters meet one of functionalism's basic criteria: the method of production helps generate form.

Functionalism, however, rarely worked as an objective, value-free design method, or as a self-contained formula for decision-making. Design strategies such as simplified form, exposed structure, and standardized elements were weighted with philosophical ideals and cultural connotations. Criteria such as faithfulness to materials and fitness to purpose rarely dictated every aspect of a design, but were supplemented with taste and intuition. Bredendieck's student lettering project was inspired by Herbert Bayer's "universal alphabet," designed at the Bauhaus between 1925 and 1928. Bayer eliminated capital letters, contending that because the uppercase/lowercase distinction does not occur in speech, it is artificial and unnecessary.[3] Bayer's reform of the alphabet belonged to the broader search for a "language" of vision at the Bauhaus.[4] His geometric letters offered a simplified medium for the written word—at the Bauhaus, writing was often viewed as an enemy of the immediate, universal structures of geometry. Bayer's alphabet was not, however, a neutral solution to a utilitarian problem but a critical gesture that uncovered a "problem" that had not existed before. His font is too radical to be explained by a strictly utilitarian definition of functionalism.

Whereas some Bauhaus exercises yielded geometric solutions, the results of others appeared random or organic. For example, a New Bauhaus object called a "hand sculpture" was a smooth, irregularly shaped piece of wood designed to be comfortably held; it gave students a "tactile experience" that could be tapped later in the design of telephones, glassware, or handles.[5] A statement in a 1939 brochure read: "Mastered Technique = Freedom of Creation... discipline merges with fantasy and genuine results for application begin to appear." (50 Jahre 114). Bauhaus design theory combined the objective criteria of functionalism with subjective experience.[6]

1 Documents related to the New Bauhaus appear in Hans M. Wingler, The Bauhaus: Weimar Dessau Berlin Chicago (Cambridge: MIT Press, 1969). See also 50 Jahre New Bauhaus: Bauhaus Nachfolge in Chicago (Berlin: Bauhaus-Archiv, 1987). James Sloan Allen describes the founding of the New Bauhaus in The Romance of Commerce and Culture.

2 See Stanford Anderson, "The Fiction of Function," Assemblage 2 (February 1987): 19-31.

3 On Herbert Bayer, see Gwen Finkel Chanzit, Herbert Bayer and Modernist Design in America, 1926-1976 (Ann Arbor, Mich.: UMI Research Press, 1987); and Mike Mills, "Herbert Bayer's Universal Type and its Historical Contexts," The Bauhaus and Design Theory, Ellen Lupton and J. Abbott Miller, eds. (New York: Princeton Architectural Press, 1991), 38-49.

4 Kandinsky develops a theory of visual "language" in Point and Line to Plane (New York: Dover, 1979); published as a Bauhaus Book in 1926. See also Clarence V. Poling, Kandinsky's Teaching at the Bauhaus (New York: Rizzoli, 1986).

5 The "hand sculpture" project is documented in 50 Jahre, 116, 117; and in Moholy-Nagy's account of the New Bauhaus, Vision in Motion (Chicago: Paul Theobald, 1947).

6 A 1945 trade article stresses the liaison of rationality and individuality at the Bauhaus. A phrase that occurs again and again in the essay is "creative and functional." See Edward J. Frey, "Postwar Graphic Arts Education: What Changes Will Come in Teaching Design?" Print 3, 4 (Fall 1945): 4-7.

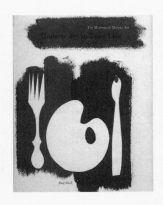

"Good Design"

FRANKLIN DELANO ROOSEVELT, HARRY S. TRUMAN

1945   Designers who came into prominence in the years
following World War II—notably Bradbury Thompson,
Paul Rand, Alvin Lustig, and Ladislav Sutnar—brought
the expressive sensibilities of the modern artist to
advertising and graphic design. Paul Rand's influential
book *Thoughts on Design* (1947) defined the designer as a
professional who tempers the instinct of the artist with
the functional requirements of advertising.[1] The
designer's role is to "restate his problem in terms of
ideas, pictures, forms, and shapes. He unifies, simpli-
fies, eliminates superfluities. He...abstracts from his
material by association and analogy" (4).

The symbols and techniques employed by Rand and
others were often derived from modernist painting and
sculpture. Designers borrowed techniques such as
collage, montage, childlike drawing, visual puns, and
biomorphic shapes from Klee, Picasso, Arp, Miró,
Chagall, and others. Rand described such forms as
"attention-getting devices," whose obscurity may need to
be balanced with "universally recognized forms" (54).
His use of abstraction and visual punning can be seen
in his 1949 cover for *Modern Art in Your Life*, shown
above left. Rand and others used techniques and motifs
from the fine arts to divorce themselves from the
"bromidic advertising (that caters to) bad taste" (136).

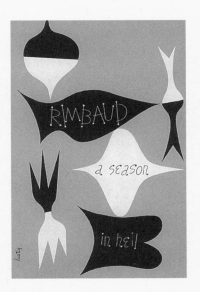

Modern art and design established a foothold in
America after the immigration of European artists,
designers, and architects in the 1930s. The spread of
modernism was also facilitated by the Museum of
Modern Art, New York, established in 1929. In a series
of exhibitions called *Useful Objects,* initiated in 1938, the
museum defined its notion of "good design." Although
the pretext of these shows was the utility and quality of
consumer goods, features such as function, durability,
and safety were secondary to appearance. Items were
generally selected for their formal affinities to modern
sculpture and painting. *Useful Objects* was followed by a
series called *Good Design,* which continued from 1950
to 1955. By advocating modern design in home furnishings, the museum hoped to influence the taste of
both manufacturers and the public.[2]

The 1949 MoMA exhibition *Modern Art in Your Life*
exemplifies the museum's attempt to elevate industrial
and graphic design by associating them with painting
and sculpture: "When the (book) jacket designer makes
up his page with a few rigorous lines against large
immaculate areas, when the package designer limits his
appeal to square-cut letters and a minimum of
rectangles, they...share Mondrian's delight in a bold and
subtle simplicity." At the same time, fine art is
democratized because it is shown to influence everyday
life. *Modern Art in Your Life* displayed the products of
the art world alongside advertisements, book covers, and
consumer goods. Shown above right is Alvin Lustig's
1947 jacket for *A Season in Hell*, which has high-culture
antecedents in the paintings of Miró and Arp.

1 Paul Rand, *Thoughts on Design* (New York:
Wittenborn, Schultz, 1947), 1.

2 Robert Goldwater and Rene d'Harnoncourt,
Modern Art in Your Life, exh. cat. (New York:
Museum of Modern Art, 1949).

 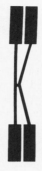 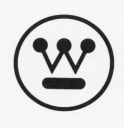

The Expansion of Corporate Identity

1949 HARRY S. TRUMAN

The CBS "eye" is the most prominent feature of that company's design program. Since 1951 it has appeared on everything from television screens and print ads to napkins, matchbooks, wallpaper, and adhesive tape. William Golden, who became art director at CBS in 1949, designed his own postal meter slugs, with colored inks to match the printing on various packages.[1]

Advertising was the main product advertised by the witty and elegant campaigns of CBS, which promoted television and radio to advertisers and account executives. Several other early corporate identity programs also used sophisticated design to sell design-related products—the Container Corporation of America began employing modernist designers in 1934, and Knoll International commissioned work from the Swiss designer Herbert Matter in the 1940s.[2]

By the end of the 1950s, however, professionally designed identity programs had been adopted by more diverse industries. The new genre was enthusiastically embraced by trade magazines, which heralded corporate "image" as a lucrative field for ad agencies and public relations departments.

A writer for *Advertising Age* in 1959 offered business as a subject for psychoanalysis: the corporation is "just as subject to neuroses and inner searchings and optimism and depression...as any single person is."[3] Psychoanalysis became popular in the 1950s, the decade when the analyst Erik Erikson coined the term "identity crisis."[4] In the midst of this popular fascination with the invisible histories behind human will, the corporation emerged as a new personality type. Designers and public relations officers were called on for diagnoses and cures.

Print magazine was particularly energetic in promoting and documenting corporate graphics. In 1953 it exchanged its bookish, scholarly image for a big, glossy format, and the editors announced a new focus on design and business. Especially well documented in *Print* at the end of the 1950s were identity programs directed by mature designers who had begun their careers in the 30s and 40s. Paul Rand and the architect Eliot Noyes collaborated on a design program for IBM, initiated in 1956. Rand, Noyes, Herbert Matter, and Charles Eames collaborated on the 1959 identity program for Westinghouse. Matter designed graphics for the New Haven Railroad in 1955, and Lester Beall established a program for International Paper in 1960.[5] Thus in the same decade that International Style architecture became the preferred idiom for new office buildings, the rise of corporate image signaled the integration of modernist graphic design into corporate culture and the expansion of the design profession.

1 On CBS see William Golden, "My Eye," *Print* 13, 3 (May-June 1957): 24-29; Cipe Pineles Golden et al., eds., *The Visual Craft of William Golden* (New York: George Braziller, 1962); and Dick Hess and Marion Muller, *Dorfsman and CBS* (New York: American Showcase, 1987).

2 On Herbert Matter's work for Knoll, see Eric Larrabee and Massimo Vignelli, *Knoll Design* (New York: Harry N. Abrams, 1981).

3 Howard Gossage, "Give Your Company A Clear, Consistent Identity, and Its Advertising Will be Easier, Better," *Advertising Age* (9 March 1959): 59.

4 Erik H. Erikson, *Childhood and Society* (New York: W.W.Norton, 1985).

5 *Print* devoted its May-June 1957 issue to corporate identity. See also "Four Major Corporate Design Programs," *Print* 14, 6 (November-December 1960): 31-50.

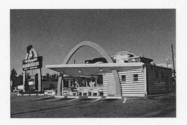

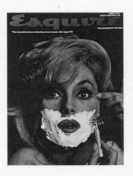

Chambers of Commerce

Visual Thinking

1953 DWIGHT D. EISENHOWER

The postwar rush to the suburbs encouraged urban retailers to establish branches outside the city equipped with large parking lots. The lifeline of many suburbs became the strip of retail stores, eateries, and movie theaters whose illuminated, blinking and revolving signs created a dense, graphic corridor of commerce.

While restaurant chains were formed as early as the 1870s, the first to standardize its architectural image was White Castle. In the early 1920s the White Castle System of Eating Houses had established a fiefdom of crenellated, rusticated, and turreted snack shops, whose stainless steel shimmer and lavatory whiteness promoted the restaurant's hygienic hamburgers.[1] McDonald's was among the first and most successful postwar chains to adopt the White Castle model of standardized food and imagery. In 1952 Richard and Maurice McDonald, working with Ray Kroc, began to franchise their successful self-service restaurant. By 1953 the yellow parabolic arches were the company's trademark. According to historian Philip Langdon, this zealous expression of technology and modernity has roots in Le Corbusier's unrealized plan for the Palace of Soviets in Moscow and other kinds of "dynamic structural modernism" (84-109).

The novelty rooflines and expressive appendages of the 1950s were attacked by environmentalists and community leaders during the late 60s. In 1969 McDonald's unveiled its first environment-conscious, restrained, brown brick buildings, with discretely illuminated ribs on a mansard roof.[2] The industry-wide shift from futuristic bombast to domestic and historical references—Colonial, Southwest, Victorian, Cape Cod—reflects the eclecticism of suburban residential architecture and the tastes of municipal zoning boards.

1 Philip Langdon, *Orange Roofs, Golden Arches: The Architecture of American Chain Restaurants* (London: Michael Joseph, 1986).

2 Regina S. Baraban, "Eat and Run," *Metropolis* 7, 8 (April 1988): 52.

1957 DWIGHT D. EISENHOWER

In a 1955 design annual, the rise of television was described as marking "a transition from word thinking to visual thinking" in magazine design.[1] The new double-imperative of magazine graphics—greater attention to images and faster delivery of information—put increasing pressure on the art director to shape content. Many of the leading art directors of this period—Henry Wolf (*Esquire* and *Harper's Bazaar*), Otto Storch (*McCall's*), and Sam Antupit (*Esquire*)—had studied with Alexey Brodovitch. Others, such as Bradbury Thompson (*Mademoiselle*), Cipe Pineles (*Charm*), Allen Hurlburt (*Look*), Alexander Liberman (*Vogue*), Art Kane (*Seventeen*), Tina Fredricks (*Glamour*), and Will Burtin and Leo Lionni (*Fortune*), also came to prominence in this era.

Magazine designers used typography, photography, and illustration to provocatively represent subject matter and editorial angle. Henry Wolf's covers for *Esquire* in the 1950s used clever visual punning to express urban, "gentlemanly" sophistication. The fusion of images and words extended from cover designs to page layouts, in staged photographs incorporating text type and in typography composed of three-dimensional objects. Such efforts to collapse the verbal and visual helped magazines compete with television's rhythmic flow of imagery overlaid with spoken and typographic texts. Wolf's techniques were pursued in a more aggressive way when *Esquire*, facing economic collapse in 1962, enlisted advertising designer George Lois to art direct covers for the magazine.[2] The 1965 cover shown above attempted to shock and titillate readers with its blunt interpretation of a feature article on the "masculin-ization of the American woman."

1 Wallace F. Hainline, "Editorial Layout," *The 34th Annual of Advertising and Editorial Art and Design* (New York: Watson-Guptill, 1955).

2 Victor Margolin situates Lois's work for *Esquire* in the context of American political graphics in "Rebellion, Reform, and Revolution: American Graphic Design for Social Change," *Design Issues* 5, 1 (Fall 1988): 59-70.

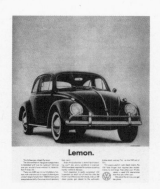

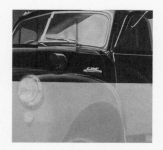

The New Advertising and the New Ad Agencies/The Old Advertising and Pop

1961

JOHN F. KENNEDY, LYNDON B. JOHNSON

"The new advertising" refers to the unorthodox strategies that transformed the character of advertising in the 1960s.[1] The campaign that became the icon of the new advertising was created by the firm Doyle Dane Bernbach (DDB) for Volkswagen. Irreverent humor, disarming wit, and a new self-consciousness about advertising were the hallmarks of the Volkswagen campaign. A simple layout, a sober black and-white photograph, and an unexpected caption were the antithesis of the hard sell; the modest appearance of the car jabbed at Detroit's obsession with styling at the expense of engineering and economy.

The creative director of DDB was Bill Bernbach, who initiated the concept of the "creative team," composed of a copywriter and an art director.[2] In his own career as a copywriter, Bernbach had found that the traditional separation between writing and art directing led to ads whose text and imagery were arbitrarily or awkwardly linked. The new advertising transformed not only the look of ads but also the structure of agencies. Previously, the copywriter and art director had served the will of an executive staff that relied heavily on market research and demographics. As the new advertising flourished, creative teams gained executive positions, and there was a proliferation of "boutiques," small agencies headed by creative teams that often had broken away from larger firms. Another result was the dismantling of the Anglo-Saxon, upper-middle-class, old-boy network of Madison Avenue.

While Doyle Dane Bernbach represented the sophisticated avant-garde of American advertising, it existed alongside a larger mainstream of commonplace commercial graphics. In London in the mid-1950s the term Pop Art was coined by a collective of artists and designers called the Independent Group; Pop named a class of objects banished from the realm of good design. Stylish Detroit automobiles, Hollywood film posters, and the routine ads of the "old" Madison Avenue were held up as symbols of freedom against the austere modernism promoted after World War II.[3]

In 1955 the critic Reyner Banham praised the American Cadillac as a paragon of Pop values—it was ephemeral, emotional, sensual, and symbolic. Banham attacked the Volkswagen in 1961 as a product of false modesty, whose lack of superficial design "styling" belied an absence of technical and aesthetic imagination: the VW's "overwhelming virtue in the eyes of men of liberal conscience was that in a world of automotive flux its appearance remained constant....In other words, it was a symbol of protest against the standards of Detroit, the mass media and the Pop Arts."[4]

In New York, Pop Art emerged in the late 1950s as a response to the heroic Abstract Expressionism of the previous decade; Pop tried to find a less personal brand of abstraction in the flat colors, halftone screens, and mechanical repetition of the mass media. Most of the commercial imagery incorporated by the American Pop artists was not modernist design or conceptually sophisticated "new" advertising, but rather the slick mainstream of fast-food, comic strips, supermarket packaging, journalistic photographs, and ordinary automobiles, as in James Rosenquist's 1963 *Untitled (Broome Street Truck)*, shown above. While celebrating the life of the present, Pop Art also provoked nostalgia for a golden age of unselfconscious, truly "American" design and media.

1 Robert Glatzer, *The New Advertising* (New York: Citadel Press, 1970): 10; and Larry Dobrow, *When Advertising Tried Harder* (New York: Friendly Press, 1984).

2 Bernbach began working directly with an art director when he teamed with Paul Rand on playful advertisements for Ohrbach's department stores in the late 1940s.

3 On the British Pop movement, see Brian Wallis, ed., *This Is Tomorrow Today: The Group and British Pop Art*, exh. cat. (New York: The Clock Tower and the Institute for Art and Urban Resources, 1987). The book includes reprints of 1950s articles by Reyner Banham, Richard Hamilton, and others.

4 Reyner Banbam, "Design by Choice," first published in *Architectural Review*, July 1961, and reprinted in Penny Sparke, ed., *Design by Choice* (New York: Rizzoli, 1981), 97-107.

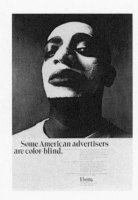

Some American advertisers are color-blind.

Ebony

Black Markets/
Black Power

1965 LYNDON B. JOHNSON In the late 1950s and 1960s, magazines directed at African-American readers, such as *Ebony, Jet, Negro Digest,* and *Tan,* encouraged national advertisers to promote their products to black markets. John H. Johnson, publisher of all four of these periodicals, helped generate national awareness of black consumers. The ad shown above ran as a full page in *The New York Times* in 1969; art directed by Herb Lubalin, the ad urged manufacturers to recognize that "the Negro is not the white man's burden....he's earning $30 billion a year;...he spends a greater percentage of his income on food, home furnishings, and personal care products than white people of comparable income do."

Whereas Johnson urged advertisers to reach the black market through black publications in ads showing black consumers, African-American models were rarely seen in "mainstream" publications such as *Time* or *Life,* whose readership was assumed to be white. In the early 60s the Congress of Racial Equality (CORE) and other civil rights groups began to call for a fairer representation of blacks in the mainstream media, countering the practice of "separate but equal" ad campaigns. In 1963 CORE pressured the ad industry to increase black representation in the advertisements, television programming, and in the composition of the ad industry itself. Efforts toward integrated advertising reflected the extension of civil rights activity beyond the primary issues of education and voting into the areas of affirmative action and anti-discrimination.

An expanded discussion of this issue appears in the essay "White on Black on Gray" included in this book.

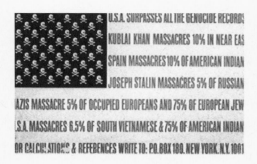

Posters and Protest

1969 RICHARD NIXON Collecting stylish Art Nouveau posters that advertised literary periodicals and cultural events was a fashionable pastime in the 1890s. The poster craze of the late 1960s and early 70s was just as fashionable, while lacking pretensions to the genteel world of the salon. This second wave of poster art had its origins in youth and pop culture, specifically in the promotion of San Francisco-area rock groups. The posters' psychedelic colors and writhing letter forms, suggestive of drug-induced hallucinations, quickly gained an audience and became commercially available through several poster houses. As their popularity increased, distributors— mostly mail-order houses—began to offer a wider selection, reflecting the disparate sources and influences of youth culture in the 1960s: themes of peace and protest, underground comics, science fiction, political heroes and despots, nineteenth-century temperance images, and pop stars.[1]

A recurring strategy was to amend the American flag. For the disillusioned of the 1960s, the flag had become a symbol of militaristic, right-wing America. Numerous protest posters used visual punning to revive an icon whose meanings had become diffuse and contradictory. The poster above was designed by George Maciunas.

While the posters collected at the end of the 1800s originally functioned as advertisements, the bulk of poster production in the 1960s and 70s did not. Most of these late twentieth-century posters had a brief public life—on board fences, kiosks, or newsstands—but were primarily intended for domestic display.

1 David Kunzle, *American Posters of Protest, 1966-70,* exh. cat. (New York; New School Art Center, 1971): 15. For a more general account of political graphics, see Robert Philippe, *Political Graphics: Art as a Weapon* (New York: Abbeville, 1982), 281.

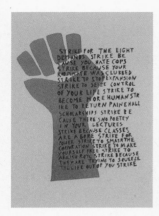

The political posters available from the retail stores and distribution houses were purchased and hung to express solidarity with a cause. They were not, like the street posters produced by student groups in the late 1960s, tools of a specific political struggle.

The popular interest in posters made them an effective medium for groups lacking access to radio, television, and newspapers. From 1968 to 1970, student demonstrations reached a peak on campuses throughout the country; two of the major issues were the struggle for minority recognition and increased student power. At Columbia, as at many other colleges and universities, students questioned the relationship between the school and the community it inhabited. The war in Vietnam—particularly as it affected the university through ROTC, on-campus recruiting, and military research—was another major issue in student protests.[2]

The 1969 poster shown above was anonymously produced in response to the violent police action taken when students occupied an administration building at Harvard University. The takeover began after negotiations to initiate a black studies program had proven ineffective. The poster employs the boldly simplified forms, terse language, and deliberately crude lettering that were hallmarks of the posters of the student/worker uprisings in Paris of May 1968.[3] For many activists in the United States, the events of May served as a model, proving that revolutionary action was possible in a modern industrial state. Few examples of student-protest posters remain, for their role was related more to the expendability and urgency of newspapers and graffiti than to interior display.

2 See *Student Protests, 1969* (Chicago: Urban Research Corporation, 1970). For the period 1968-1970, see Ronald Fraser et al., *1968: A Student Generation in Revolt* (New York: Pantheon, 1988).

3 The posters produced during the Paris uprisings were the collective effort of the Atelier Populaire, a group of art students who had seized their schools' printing studios and produced as many as five hundred posters a day. The posters were statements of resistance, daily news reports of factory strikes, and notices of police brutality. See James C. Douglass, "The Graphics of Revolution," *Print* 22, 5 (September-October 1968): 1, 5-20.

1973

RICHARD NIXON, GERALD FORD

Signature Styles/International Styles

By the end of the 1960s a major movement had emerged in American graphic design, which coincided with a widespread reaction against modernism or the International Style among architects. A group of graphic designers, including Milton Glaser, Seymour Chwast, and Herb Lubalin, rejected such ideals as functionalism and neutrality in favor of a witty, eclectic style, assembled out of bits and pieces of art history, popular culture, and personal experience.[1]

Milton Glaser, after attending The Cooper Union School of Art in New York in the early 1950s, studied etching in Italy with Giorgio Morandi, a classical artist who had worked with the avant-garde "metaphysical" painters early in the century. This experience in Italy would inform his lifelong commitment to drawing as a tool for design. As early as 1960 he criticized designers who depend on collaging together existing images: "A designer who must rely on cutouts and rearranging to create effects, who cannot achieve the specific image or idea he wants by drawing, is in trouble."[2]

Glaser founded the Push Pin Studios with Seymour Chwast, Reynold Ruffins, and Edward Sorel in 1954. Although the studio's early work employed expressionist mannerisms typical of 1950s design, the "Push Pin style" came into its own in the 1960s, yielding images that were personal yet highly controlled, characterized by bright colors, flattening outlines, exaggerated, fattened forms, and clever, sometimes bizarre juxtapositions. According to Glaser, designers should work within a "vernacular language," manipulating culturally familiar elements in a new way.

1 *The Push Pin Styles* (Palo Alto: Communication Arts Magazine, 1970); Seymour Chwast, *The Left-Handed Designer* (New York: Harry N. Abrams, 1985); Milton Glaser, *Graphic Design* (Woodstock: Overlook Press, 1973); and Gertrude Snyder and Alan Peckolick, *Herb Lubalin: Art Director, Graphic Designer, and Typographer* (New York: American Showcase, 1985). Other artists who worked with the Push Pin Studios include John Alcorn, Sam Antupit, Paul Davis, Herb Levitt, Reynold Ruffins, and Barry Zaid.

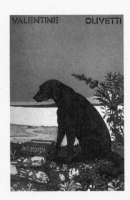

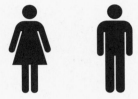

Whereas the camera and scissors have dominated avant-garde design since the 1920s, the Push Pin designers celebrated an aesthetic of the hand. In the 1968 poster shown above, Glaser inserted the client's product—a portable Olivetti typewriter designed by Ettore Sottsass—into a landscape borrowed from the fifteenth-century painter Piero di Cosimo. Glaser thus depicted Pop-inspired Italian design with references to Renaissance classicism, metaphysical surrealism, and American comic book illustration.[3]

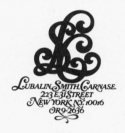

Like the illustrations of Glaser and Chwast, the typography of Herb Lubalin shows a love for exaggerating the familiar. Lubalin abandoned modernist standards of "invisible" text and classical proportions in favor of intensifying the distinctive features of an alphabet—thinner thin strokes, rounder "o's," sharper serifs, and inventive ligatures. Lubalin's own corporate logo, designed in 1967 with his partner Tom Carnase, has sinuous swashes that recall Victorian engraving, but whose fat, almost uniform weight makes the mark bold and "contemporary."

While Glaser, Lubalin, and others appealed to the changeable tastes of middle-class consumers, another segment of the American design profession searched for a universal style that would communicate through a neutral vocabulary of photography, geometry, schematic drawings, systematically applied grids, and spare, sans-serif typefaces. Although the notion of an "International Style" seemed inappropriate in the U.S. for the design of popular media or for promoting consumer goods, it was embraced in the 1960s as the official visual "language" of corporate, institutional, and governmental communications, in the tradition of design for the public good.

In 1974 a set of pictorial symbols, designed for use in airports, hospitals, and office buildings, was endorsed by the United States Department of Transportation (DOT) and the American Institute of Graphic Arts (AIGA). The project was overseen by a committee of prominent designers, including Thomas Geismar, Rudolph de Harak, and Massimo Vignelli, each of whom had built successful businesses during the 1960s designing signage and identity programs based on modernist principles. Seymour Chwast also belonged to the committee—for the rigorously eclectic Chwast, modernism, like any historical style, had its appropriate uses.[4]

The project aimed to express objective scientific methods rather than the personalities of individual designers. The group analyzed past examples and instructed the firm Cook & Shanosky to design a new set of symbols. The committee used semiotic terminology to phrase its recommendations, adding to the "scientific" authority of its report. Although the DOT symbols aspired to rational universality, their plump, sausage-like forms carry the faint yet unmistakable flavor of the Pop design culture of the 1970s.

For a more detailed discussion of international symbols, see the essay "Modern Hieroglyphs" included in this book.

2 Glaser is quoted in Sterling McIlhany, "Milton Glaser," *Graphis* 16, 93 (November-December 1960): 508. For a more recent statement of the same idea, see Milton Glaser, "Some Thoughts on Modernism: Past, Present and Future," *AIGA Journal of Graphic Design* 5, 2 (1987): 6.

3 Glaser connects his work to comic book art in "Comics, Advertising, and Illustration," *Graphis* 28, 160 (1972-1973): 104-117. On the historicism in 1960s design, see "Art Nouveau: Then and Now," *Print* 18, 6 (November-December 1964).

4 American Institute of Graphic Arts, *Symbol Signs* (New York: Hastings House, 1981).

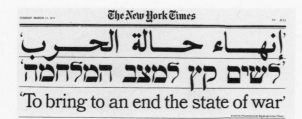

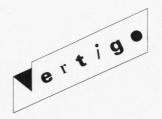

Designing Newspapers

New Wave, Neo-Conservative

1977 JIMMY CARTER

In the 1930s and 1940s many newspapers adopted modern headline typography. Flush-left lines, lowercase letters, and limited type families yielded clean, orderly designs that echoed the journalistic ideal of objectivity. In contrast, tabloids continued to use mixed typography and sensationally scaled, boldly presented images.[1] Several papers changed more dramatically during the 1960s, a period when labor disputes and intense competition with magazines and television devastated many papers—*The New York Herald Tribune* was redesigned by Peter Palazzo with large, magazine-style photographs and assertive typography, but the paper did not survive the decade.[2]

The notoriously conservative *New York Times* developed an entirely new graphic image during the mid-1970s. Louis Silverstein, an advertising designer who had been head of *The Times*'s promotion department since 1952, brought techniques from progressive advertising, such as large type and photographs and witty juxtapositions of image and text, to the newspaper. Silverstein's imaginative use of typography in the newspaper headline above infused the journalistic message with emotional power.[3]

The national daily paper *USA Today,* founded in 1982, exemplifies current trends in newspaper design. *USA Today*'s full-color photography, bold information graphics, and telegraphic editorial style brought the spirit of network television to the newspaper industry, condensing events into an easy-to-read, ready-to-serve, nationally uniform package.[4]

Contemporary newspaper design is described in greater detail in the essay "McPaper" included in this book.

1981 RONALD REAGAN

For the classic Swiss Modernism of the 1950s and 60s, grids, sans-serif type, and photography represented such values as objectivity and universality. By the early 1980s members of a younger generation were using the same elements to express an apparently contradictory set of values: ambiguity, complexity, and individuality. Proponents of "Postmodernism" or the "new wave" working in the U.S. included April Greiman, Dan Friedman, and Willi Kunz.[1]

The logo for the retailer Vertigo, designed by April Greiman and Jayme Odgers, is composed of rules, geometric letter forms, and primary shapes—the ingredients of classic Modernism. But here the elements form a free-floating series of marks held together by an external frame. Whereas classic modernist design aimed to produce unified, "organic" wholes, the Vertigo logo consists of discontinuous parts.

 Compare, for example, Lester Beall's 1960 mark for International Paper, where the framing element is formally consistent with the interior symbol, having the same heavy line weight and geometric clarity.

The clientele for new wave design in the early 80s consisted largely of art- and fashion-oriented businesses—clothing stores, architectural firms, restaurants, museums, and the art schools where the style was taught. As the decade progressed, however, the new wave became attractive to corporate clients.[2] For a growing population of "young urban professionals," new wave graphics offered a fresh, forward-looking companion to fashionable Postmodern architecture, established as a corporate idiom during the age of Ronald Reagan and George Bush.

---

1 Developments in newspaper design during the 30s and 40s can be seen by comparing John E. Allen's *Newspaper Makeup* (New York: Harper and Brothers, 1936) with his later book *Newspaper Designing* (New York: Harper and Brothers, 1947).

2 Peter Palazzo, "Behind the Trib's New Look," *Print* 17, 5 (September-October 1964): 32-35.

1 An early article to use the terms Postmodern, new wave, and Swiss-punk in reference to graphic design is Jean W. Progner, "Play and Dismay in Post-Modern Graphics," *ID* 27, 2 (1980): 42-47.

2 On new wave corporate graphics, see Michael Bierut, "Corporate Design: A Cutting Edge in the Age of Entropy?" *ID* 35, 2 (1988): 30-33.

THE NEW PriMitiVES

Electronic Publishing: Off-line and On-line

1985 RONALD REAGAN

During the 1980s the microcomputer became a commonplace office machine. By making typographic production less expensive and by centering many tasks in an accessible network of machines and services, the system of "desktop publishing" (whose equipment rarely sits on a single desk) has enabled many designers to establish small studios. Computers have also encouraged more people to publish more documents—with or without help from professional designers.

Microcomputer typography can closely approximate the appearance of traditional typesetting, or it can be emphatically crude. In the mid-80s designers Zuzana Licko and Rudy VanderLans dramatized the potential harshness of bit-mapped typefaces. Calling themselves "the new primitives," they refused to use the computer as an instrument for imitating typographic norms.[1] They founded the digital type foundry Emigre in 1984, anticipating the proliferation of numerous small, independent distributors of typefaces in the early 90s. In addition to transforming design for print, the rise of the microcomputer spurred the growth of on-line communication, in which documents are stored and disseminated electronically.[2] Since the 1970s, database services have transmitted centrally-stored information to terminals in libraries and offices. Networks such as the Internet, once restricted to university and government employees, became increasingly accessible during the mid-90s, while smaller databases and interactive publications were available on CD-ROMs and other media.

The design considerations involved in on-line publishing are different from those of print. How many ways will a document be output? How is the information organized and accessed? How is the user oriented within the document? Does the interface imitate a familiar environment—such as an office desktop—or does it try to develop a new "vernacular" for an electronic culture?

1 Zuzana Licko and Rudy VanderLans, "The New Primitives," *ID* 35, 2 (March-April 1988): 60.

2 An early work on this subject is Stephen T. Kerr, "Instructional Text: The Transition from Page to Screen," *Visible Language* 20, 4 (1986): 368-392.

History of Design/Design as History

1989 GEORGE BUSH

Graphic design has been established as a relatively unified "profession" for several decades, with tacitly understood aims and limits. Graphic design has emerged as a humanistic discipline which, like painting and architecture, aims to transcend utility to enrich sensual and intellectual experience. Some critics, however, have recently noted that graphic design lacks the historical self-awareness common to other humanist disciplines, which have long traditions of debate over theory, style, and purpose.[1]

Some design historians have worked to identify a base of important movements and individuals: a humanist discipline needs a humanist heritage. Philip Meggs produced the first encyclopedic history of graphic design in 1983. His narrative begins with cave painting and progresses toward the modern profession and the work of individual designers.[2]

A history of the design profession could be fortified, complemented, or even engulfed by a study of those forms existing beyond or beneath the domain of "graphic design"—the bulk of graphic communication, from interoffice mail to anonymous soapboxes, does not appear in the annuals of professional societies. Scholarship that fits this more inclusive view includes Adrian Forty's 1986 *Objects of Desire*, which analyzes the politics and economics of design through case studies of the sewing machine, the automated office, and the graphics of the London Underground.[3] For history to be valuable to contemporary designers, it should address the origins and aims of the profession; this orientation helps make scholarship relevant to practice. But the profession can be studied as a changing institution that has interacted with and defined itself against other modes of expression.

1 See Victor Margolin, "A Decade of Design History in the United States, 1977-87," *Journal of Design History* 1, 1 (1988): 51-72.

2 Philip B. Meggs, *A History of Graphic Design* (New York: Van Nostrand Reinhold, 1983).

3 Adrian Forty, *Objects of Desire: Design and Society from Wedgewood to IBM* (New York: Pantheon Books, 1986).

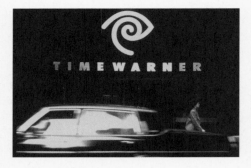

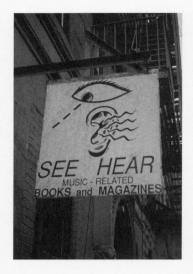

Mass Media/Micro Media

1993 BILL CLINTON

The 1980s and early 90s witnessed the growth of huge global corporations that own hundreds and even thousands of media properties in film, publishing, music, and television. Perhaps the most spectacular corporate takeover of the period was the merger of Warner Communications and Time Inc., which made Time Warner one of the largest media owners in the world. In 1990 Time Warner commissioned Chermayeff & Geismar Associates to design a symbol for the new conglomerate. Steff Geissbuhler, an associate at the firm, designed a hieroglyph that combined schematic drawings of an eye and an ear to symbolize Time Warner's conquest of the senses.

The daring attitude of the new logo was matched by a series of annual reports designed by Frankfurt Gips Balkind, who incorporated elements from pop culture—from the typography of surfing magazines to the info-graphics of *Spy*—into the conservative realm of annual reports.

In 1993, shortly after the death of CEO Steven Ross, whose flashy West Coast persona had embodied Warner Communications' corporate culture, Time Warner replaced the eye/ear hieroglyph with a bland typographic mark, explaining that Geissbuhler's symbol had overpowered the brand identity of the individual companies that make up Time Warner. The corporation also returned to more conventional design in its annual reports.

While major corporations have extended their reach during the past fifteen years, there has also been a proliferation of independent producers across the media industries. The birth of "desktop publishing" and the growing accessibility of inexpensive printing and photocopying services has encouraged the spread of "zines" or "fanzines"—small, crudely produced, sporadically issued journals aimed at narrow audiences. Zines have charted the philosophy and style of numerous subcultural movements, feeding fandom in the realms of music, film, sexuality, fashion, literature, sports, and countless other areas. The store See/Hear in New York's East Village specializes in music zines and small-issue recordings.

Fanzine publishers, independent music producers, club promoters, and other makers of contemporary urban life draw imagery from a vast range of sources, from local graffiti to national brand identities. Such underground activity is carefully monitored by huge entertainment companies like Time Warner, who frequently convert the energy of the street into products for mass consumption.

BIBLIOGRAPHY

SOURCES OF ESSAYS IN THIS VOLUME

DECONSTRUCTION AND
GRAPHIC DESIGN
First published as "Deconstruction
and Graphic Design: History Meets
Theory," *Visible Language* 28, 4
(1994): 345-65. Edited by Andrew
Blauvelt. Written by Ellen Lupton
and J. Abbott Miller. Substantially
revised.

PERIOD STYLES
First published in *Period Styles:
A History of Punctuation.* New York:
The Cooper Union, 1988.
Exhibition monograph. Written by
Ellen Lupton.

COUNTING SHEEP
First published as "Object
Lessons," in *Numbers.* New York:
The Cooper Union, 1989.
Exhibition monograph. Written by
Ellen Lupton.

MODERN HIEROGLYPHS
This essay draws on research for
the exhibition *Global Signage:
Semiotics and the Language of
International Pictures,* curated by
Ellen Lupton at The Cooper Union,
1986. Her essay "Reading Isotype"
was published in *Design Issues* 3, 2
(1986): 47-58. It later appeared in
Design Discourse. Ed. Victor
Margolin. Chicago: University of
Chicago Press, 1989.

LANGUAGE OF DREAMS
First published as "The Language
of Dreams." *Typography in Asia:
A View from Tokyo.* New York:
The Cooper Union, 1990.
Exhibition monograph. Written by
Ellen Lupton.

BODY OF THE BOOK
First published as "Appendix,"
Writing and the Body. New York:
The Cooper Union, 1990.
Exhibition monograph. Written by
Ellen Lupton.

LANGUAGE OF VISION
First published as "The Mystique
of Visual Language." *AIGA
Journal of Graphic Design* 5, 3
(1987): 9. Written by Ellen
Lupton.

LAWS OF THE LETTER
First published as "Type Writing:
Structuralism and Typography."
Emigre 15 (1990): i-viii. Also
published in *Printed Letters:
The Natural History of Typo-
graphy.* Exhibition monograph.
Ed. J. Abbott Miller. Jersey City:
Jersey City Museum, 1992.
Written by Ellen Lupton and
J. Abbott Miller. Substantially
revised.

DISCIPLINES OF DESIGN
Written by Ellen Lupton.

LINE ART
First published as "Line Art:
Andy Warhol's Commercial Art
World." *Success is a Job in New
York: The Early Art and Business
of Andy Warhol.* Ed. Donna de
Salvo. Exhibition catalogue. New
York: Grey Art Gallery, 1989.
Written by J. Abbott Miller and
Ellen Lupton.

MCLUHAN/FIORE
First published as "Quentin
Fiore: Massaging the Message."
Eye 8, 2 (1993): 46-55. Written
by J. Abbott Miller.

WHITE ON BLACK ON GRAY
Written by J. Abbott Miller.

PICTURES FOR RENT
First published as "Pictures for
Rent." *Eye* 14, 4 (1994): 68-77.
Written by J. Abbott Miller.
Substantially revised.

SUBLIMINAL SEDUCTION
Written by J. Abbott Miller.

MCPAPER
First published as "USA Today:
Learning from Las Vegas." *Print* 44, 6
(1990): 90-97. Written by J. Abbott
Miller. Substantially revised.

LOW AND HIGH
First published as "High and Low."
Eye 2, 7 (1992): 72-77. Written by Ellen
Lupton. Substantially revised.

GRAPHIC DESIGN IN AMERICA
First published as "A Time Line of
American Graphic Design, 1829-1989."
*Graphic Design in America: A Visual
Language History.* Ed. Mildred
Friedman. Minneapolis: Walker Art
Center, 1989. 24-65. Written by
Ellen Lupton and J. Abbott Miller.
Significantly condensed.

204 DESIGN WRITING RESEARCH

Ellen Lupton. *Mechanical Brides: Women and Machines from Home to Office.* New York: Cooper-Hewitt, National Design Museum and Princeton Architectural Press, 1993.

Ellen Lupton and J. Abbott Miller. *The Bathroom, the Kitchen, and the Aesthetics of Waste: A Process of Elimination.* Cambridge and New York: MIT List Visual Arts Center and Princeton Architectural Press, 1992.

Ellen Lupton, ed. *Graphic Design and Typography in the Netherlands: A View of Recent Work.* New York: The Cooper Union and Princeton Architectural Press, 1992.

Ellen Lupton and J. Abbott Miller. *The ABCs of* ▲■●: *The Bauhaus and Design Theory.* New York: The Cooper Union and Princeton Architectural Press, 1991.

"Design and Cultural Identity: A Study in Mixing Messages." *Graphic Design USA 16.* New York: American Institute of Graphic Arts, 1995. 26-33. Ellen Lupton.

"Fabien Baron." Interview with J. Abbott Miller. *Eye* 5, 18 (1995): 10-16.

"Words Made Flesh: Johanna Drucker." *Eye* 5, 18 (1995): 72-77. Ellen Lupton.

"Archive: Elaine Lustig Cohen." *Eye* 17, 5 (1995): 8-9. Ellen Lupton.

"Underground Matriarchy." *Eye* 4, 14 (1994): 42-47. Ellen Lupton and Laurie Haycock Makela.

"Word Art." *Eye* 3, 11 (1994): 34-43. J. Abbott Miller.

"A Post-Mortem on Deconstruction?" *AIGA Journal of Graphic Design* 12, 2 (1994): 24-26. Ellen Lupton.

"Design as Research." *The 100 Show: The Sixteenth Annual of the American Center for Design.* Chicago: American Center for Design, 1994. 7-14. Ellen Lupton and J. Abbott Miller.

"Case Study House: Comfort and Convenience." *Assemblage* 24 (1994): 86-89. Special issue on *House Rules* exhibition, Wexner Center, Ohio State University; curated by Mark Robbins. Ellen Lupton and Jane Murphy.

"The Idea is the Machine." *Eye* 3, 10 (1993): 58-65. J. Abbott Miller.

"Critical Wayfinding." *The Edge of the Millennium.* Ed. Susan Yelavich. New York: Whitney Library of Design, 1993. 220-232. Ellen Lupton and J. Abbott Miller.

"Sheila Levrant De Bretteville." Interview with Ellen Lupton. *Eye* 2, 8 (1993): 10-16.

"Hygiene, Cuisine, and the Product World of Early Twentieth-Century America." *Zone 6: Incorporations.* Ed. Jonathan Crary and Sanford Kwinter. New York: Zone Books, 1992. 495-515. Ellen Lupton and J. Abbott Miller.

"Archives and Collections: The Herb Lubalin Study Center, New York." *Journal of Design History* 5, 1 (1992): 91-93. Ellen Lupton.

"Cranbrook: The Academy of Deconstruction." *Eye* 2, 1 (1991): 44-52. Ellen Lupton.

"Good History/Bad History." *Print* 45, 2 (1991): 114-123. J. Abbott Miller, Karrie Jacobs, and Tibor Kalman.

"Post *Saturday Evening Post*: Magazine Design and Its Discontents." *Print* 44, 4 (1990): 58-67. Ellen Lupton.

"Writing About Design." *AIGA Journal of Graphic Design* 8, 2 (1990): 10-11. Ellen Lupton.

"1980s: Postmodern, Postmerger, PostScript." *Print* 43, 6 (December 1989): 162-185. J. Abbott Miller.

"1970s: Age of the Sign." *Print* 43, 6 (December 1989): 138-161. Ellen Lupton.

"Apocalypse Now and Then: Excavating the 1980s." *AIGA Journal of Graphic Design* 7, 3 (1989): 4-5. J. Abbott Miller and Ellen Lupton.

"Toddler Modern: The Bauhaus as Elementary School." *AIGA Journal of Graphic Design* 7, 1 (1989): 4. J. Abbott Miller.

"Tracking the Elusive Time Line." *AIGA Journal of Graphic Design* 6, 2 (1988): 7. J. Abbott Miller.

Design Papers 5: Rhetorical Handbook. Halifax: Nova Scotia College of Art and Design, 1988. Hanno Ehses and Ellen Lupton.

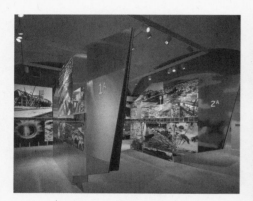

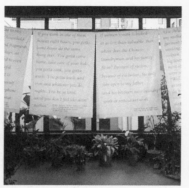

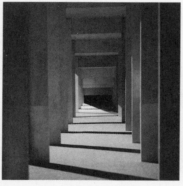

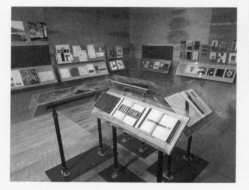

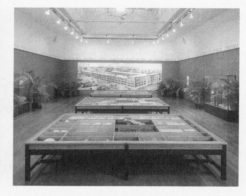

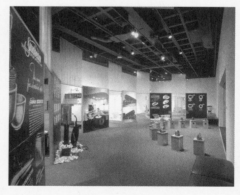

World War II and the American Dream, 1994.
National Building Museum, Washington, D.C.
Photo by Paul Warchol.

*Elaine Lustig Cohen, Modern Graphic
Designer*, 1995. Cooper-Hewitt, National
Design Museum, New York City. Photo by
Joshua McHugh.

*Mechanical Brides: Women and Machines
from Home to Office*, 1993. Cooper-Hewitt,
National Design Museum, New York City.
Photo by Bill Jacobson.

Geoffrey Beene Unbound. Spring 1994.
The Museum at FIT, New York City.
Photo by Jack Deutsch.

*Printed Letters: The Natural History of
Typography*, 1992. Jersey City Museum, Jersey
City, New Jersey. Photo by Kit Latham.

*The Bathroom, the Kitchen, and the Aesthetics
of Waste: A Process of Elimination*, 1992.
MIT List Visual Arts Center, Cambridge,
Massachusetts. Photo by Charles Mayer.

Elaine Lustig Cohen, Modern Graphic Designer. Winter 1995. Cooper-Hewitt, National Design Museum, New York. Exhibition about a modernist American designer active in the 1950s and 60s. Curated and designed by Ellen Lupton.

World War II and the American Dream. Fall 1994—Winter 1996. National Building Museum, Washington, D.C. Exhibition documenting the impact of wartime technologies on domestic architecture and product design. Curated by Donald Albrecht. Designed by J. Abbott Miller and Michael Sorkin.

Geoffrey Beene Unbound. Spring 1994. The Museum at FIT, New York. Thirty-year retrospective of the great American designer. Curated by Dorothy Twining Globus. Designed by J. Abbott Miller.

Mechanical Brides: Women and Machines, from Home to Office. Fall 1993. Cooper-Hewitt, National Design Museum, New York. Exhibition about objects central to women's work in the twentieth century, including the telephone, typewriter, and washing machine. Curated by Ellen Lupton. Designed by Ellen Lupton, Constantin Boym, and Laurene Leon.

Printed Letters: The Natural History of Typography. Winter 1992-93. Jersey City Museum, Jersey City, New Jersey. Installation compared the preservation of words on the pages of books to the preservation of specimens in museums of natural history. Curated and designed by J. Abbott Miller.

The Process of Elimination: The Bathroom, the Kitchen, and the Aesthetics of Waste. May 1992. MIT List Visual Arts Center, Cambridge. Exhibition related the history of the American bathroom and kitchen, 1890-1940, to the rise of a consumer economy. Curated and designed by J. Abbott Miller and Ellen Lupton.

Graphic Design in the Netherlands: A View of Recent Work. January 1992. Herb Lubalin Study Center, The Cooper Union, New York. Exhibition of work by emerging Dutch designers. Curated by Ellen Lupton.

The Bauhaus and Design Theory, from Preschool to Post-Modernism. Herb Lubalin Study Center, The Cooper Union, New York. April 1991. Exhibition about the origins of Bauhaus design theory in children's education and the legacy of the search for an elementary "language of vision." Curated and designed by Ellen Lupton, J. Abbott Miller, and Mike Mills.

Dennis Livingston: Social Graphics. October 1990. Herb Lubalin Study Center, The Cooper Union, New York. Exhibition about the information graphics of a social activist. Curated by Ellen Lupton.

Writing and the Body. April 1990. Herb Lubalin Study Center, The Cooper Union, New York. Curated with three design students, who examined the history of writing, sign language for the deaf, and AIDS in advertising. Curated and designed by Ellen Lupton, Ann Antoshak, Brian Boyce, and Chris Evans.

Anthon Beeke's Stage: Holland's Illusionist Poster Designer. February 1990. Herb Lubalin Study Center, The Cooper Union, New York. Exhibition of posters, magazines, and other graphics from the 1970s and 80s. Curated by Ellen Lupton.

Numbers. September 1989. Herb Lubalin Study Center, The Cooper Union, New York. Interactive, multimedia exhibition about the culture and science of numbers. Curated by Ellen Lupton and Alan Wolf.

MIT/Casey. April 1989. Herb Lubalin Study Center, The Cooper Union, New York. Retrospective of work by Jacqueline Casey for MIT. Curated by Ellen Lupton.

Period Styles: A History of Punctuation. March 1988. Herb Lubalin Study Center, The Cooper Union, New York. A typographic, grammatical, and literary history. Curated by Ellen Lupton.

Global Signage: Semiotics and the Language of International Pictures. March 1986. Herb Lubalin Study Center, The Cooper Union, New York. The history and theory of modern pictographic sign systems. Curated by Ellen Lupton.

Meta Metafont. December 1985. Herb Lubalin Study Center, The Cooper Union, New York. Exhibition about the typographical and philosophical implications of Donald Knuth's computer language Metafont. Curated by Ellen Lupton.

REPRODUCTION CREDITS

pp. 72, 74, 77 (upper left), 78: © 1995 The Andy Warhol Foundation, Inc.

pp. 75, 76, 77 (bottom), 81, 82, 84, 89: Previously appeared in the catalogue from the exhibition, *"Success is a job in New York ..." The Early Art and Business of Andy Warhol*. Courtesy Grey Art Gallery & Study Center, New York University. Collection of the Andy Warhol Foundation, Inc.

p. 105 (lower right): © 1978 Matt Heron/ Take Stock

p. 170 (left): Collection of the New York Historical Society; (right): Clarence P. Hornung and George Braziller, Inc., New York

p. 172: Jim Frank, courtesy Merrill Berman

p. 173 (top): *An American Railway Scene at Homellsville, Erie Railway*. Drawn on stone by Parsons & Atwater Lithography firm of Currier & Ives. Chromolithograph, 1874. Amon Carter Museum, Fort Worth, Texas 1970.190 (middle): Earl F. Lundgren, Professor Emeritus, University of Missouri, Columbia

p. 174: Collection of the New York Historical Society

p. 175 (left & center): The Lincoln Museum, Fort Wayne, Indiana, Nos. 2622 & 2258; (right): Library of Congress, Washington, D.C.

p. 176 (right): Jim Frank, courtesy Merrill Berman; (lower right): Rob Roy Kelly *American Wood Type, 1828-1900*

p. 177: ™ and © The Quaker Oats Company. All rights reserved.

pp. 178, 179: General Research Division, The New York Public Library, Astor, Lenox and Tilden Foundations, New York

p. 180 (left): From *Chicago Inter-Ocean*, Illustrated Supplement, June 7, 1893; (right): Chicago Historical Society

p. 181 (left): Courtesy of Norwest Corporation; (right): Library of Congress, Washington, D.C.

p. 182: H.J. Heinz Company

p. 183: Trefoil Publications, London

p. 184 (left): *The Saturday Evening Post*, © 1920 The Curtis Publishing Co., Indianapolis; (right): Rare Book and Manuscript Division, The New York Public Library, Astor, Lenox and Tilden Foundations, New York

p. 185: The Schlesinger Library, Radcliffe College

p. 186 (left): American Red Cross; (right): Yale Collection of American Literature, The Beineke Rare Book and Manuscript Library, Yale University, New Haven, CT

p. 187: Art Directors Club, Inc., New York

p. 188: © Walter Dorwin Teague, Shop Front, Design for the Machine, 1932, Philadelphia Museum of Art

p. 189: © 1934 The Hearst Corporation, courtesy *Harper's Bazaar*

p. 190 (left): Library of Congress, Washington, D.C.; (right): Lester Beall, *Cross Out Slums*, 1941. Offset lithograph, printed in color, 39 1/2 x 29 1/8 in. The Museum of Modern Art, New York. Gift of the designer. © 1995 The Museum of Modern Art, New York

p. 191 (right): Herbert Bayer Collection and Archive, Denver Art Museum, #1986.787 (center): Jefferson Smurfit Corporation (right): National Museum of American Art, Washington, D.C./Art Resource, New York

p. 192 (left): Bauhaus-Archiv, Museum für Gestaltung, Berlin, © Hin Brendendieck; (right): Herbert Bayer Collection and Archive, Denver Art Museum

p. 193 (left): Paul Rand. Cover of exhibition catalogue "Modern Art in Your Life." New York: The Museum of Modern Art, New York, 1949. Offset lithograph, print ed in color, page size 9 15/16 x 7 1/2 in. The Library, The Museum of Modern Art, New York. Photograph © The Museum of Modern Art, New York; (right): © Alvin Lustig, book cover for Rimbaud's *A Season in Hell* (Norfolk, CT: New Directions, 1947)

p. 194 (left to right): © William Golden, 1951; IBM and the IBM logotype are registered trademarks of International Business Machines Corporation; © Herbert Matter; © Paul Rand, Eliot Noyes, Herbert Matter and Charles Eames, 1959

p. 195: © Esquire Magazine and The Hearst Corporation

p. 196 (left): © Volkswagen United States, Inc., Troy Michigan; (right): Collection of Whitney Museum of American Art © 1995 Whitney Museum of American Art

p. 197 (left): Ebony Magazine and Johnson Publishing Company, Chicago;

p. 198: Courtesy Ray Frieden

p. 199 (left): Milton Glaser; (middle): © Herb Lubalin and Tom Carnase; (right): © Cook & Shanasky, 1974

p. 200 (left): The New York Times; (right): © April Greiman; (lower right): © Lester Beall

p. 201: © Zuzana Licko and Rudy VanderLans

INDEX

COLOPHON

DESIGN & EDITORIAL DIRECTORS
Ellen Lupton and J. Abbott Miller

BOOK DESIGN
Design/Writing/Research, New York
J. Abbott Miller, Ellen Lupton, Steve
Hoskins, Deborah Drodvillo, Paul Carlos,
Anthony Inciong

MANAGING EDITOR
Tracey Hummer

PUBLISHING CONSULTANT
Jane Rosch

TYPOGRAPHY
Scala (1990) and Scala Sans (1993)
Designed by Martin Majoor
Distributed by FontShop

STILL-LIFE PHOTOGRAPHY
Kevin Downs

PRODUCTION AND PRINTING
Studley Press
Dalton, Massachusetts

PAPER
Mohawk Paper Mills
Theory, Mohawk Options
Media, Mohawk Innovation
History, Mohawk Vellum

COVER DESIGN
Luke Hayman, J. Abbott Miller

COVER PHOTOGRAPH
Detail of spread from *The Medium is the
Massage*, by Marshall McLuhan and Quentin
Fiore. Used by permission of Jerome Agel.
Re-photographed by Kevin Downs.